C-4110   CAREER EXAMINATION SERIES

This is your
PASSBOOK for...

Certified Alcohol & Substance Abuse Counselor (CASAC)

Test Preparation Study Guide
Questions & Answers

NATIONAL LEARNING CORPORATION®

COPYRIGHT NOTICE

This book is SOLELY intended for, is sold ONLY to, and its use is RESTRICTED to individual, bona fide applicants or candidates who qualify by virtue of having seriously filed applications for appropriate license, certificate, professional and/or promotional advancement, higher school matriculation, scholarship, or other legitimate requirements of education and/or governmental authorities.

This book is NOT intended for use, class instruction, tutoring, training, duplication, copying, reprinting, excerption, or adaptation, etc., by:

1) Other publishers
2) Proprietors and/or Instructors of "Coaching" and/or Preparatory Courses
3) Personnel and/or Training Divisions of commercial, industrial, and governmental organizations
4) Schools, colleges, or universities and/or their departments and staffs, including teachers and other personnel
5) Testing Agencies or Bureaus
6) Study groups which seek by the purchase of a single volume to copy and/or duplicate and/or adapt this material for use by the group as a whole without having purchased individual volumes for each of the members of the group
7) Et al.

Such persons would be in violation of appropriate Federal and State statutes.

PROVISION OF LICENSING AGREEMENTS – Recognized educational, commercial, industrial, and governmental institutions and organizations, and others legitimately engaged in educational pursuits, including training, testing, and measurement activities, may address request for a licensing agreement to the copyright owners, who will determine whether, and under what conditions, including fees and charges, the materials in this book may be used them. In other words, a licensing facility exists for the legitimate use of the material in this book on other than an individual basis. However, it is asseverated and affirmed here that the material in this book CANNOT be used without the receipt of the express permission of such a licensing agreement from the Publishers. Inquiries re licensing should be addressed to the company, attention rights and permissions department.

All rights reserved, including the right of reproduction in whole or in part, in any form or by any means, electronic or mechanical, including photocopying, recording, or by any information storage and retrieval system, without permission in writing from the Publisher.

Copyright © 2024 by
National Learning Corporation

212 Michael Drive, Syosset, NY 11791
(516) 921-8888 • www.passbooks.com
E-mail: info@passbooks.com

PUBLISHED IN THE UNITED STATES OF AMERICA

PASSBOOK® SERIES

THE *PASSBOOK® SERIES* has been created to prepare applicants and candidates for the ultimate academic battlefield – the examination room.

At some time in our lives, each and every one of us may be required to take an examination – for validation, matriculation, admission, qualification, registration, certification, or licensure.

Based on the assumption that every applicant or candidate has met the basic formal educational standards, has taken the required number of courses, and read the necessary texts, the *PASSBOOK® SERIES* furnishes the one special preparation which may assure passing with confidence, instead of failing with insecurity. Examination questions – together with answers – are furnished as the basic vehicle for study so that the mysteries of the examination and its compounding difficulties may be eliminated or diminished by a sure method.

This book is meant to help you pass your examination provided that you qualify and are serious in your objective.

The entire field is reviewed through the huge store of content information which is succinctly presented through a provocative and challenging approach – the question-and-answer method.

A climate of success is established by furnishing the correct answers at the end of each test.

You soon learn to recognize types of questions, forms of questions, and patterns of questioning. You may even begin to anticipate expected outcomes.

You perceive that many questions are repeated or adapted so that you can gain acute insights, which may enable you to score many sure points.

You learn how to confront new questions, or types of questions, and to attack them confidently and work out the correct answers.

You note objectives and emphases, and recognize pitfalls and dangers, so that you may make positive educational adjustments.

Moreover, you are kept fully informed in relation to new concepts, methods, practices, and directions in the field.

You discover that you are actually taking the examination all the time: you are preparing for the examination by "taking" an examination, not by reading extraneous and/or supererogatory textbooks.

In short, this PASSBOOK®, used directedly, should be an important factor in helping you to pass your test.

CERTIFIED ALCOHOL & SUBSTANCE ABUSE COUNSELOR (CASAC)

DUTIES

As a Certified Alcohol & Substance Abuse Counselor, you would work in a specific area such as a court, an agency office, a correctional facility or private community treatment program providing client intake, assessment, referral and counseling services to individuals identified as substance abusers. Your degree of direct involvement with the counseling of substance abusers may vary depending on which area of the state or work site you are employed. You would interview and provide referral services to releasees with alcohol and/or substance abuse problems. As requested, you would also consult with and provide advice to parole officers regarding releasees' treatment needs and resources. You may also participate in group educational sessions as a leader or observer and provide training in alcohol or substance abuse issues. You would be responsible for making a thorough psychosocial assessment of clients' problems, needs and drug dependency, and determining the appropriate treatment modality.

The Certified Alcohol & Substance Abuse Counselor implements an established program to offer guidance, counsel and rehabilitation opportunities to participants, whose use of narcotics and/or intemperate drinking results in employability, job, social, and other problems; interviews and screens drug abusers seeking admission to addiction treatment programs; counsels patients in job training and placement, advises them of available social services and refers them to other agencies as needed; consults and confers with professional superiors regarding patient progress and services; conducts education and information sessions with drug abusers and members rapport; provides counseling and related services to alcoholics, alcohol abusers and members of the families; plans, implements and evaluates an individualized treatment plan for each client; consults clients individually and also by organizing and conducting group therapy sessions; participates in and conducts education programs for clients, their families and interested community members; maintains records and prepares statistical reports; and performs related work as required.

KNOWLEDGE, EDUCATION AND TRAINING

In order to best prepare for the written examination, it is strongly encouraged that you complete education and training in the following areas: Knowledge of the variety of models and theories of addiction and other chemical abuse and/or dependence related problems; Knowledge of the social, political, economic and cultural context within which chemical abuse and/or dependence exists; Knowledge of the behavioral, psychological, physical health and social effects of chemical abuse and/or dependence on the patient and significant others; Skill in recognizing the potential for chemical abuse and/or dependence disorders to mimic a variety of medical and psychological disorders and the potential for medical and psychological disorders to coexist with chemical abuse and/or dependence; Knowledge of the philosophies, practices, policies and outcomes of the most generally accepted models of treatment, recovery, relapse prevention and continuing care for chemical abuse and/or dependence related problems; Knowledge of the importance of family, social networks and community systems in the treatment and recovery process; Understanding of the value of an interdisciplinary approach to chemical abuse and/or dependence treatment; Skill in using the established diagnostic criteria for chemical abuse and/or dependence and understanding of the variety of treatment options and placement criteria within the continuum of care; Ability to utilize various counseling strategies and develop treatment plans based on the patient's stage of dependence or recovery; Knowledge of the medical and pharmaceutical resources in the treatment of chemical abuse and/or dependence; Ability to incorporate the special needs of diverse racial and ethnic cultures and special populations into clinical practice, including their distinct patterns of communication; Understanding of the obligation of the CASAC to engage in prevention as well as treatment techniques; Knowledge of the obligations of a CASAC to adhere to generally accepted ethical and behavioral standards of conduct in the counseling relationship; Proficiency in English including the ability to speak, write, comprehend aurally and read at a minimum level necessary to perform as a CASAC.

SCOPE OF THE EXAMINATION
The written test will cover knowledge, skills and/or abilities in such areas as:

1. Alcoholism and substance abuse;
2. Alcoholism and substance abuse counseling;
3. Assessment, clinical evaluation, treatment planning, case management, and patient, family and community education; and
4. Professional and ethical responsibilities.

HOW TO TAKE A TEST

I. YOU MUST PASS AN EXAMINATION

A. WHAT EVERY CANDIDATE SHOULD KNOW

Examination applicants often ask us for help in preparing for the written test. What can I study in advance? What kinds of questions will be asked? How will the test be given? How will the papers be graded?

As an applicant for a civil service examination, you may be wondering about some of these things. Our purpose here is to suggest effective methods of advance study and to describe civil service examinations.

Your chances for success on this examination can be increased if you know how to prepare. Those "pre-examination jitters" can be reduced if you know what to expect. You can even experience an adventure in good citizenship if you know why civil service exams are given.

B. WHY ARE CIVIL SERVICE EXAMINATIONS GIVEN?

Civil service examinations are important to you in two ways. As a citizen, you want public jobs filled by employees who know how to do their work. As a job seeker, you want a fair chance to compete for that job on an equal footing with other candidates. The best-known means of accomplishing this two-fold goal is the competitive examination.

Exams are widely publicized throughout the nation. They may be administered for jobs in federal, state, city, municipal, town or village governments or agencies.

Any citizen may apply, with some limitations, such as the age or residence of applicants. Your experience and education may be reviewed to see whether you meet the requirements for the particular examination. When these requirements exist, they are reasonable and applied consistently to all applicants. Thus, a competitive examination may cause you some uneasiness now, but it is your privilege and safeguard.

C. HOW ARE CIVIL SERVICE EXAMS DEVELOPED?

Examinations are carefully written by trained technicians who are specialists in the field known as "psychological measurement," in consultation with recognized authorities in the field of work that the test will cover. These experts recommend the subject matter areas or skills to be tested; only those knowledges or skills important to your success on the job are included. The most reliable books and source materials available are used as references. Together, the experts and technicians judge the difficulty level of the questions.

Test technicians know how to phrase questions so that the problem is clearly stated. Their ethics do not permit "trick" or "catch" questions. Questions may have been tried out on sample groups, or subjected to statistical analysis, to determine their usefulness.

Written tests are often used in combination with performance tests, ratings of training and experience, and oral interviews. All of these measures combine to form the best-known means of finding the right person for the right job.

II. HOW TO PASS THE WRITTEN TEST

A. NATURE OF THE EXAMINATION

To prepare intelligently for civil service examinations, you should know how they differ from school examinations you have taken. In school you were assigned certain definite pages to read or subjects to cover. The examination questions were quite detailed and usually emphasized memory. Civil service exams, on the other hand, try to discover your present ability to perform the duties of a position, plus your potentiality to learn these duties. In other words, a civil service exam attempts to predict how successful you will be. Questions cover such a broad area that they cannot be as minute and detailed as school exam questions.

In the public service similar kinds of work, or positions, are grouped together in one "class." This process is known as *position-classification*. All the positions in a class are paid according to the salary range for that class. One class title covers all of these positions, and they are all tested by the same examination.

B. FOUR BASIC STEPS

1) Study the announcement

How, then, can you know what subjects to study? Our best answer is: "Learn as much as possible about the class of positions for which you've applied." The exam will test the knowledge, skills and abilities needed to do the work.

Your most valuable source of information about the position you want is the official exam announcement. This announcement lists the training and experience qualifications. Check these standards and apply only if you come reasonably close to meeting them.

The brief description of the position in the examination announcement offers some clues to the subjects which will be tested. Think about the job itself. Review the duties in your mind. Can you perform them, or are there some in which you are rusty? Fill in the blank spots in your preparation.

Many jurisdictions preview the written test in the exam announcement by including a section called "Knowledge and Abilities Required," "Scope of the Examination," or some similar heading. Here you will find out specifically what fields will be tested.

2) Review your own background

Once you learn in general what the position is all about, and what you need to know to do the work, ask yourself which subjects you already know fairly well and which need improvement. You may wonder whether to concentrate on improving your strong areas or on building some background in your fields of weakness. When the announcement has specified "some knowledge" or "considerable knowledge," or has used adjectives like "beginning principles of..." or "advanced ... methods," you can get a clue as to the number and difficulty of questions to be asked in any given field. More questions, and hence broader coverage, would be included for those subjects which are more important in the work. Now weigh your strengths and weaknesses against the job requirements and prepare accordingly.

3) Determine the level of the position

Another way to tell how intensively you should prepare is to understand the level of the job for which you are applying. Is it the entering level? In other words, is this the position in which beginners in a field of work are hired? Or is it an intermediate or advanced level? Sometimes this is indicated by such words as "Junior" or "Senior" in the class title. Other jurisdictions use Roman numerals to designate the level – Clerk I, Clerk II, for example. The word "Supervisor" sometimes appears in the title. If the level is not indicated by the title, check the description of duties. Will you be working under very close supervision, or will you have responsibility for independent decisions in this work?

4) Choose appropriate study materials

Now that you know the subjects to be examined and the relative amount of each subject to be covered, you can choose suitable study materials. For beginning level jobs, or even advanced ones, if you have a pronounced weakness in some aspect of your training, read a modern, standard textbook in that field. Be sure it is up to date and has general coverage. Such books are normally available at your library, and the librarian will be glad to help you locate one. For entry-level positions, questions of appropriate difficulty are chosen – neither highly advanced questions, nor those too simple. Such questions require careful thought but not advanced training.

If the position for which you are applying is technical or advanced, you will read more advanced, specialized material. If you are already familiar with the basic principles of your field, elementary textbooks would waste your time. Concentrate on advanced textbooks and technical periodicals. Think through the concepts and review difficult problems in your field.

These are all general sources. You can get more ideas on your own initiative, following these leads. For example, training manuals and publications of the government agency which employs workers in your field can be useful, particularly for technical and professional positions. A letter or visit to the government department involved may result in more specific study suggestions, and certainly will provide you with a more definite idea of the exact nature of the position you are seeking.

III. KINDS OF TESTS

Tests are used for purposes other than measuring knowledge and ability to perform specified duties. For some positions, it is equally important to test ability to make adjustments to new situations or to profit from training. In others, basic mental abilities not dependent on information are essential. Questions which test these things may not appear as pertinent to the duties of the position as those which test for knowledge and information. Yet they are often highly important parts of a fair examination. For very general questions, it is almost impossible to help you direct your study efforts. What we can do is to point out some of the more common of these general abilities needed in public service positions and describe some typical questions.

1) General information

Broad, general information has been found useful for predicting job success in some kinds of work. This is tested in a variety of ways, from vocabulary lists to questions about current events. Basic background in some field of work, such as sociology or economics, may be sampled in a group of questions. Often these are principles which have become familiar to most persons through exposure rather than through formal training. It is difficult to advise you how to study for these questions; being alert to the world around you is our best suggestion.

2) Verbal ability

An example of an ability needed in many positions is verbal or language ability. Verbal ability is, in brief, the ability to use and understand words. Vocabulary and grammar tests are typical measures of this ability. Reading comprehension or paragraph interpretation questions are common in many kinds of civil service tests. You are given a paragraph of written material and asked to find its central meaning.

3) Numerical ability

Number skills can be tested by the familiar arithmetic problem, by checking paired lists of numbers to see which are alike and which are different, or by interpreting charts and graphs. In the latter test, a graph may be printed in the test booklet which you are asked to use as the basis for answering questions.

4) Observation

A popular test for law-enforcement positions is the observation test. A picture is shown to you for several minutes, then taken away. Questions about the picture test your ability to observe both details and larger elements.

5) Following directions

In many positions in the public service, the employee must be able to carry out written instructions dependably and accurately. You may be given a chart with several columns, each column listing a variety of information. The questions require you to carry out directions involving the information given in the chart.

6) Skills and aptitudes

Performance tests effectively measure some manual skills and aptitudes. When the skill is one in which you are trained, such as typing or shorthand, you can practice. These tests are often very much like those given in business school or high school courses. For many of the other skills and aptitudes, however, no short-time preparation can be made. Skills and abilities natural to you or that you have developed throughout your lifetime are being tested.

Many of the general questions just described provide all the data needed to answer the questions and ask you to use your reasoning ability to find the answers. Your best preparation for these tests, as well as for tests of facts and ideas, is to be at your physical and mental best. You, no doubt, have your own methods of getting into an exam-taking mood and keeping "in shape." The next section lists some ideas on this subject.

IV. KINDS OF QUESTIONS

Only rarely is the "essay" question, which you answer in narrative form, used in civil service tests. Civil service tests are usually of the short-answer type. Full instructions for answering these questions will be given to you at the examination. But in case this is your first experience with short-answer questions and separate answer sheets, here is what you need to know:

1) Multiple-choice Questions

Most popular of the short-answer questions is the "multiple choice" or "best answer" question. It can be used, for example, to test for factual knowledge, ability to solve problems or judgment in meeting situations found at work.

A multiple-choice question is normally one of three types—
- It can begin with an incomplete statement followed by several possible endings. You are to find the one ending which *best* completes the statement, although some of the others may not be entirely wrong.
- It can also be a complete statement in the form of a question which is answered by choosing one of the statements listed.

- It can be in the form of a problem – again you select the best answer.

Here is an example of a multiple-choice question with a discussion which should give you some clues as to the method for choosing the right answer:

When an employee has a complaint about his assignment, the action which will *best* help him overcome his difficulty is to
  A. discuss his difficulty with his coworkers
  B. take the problem to the head of the organization
  C. take the problem to the person who gave him the assignment
  D. say nothing to anyone about his complaint

In answering this question, you should study each of the choices to find which is best. Consider choice "A" – Certainly an employee may discuss his complaint with fellow employees, but no change or improvement can result, and the complaint remains unresolved. Choice "B" is a poor choice since the head of the organization probably does not know what assignment you have been given, and taking your problem to him is known as "going over the head" of the supervisor. The supervisor, or person who made the assignment, is the person who can clarify it or correct any injustice. Choice "C" is, therefore, correct. To say nothing, as in choice "D," is unwise. Supervisors have and interest in knowing the problems employees are facing, and the employee is seeking a solution to his problem.

2) True/False Questions

The "true/false" or "right/wrong" form of question is sometimes used. Here a complete statement is given. Your job is to decide whether the statement is right or wrong.

SAMPLE: A roaming cell-phone call to a nearby city costs less than a non-roaming call to a distant city.

This statement is wrong, or false, since roaming calls are more expensive.

This is not a complete list of all possible question forms, although most of the others are variations of these common types. You will always get complete directions for answering questions. Be sure you understand *how* to mark your answers – ask questions until you do.

V. RECORDING YOUR ANSWERS

Computer terminals are used more and more today for many different kinds of exams.

For an examination with very few applicants, you may be told to record your answers in the test booklet itself. Separate answer sheets are much more common. If this separate answer sheet is to be scored by machine – and this is often the case – it is highly important that you mark your answers correctly in order to get credit.

An electronic scoring machine is often used in civil service offices because of the speed with which papers can be scored. Machine-scored answer sheets must be marked with a pencil, which will be given to you. This pencil has a high graphite content which responds to the electronic scoring machine. As a matter of fact, stray dots may register as answers, so do not let your pencil rest on the answer sheet while you are pondering the correct answer. Also, if your pencil lead breaks or is otherwise defective, ask for another.

Since the answer sheet will be dropped in a slot in the scoring machine, be careful not to bend the corners or get the paper crumpled.

The answer sheet normally has five vertical columns of numbers, with 30 numbers to a column. These numbers correspond to the question numbers in your test booklet. After each number, going across the page are four or five pairs of dotted lines. These short dotted lines have small letters or numbers above them. The first two pairs may also have a "T" or "F" above the letters. This indicates that the first two pairs only are to be used if the questions are of the true-false type. If the questions are multiple choice, disregard the "T" and "F" and pay attention only to the small letters or numbers.

Answer your questions in the manner of the sample that follows:

32. The largest city in the United States is
     A. Washington, D.C.
     B. New York City
     C. Chicago
     D. Detroit
     E. San Francisco

1) Choose the answer you think is best. (New York City is the largest, so "B" is correct.)
2) Find the row of dotted lines numbered the same as the question you are answering. (Find row number 32)
3) Find the pair of dotted lines corresponding to the answer. (Find the pair of lines under the mark "B.")
4) Make a solid black mark between the dotted lines.

VI. BEFORE THE TEST

Common sense will help you find procedures to follow to get ready for an examination. Too many of us, however, overlook these sensible measures. Indeed, nervousness and fatigue have been found to be the most serious reasons why applicants fail to do their best on civil service tests. Here is a list of reminders:

- Begin your preparation early – Don't wait until the last minute to go scurrying around for books and materials or to find out what the position is all about.
- Prepare continuously – An hour a night for a week is better than an all-night cram session. This has been definitely established. What is more, a night a week for a month will return better dividends than crowding your study into a shorter period of time.
- Locate the place of the exam – You have been sent a notice telling you when and where to report for the examination. If the location is in a different town or otherwise unfamiliar to you, it would be well to inquire the best route and learn something about the building.
- Relax the night before the test – Allow your mind to rest. Do not study at all that night. Plan some mild recreation or diversion; then go to bed early and get a good night's sleep.
- Get up early enough to make a leisurely trip to the place for the test – This way unforeseen events, traffic snarls, unfamiliar buildings, etc. will not upset you.
- Dress comfortably – A written test is not a fashion show. You will be known by number and not by name, so wear something comfortable.

- Leave excess paraphernalia at home – Shopping bags and odd bundles will get in your way. You need bring only the items mentioned in the official notice you received; usually everything you need is provided. Do not bring reference books to the exam. They will only confuse those last minutes and be taken away from you when in the test room.
- Arrive somewhat ahead of time – If because of transportation schedules you must get there very early, bring a newspaper or magazine to take your mind off yourself while waiting.
- Locate the examination room – When you have found the proper room, you will be directed to the seat or part of the room where you will sit. Sometimes you are given a sheet of instructions to read while you are waiting. Do not fill out any forms until you are told to do so; just read them and be prepared.
- Relax and prepare to listen to the instructions
- If you have any physical problem that may keep you from doing your best, be sure to tell the test administrator. If you are sick or in poor health, you really cannot do your best on the exam. You can come back and take the test some other time.

VII. AT THE TEST

The day of the test is here and you have the test booklet in your hand. The temptation to get going is very strong. Caution! There is more to success than knowing the right answers. You must know how to identify your papers and understand variations in the type of short-answer question used in this particular examination. Follow these suggestions for maximum results from your efforts:

1) Cooperate with the monitor

The test administrator has a duty to create a situation in which you can be as much at ease as possible. He will give instructions, tell you when to begin, check to see that you are marking your answer sheet correctly, and so on. He is not there to guard you, although he will see that your competitors do not take unfair advantage. He wants to help you do your best.

2) Listen to all instructions

Don't jump the gun! Wait until you understand all directions. In most civil service tests you get more time than you need to answer the questions. So don't be in a hurry. Read each word of instructions until you clearly understand the meaning. Study the examples, listen to all announcements and follow directions. Ask questions if you do not understand what to do.

3) Identify your papers

Civil service exams are usually identified by number only. You will be assigned a number; you must not put your name on your test papers. Be sure to copy your number correctly. Since more than one exam may be given, copy your exact examination title.

4) Plan your time

Unless you are told that a test is a "speed" or "rate of work" test, speed itself is usually not important. Time enough to answer all the questions will be provided, but this does not mean that you have all day. An overall time limit has been set. Divide the total time (in minutes) by the number of questions to determine the approximate time you have for each question.

5) Do not linger over difficult questions

If you come across a difficult question, mark it with a paper clip (useful to have along) and come back to it when you have been through the booklet. One caution if you do this – be sure to skip a number on your answer sheet as well. Check often to be sure that you have not lost your place and that you are marking in the row numbered the same as the question you are answering.

6) Read the questions

Be sure you know what the question asks! Many capable people are unsuccessful because they failed to *read* the questions correctly.

7) Answer all questions

Unless you have been instructed that a penalty will be deducted for incorrect answers, it is better to guess than to omit a question.

8) Speed tests

It is often better NOT to guess on speed tests. It has been found that on timed tests people are tempted to spend the last few seconds before time is called in marking answers at random – without even reading them – in the hope of picking up a few extra points. To discourage this practice, the instructions may warn you that your score will be "corrected" for guessing. That is, a penalty will be applied. The incorrect answers will be deducted from the correct ones, or some other penalty formula will be used.

9) Review your answers

If you finish before time is called, go back to the questions you guessed or omitted to give them further thought. Review other answers if you have time.

10) Return your test materials

If you are ready to leave before others have finished or time is called, take ALL your materials to the monitor and leave quietly. Never take any test material with you. The monitor can discover whose papers are not complete, and taking a test booklet may be grounds for disqualification.

VIII. EXAMINATION TECHNIQUES

1) Read the general instructions carefully. These are usually printed on the first page of the exam booklet. As a rule, these instructions refer to the timing of the examination; the fact that you should not start work until the signal and must stop work at a signal, etc. If there are any *special* instructions, such as a choice of questions to be answered, make sure that you note this instruction carefully.

2) When you are ready to start work on the examination, that is as soon as the signal has been given, read the instructions to each question booklet, underline any key words or phrases, such as *least, best, outline, describe* and the like. In this way you will tend to answer as requested rather than discover on reviewing your paper that you *listed without describing*, that you selected the *worst* choice rather than the *best* choice, etc.

3) If the examination is of the objective or multiple-choice type – that is, each question will also give a series of possible answers: A, B, C or D, and you are called upon to select the best answer and write the letter next to that answer on your answer paper – it is advisable to start answering each question in turn. There may be anywhere from 50 to 100 such questions in the three or four hours allotted and you can see how much time would be taken if you read through all the questions before beginning to answer any. Furthermore, if you come across a question or group of questions which you know would be difficult to answer, it would undoubtedly affect your handling of all the other questions.

4) If the examination is of the essay type and contains but a few questions, it is a moot point as to whether you should read all the questions before starting to answer any one. Of course, if you are given a choice – say five out of seven and the like – then it is essential to read all the questions so you can eliminate the two that are most difficult. If, however, you are asked to answer all the questions, there may be danger in trying to answer the easiest one first because you may find that you will spend too much time on it. The best technique is to answer the first question, then proceed to the second, etc.

5) Time your answers. Before the exam begins, write down the time it started, then add the time allowed for the examination and write down the time it must be completed, then divide the time available somewhat as follows:
   - If 3-1/2 hours are allowed, that would be 210 minutes. If you have 80 objective-type questions, that would be an average of 2-1/2 minutes per question. Allow yourself no more than 2 minutes per question, or a total of 160 minutes, which will permit about 50 minutes to review.
   - If for the time allotment of 210 minutes there are 7 essay questions to answer, that would average about 30 minutes a question. Give yourself only 25 minutes per question so that you have about 35 minutes to review.

6) The most important instruction is to *read each question* and make sure you know what is wanted. The second most important instruction is to *time yourself properly* so that you answer every question. The third most important instruction is to *answer every question*. Guess if you have to but include something for each question. Remember that you will receive no credit for a blank and will probably receive some credit if you write something in answer to an essay question. If you guess a letter – say "B" for a multiple-choice question – you may have guessed right. If you leave a blank as an answer to a multiple-choice question, the examiners may respect your feelings but it will not add a point to your score. Some exams may penalize you for wrong answers, so in such cases *only*, you may not want to guess unless you have some basis for your answer.

7) Suggestions
   a. Objective-type questions
      1. Examine the question booklet for proper sequence of pages and questions
      2. Read all instructions carefully
      3. Skip any question which seems too difficult; return to it after all other questions have been answered
      4. Apportion your time properly; do not spend too much time on any single question or group of questions

5. Note and underline key words – *all, most, fewest, least, best, worst, same, opposite*, etc.
6. Pay particular attention to negatives
7. Note unusual option, e.g., unduly long, short, complex, different or similar in content to the body of the question
8. Observe the use of "hedging" words – *probably, may, most likely*, etc.
9. Make sure that your answer is put next to the same number as the question
10. Do not second-guess unless you have good reason to believe the second answer is definitely more correct
11. Cross out original answer if you decide another answer is more accurate; do not erase until you are ready to hand your paper in
12. Answer all questions; guess unless instructed otherwise
13. Leave time for review

  b. Essay questions
    1. Read each question carefully
    2. Determine exactly what is wanted. Underline key words or phrases.
    3. Decide on outline or paragraph answer
    4. Include many different points and elements unless asked to develop any one or two points or elements
    5. Show impartiality by giving pros and cons unless directed to select one side only
    6. Make and write down any assumptions you find necessary to answer the questions
    7. Watch your English, grammar, punctuation and choice of words
    8. Time your answers; don't crowd material

8) Answering the essay question

Most essay questions can be answered by framing the specific response around several key words or ideas. Here are a few such key words or ideas:

M's: manpower, materials, methods, money, management
P's: purpose, program, policy, plan, procedure, practice, problems, pitfalls, personnel, public relations

  a. Six basic steps in handling problems:
    1. Preliminary plan and background development
    2. Collect information, data and facts
    3. Analyze and interpret information, data and facts
    4. Analyze and develop solutions as well as make recommendations
    5. Prepare report and sell recommendations
    6. Install recommendations and follow up effectiveness

  b. Pitfalls to avoid
    1. *Taking things for granted* – A statement of the situation does not necessarily imply that each of the elements is necessarily true; for example, a complaint may be invalid and biased so that all that can be taken for granted is that a complaint has been registered

2. *Considering only one side of a situation* – Wherever possible, indicate several alternatives and then point out the reasons you selected the best one
3. *Failing to indicate follow up* – Whenever your answer indicates action on your part, make certain that you will take proper follow-up action to see how successful your recommendations, procedures or actions turn out to be
4. *Taking too long in answering any single question* – Remember to time your answers properly

IX. AFTER THE TEST

Scoring procedures differ in detail among civil service jurisdictions although the general principles are the same. Whether the papers are hand-scored or graded by machine we have described, they are nearly always graded by number. That is, the person who marks the paper knows only the number – never the name – of the applicant. Not until all the papers have been graded will they be matched with names. If other tests, such as training and experience or oral interview ratings have been given, scores will be combined. Different parts of the examination usually have different weights. For example, the written test might count 60 percent of the final grade, and a rating of training and experience 40 percent. In many jurisdictions, veterans will have a certain number of points added to their grades.

After the final grade has been determined, the names are placed in grade order and an eligible list is established. There are various methods for resolving ties between those who get the same final grade – probably the most common is to place first the name of the person whose application was received first. Job offers are made from the eligible list in the order the names appear on it. You will be notified of your grade and your rank as soon as all these computations have been made. This will be done as rapidly as possible.

People who are found to meet the requirements in the announcement are called "eligibles." Their names are put on a list of eligible candidates. An eligible's chances of getting a job depend on how high he stands on this list and how fast agencies are filling jobs from the list.

When a job is to be filled from a list of eligibles, the agency asks for the names of people on the list of eligibles for that job. When the civil service commission receives this request, it sends to the agency the names of the three people highest on this list. Or, if the job to be filled has specialized requirements, the office sends the agency the names of the top three persons who meet these requirements from the general list.

The appointing officer makes a choice from among the three people whose names were sent to him. If the selected person accepts the appointment, the names of the others are put back on the list to be considered for future openings.

That is the rule in hiring from all kinds of eligible lists, whether they are for typist, carpenter, chemist, or something else. For every vacancy, the appointing officer has his choice of any one of the top three eligibles on the list. This explains why the person whose name is on top of the list sometimes does not get an appointment when some of the persons lower on the list do. If the appointing officer chooses the second or third eligible, the No. 1 eligible does not get a job at once, but stays on the list until he is appointed or the list is terminated.

X. HOW TO PASS THE INTERVIEW TEST

The examination for which you applied requires an oral interview test. You have already taken the written test and you are now being called for the interview test – the final part of the formal examination.

You may think that it is not possible to prepare for an interview test and that there are no procedures to follow during an interview. Our purpose is to point out some things you can do in advance that will help you and some good rules to follow and pitfalls to avoid while you are being interviewed.

What is an interview supposed to test?

The written examination is designed to test the technical knowledge and competence of the candidate; the oral is designed to evaluate intangible qualities, not readily measured otherwise, and to establish a list showing the relative fitness of each candidate – as measured against his competitors – for the position sought. Scoring is not on the basis of "right" and "wrong," but on a sliding scale of values ranging from "not passable" to "outstanding." As a matter of fact, it is possible to achieve a relatively low score without a single "incorrect" answer because of evident weakness in the qualities being measured.

Occasionally, an examination may consist entirely of an oral test – either an individual or a group oral. In such cases, information is sought concerning the technical knowledges and abilities of the candidate, since there has been no written examination for this purpose. More commonly, however, an oral test is used to supplement a written examination.

Who conducts interviews?

The composition of oral boards varies among different jurisdictions. In nearly all, a representative of the personnel department serves as chairman. One of the members of the board may be a representative of the department in which the candidate would work. In some cases, "outside experts" are used, and, frequently, a businessman or some other representative of the general public is asked to serve. Labor and management or other special groups may be represented. The aim is to secure the services of experts in the appropriate field.

However the board is composed, it is a good idea (and not at all improper or unethical) to ascertain in advance of the interview who the members are and what groups they represent. When you are introduced to them, you will have some idea of their backgrounds and interests, and at least you will not stutter and stammer over their names.

What should be done before the interview?

While knowledge about the board members is useful and takes some of the surprise element out of the interview, there is other preparation which is more substantive. It *is* possible to prepare for an oral interview – in several ways:

1) Keep a copy of your application and review it carefully before the interview

This may be the only document before the oral board, and the starting point of the interview. Know what education and experience you have listed there, and the sequence and dates of all of it. Sometimes the board will ask you to review the highlights of your experience for them; you should not have to hem and haw doing it.

2) Study the class specification and the examination announcement

Usually, the oral board has one or both of these to guide them. The qualities, characteristics or knowledges required by the position sought are stated in these documents. They offer valuable clues as to the nature of the oral interview. For example, if the job involves supervisory responsibilities, the announcement will usually indicate that knowledge of modern supervisory methods and the qualifications of the candidate as a supervisor will be tested. If so, you can expect such questions, frequently in the form of a hypothetical situation which you are expected to solve. NEVER go into an oral without knowledge of the duties and responsibilities of the job you seek.

3) Think through each qualification required

Try to visualize the kind of questions you would ask if you were a board member. How well could you answer them? Try especially to appraise your own knowledge and background in each area, *measured against the job sought*, and identify any areas in which you are weak. Be critical and realistic – do not flatter yourself.

4) Do some general reading in areas in which you feel you may be weak

For example, if the job involves supervision and your past experience has NOT, some general reading in supervisory methods and practices, particularly in the field of human relations, might be useful. Do NOT study agency procedures or detailed manuals. The oral board will be testing your understanding and capacity, not your memory.

5) Get a good night's sleep and watch your general health and mental attitude

You will want a clear head at the interview. Take care of a cold or any other minor ailment, and of course, no hangovers.

What should be done on the day of the interview?

Now comes the day of the interview itself. Give yourself plenty of time to get there. Plan to arrive somewhat ahead of the scheduled time, particularly if your appointment is in the fore part of the day. If a previous candidate fails to appear, the board might be ready for you a bit early. By early afternoon an oral board is almost invariably behind schedule if there are many candidates, and you may have to wait. Take along a book or magazine to read, or your application to review, but leave any extraneous material in the waiting room when you go in for your interview. In any event, relax and compose yourself.

The matter of dress is important. The board is forming impressions about you – from your experience, your manners, your attitude, and your appearance. Give your personal appearance careful attention. Dress your best, but not your flashiest. Choose conservative, appropriate clothing, and be sure it is immaculate. This is a business interview, and your appearance should indicate that you regard it as such. Besides, being well groomed and properly dressed will help boost your confidence.

Sooner or later, someone will call your name and escort you into the interview room. *This is it.* From here on you are on your own. It is too late for any more preparation. But remember, you asked for this opportunity to prove your fitness, and you are here because your request was granted.

What happens when you go in?

The usual sequence of events will be as follows: The clerk (who is often the board stenographer) will introduce you to the chairman of the oral board, who will introduce you to the other members of the board. Acknowledge the introductions before you sit down. Do not be surprised if you find a microphone facing you or a stenotypist sitting by. Oral interviews are usually recorded in the event of an appeal or other review.

Usually the chairman of the board will open the interview by reviewing the highlights of your education and work experience from your application – primarily for the benefit of the other members of the board, as well as to get the material into the record. Do not interrupt or comment unless there is an error or significant misinterpretation; if that is the case, do not hesitate. But do not quibble about insignificant matters. Also, he will usually ask you some question about your education, experience or your present job – partly to get you to start talking and to establish the interviewing "rapport." He may start the actual questioning, or turn it over to one of the other members. Frequently, each member undertakes the questioning on a particular area, one in which he is perhaps most competent, so you can expect each member to participate in the examination. Because time is limited, you may also expect some rather abrupt switches in the direction the questioning takes, so do not be upset by it. Normally, a board member will not pursue a single line of questioning unless he discovers a particular strength or weakness.

After each member has participated, the chairman will usually ask whether any member has any further questions, then will ask you if you have anything you wish to add. Unless you are expecting this question, it may floor you. Worse, it may start you off on an extended, extemporaneous speech. The board is not usually seeking more information. The question is principally to offer you a last opportunity to present further qualifications or to indicate that you have nothing to add. So, if you feel that a significant qualification or characteristic has been overlooked, it is proper to point it out in a sentence or so. Do not compliment the board on the thoroughness of their examination – they have been sketchy, and you know it. If you wish, merely say, "No thank you, I have nothing further to add." This is a point where you can "talk yourself out" of a good impression or fail to present an important bit of information. Remember, *you close the interview yourself*.

The chairman will then say, "That is all, Mr. _____, thank you." Do not be startled; the interview is over, and quicker than you think. Thank him, gather your belongings and take your leave. Save your sigh of relief for the other side of the door.

How to put your best foot forward

Throughout this entire process, you may feel that the board individually and collectively is trying to pierce your defenses, seek out your hidden weaknesses and embarrass and confuse you. Actually, this is not true. They are obliged to make an appraisal of your qualifications for the job you are seeking, and they want to see you in your best light. Remember, they must interview all candidates and a non-cooperative candidate may become a failure in spite of their best efforts to bring out his qualifications. Here are 15 suggestions that will help you:

1) Be natural – Keep your attitude confident, not cocky

If you are not confident that you can do the job, do not expect the board to be. Do not apologize for your weaknesses, try to bring out your strong points. The board is interested in a positive, not negative, presentation. Cockiness will antagonize any board member and make him wonder if you are covering up a weakness by a false show of strength.

2) Get comfortable, but don't lounge or sprawl

Sit erectly but not stiffly. A careless posture may lead the board to conclude that you are careless in other things, or at least that you are not impressed by the importance of the occasion. Either conclusion is natural, even if incorrect. Do not fuss with your clothing, a pencil or an ashtray. Your hands may occasionally be useful to emphasize a point; do not let them become a point of distraction.

3) Do not wisecrack or make small talk

This is a serious situation, and your attitude should show that you consider it as such. Further, the time of the board is limited – they do not want to waste it, and neither should you.

4) Do not exaggerate your experience or abilities

In the first place, from information in the application or other interviews and sources, the board may know more about you than you think. Secondly, you probably will not get away with it. An experienced board is rather adept at spotting such a situation, so do not take the chance.

5) If you know a board member, do not make a point of it, yet do not hide it

Certainly you are not fooling him, and probably not the other members of the board. Do not try to take advantage of your acquaintanceship – it will probably do you little good.

6) Do not dominate the interview

Let the board do that. They will give you the clues – do not assume that you have to do all the talking. Realize that the board has a number of questions to ask you, and do not try to take up all the interview time by showing off your extensive knowledge of the answer to the first one.

7) Be attentive

You only have 20 minutes or so, and you should keep your attention at its sharpest throughout. When a member is addressing a problem or question to you, give him your undivided attention. Address your reply principally to him, but do not exclude the other board members.

8) Do not interrupt

A board member may be stating a problem for you to analyze. He will ask you a question when the time comes. Let him state the problem, and wait for the question.

9) Make sure you understand the question

Do not try to answer until you are sure what the question is. If it is not clear, restate it in your own words or ask the board member to clarify it for you. However, do not haggle about minor elements.

10) Reply promptly but not hastily

A common entry on oral board rating sheets is "candidate responded readily," or "candidate hesitated in replies." Respond as promptly and quickly as you can, but do not jump to a hasty, ill-considered answer.

11) Do not be peremptory in your answers

A brief answer is proper – but do not fire your answer back. That is a losing game from your point of view. The board member can probably ask questions much faster than you can answer them.

12) Do not try to create the answer you think the board member wants

He is interested in what kind of mind you have and how it works – not in playing games. Furthermore, he can usually spot this practice and will actually grade you down on it.

13) Do not switch sides in your reply merely to agree with a board member

Frequently, a member will take a contrary position merely to draw you out and to see if you are willing and able to defend your point of view. Do not start a debate, yet do not surrender a good position. If a position is worth taking, it is worth defending.

14) Do not be afraid to admit an error in judgment if you are shown to be wrong

The board knows that you are forced to reply without any opportunity for careful consideration. Your answer may be demonstrably wrong. If so, admit it and get on with the interview.

15) Do not dwell at length on your present job

The opening question may relate to your present assignment. Answer the question but do not go into an extended discussion. You are being examined for a *new* job, not your present one. As a matter of fact, try to phrase ALL your answers in terms of the job for which you are being examined.

Basis of Rating

Probably you will forget most of these "do's" and "don'ts" when you walk into the oral interview room. Even remembering them all will not ensure you a passing grade. Perhaps you did not have the qualifications in the first place. But remembering them will help you to put your best foot forward, without treading on the toes of the board members.

Rumor and popular opinion to the contrary notwithstanding, an oral board wants you to make the best appearance possible. They know you are under pressure – but they also want to see how you respond to it as a guide to what your reaction would be under the pressures of the job you seek. They will be influenced by the degree of poise you display, the personal traits you show and the manner in which you respond.

ABOUT THIS BOOK

This book contains tests divided into Examination Sections. Go through each test, answering every question in the margin. We have also attached a sample answer sheet at the back of the book that can be removed and used. At the end of each test look at the answer key and check your answers. On the ones you got wrong, look at the right answer choice and learn. Do not fill in the answers first. Do not memorize the questions and answers, but understand the answer and principles involved. On your test, the questions will likely be different from the samples. Questions are changed and new ones added. If you understand these past questions you should have success with any changes that arise. Tests may consist of several types of questions. We have additional books on each subject should more study be advisable or necessary for you. Finally, the more you study, the better prepared you will be. This book is intended to be the last thing you study before you walk into the examination room. Prior study of relevant texts is also recommended. NLC publishes some of these in our Fundamental Series. Knowledge and good sense are important factors in passing your exam. Good luck also helps. So now study this Passbook, absorb the material contained within and take that knowledge into the examination. Then do your best to pass that exam.

EXAMINATION SECTION

EXAMINATION SECTION
TEST 1

DIRECTIONS: Each question or incomplete statement is followed by several suggested answers or completions. Select the one that BEST answers the question or completes the statement. *PRINT THE LETTER OF THE CORRECT ANSWER IN THE SPACE AT THE RIGHT.*

1. Which of the following is NOT an inherent characteristic of addiction? 1.____

    A. Tolerance changes
    B. Dissolution of relationships
    C. Physiological dependence
    D. Loss of self-control

2. Which type of factor in an individual's predisposition to addiction has the GREATEST potential to increase the risk of addiction after exposure to a substance? 2.____

    A. Genetic   B. Constitutional   C. Psychological   D. Sociocultural

3. The enabling behavior MOST likely practiced by the addicted person's family members in the early stages of addiction are 3.____

    A. cooperation and collaboration
    B. protecting and shielding
    C. codependence and cohabitation
    D. control and guilt

4. When making initial inquiries about an addicted person's drug or alcohol abuse patterns and history, which of the following is probably the LEAST reliable? 4.____

    A. Information provided by the subject's friends and relatives
    B. Information provided by the patient or subject
    C. Medical histories of subject's family members
    D. Subject's medical record

5. Which of the following is NOT one of the physical factors influencing addiction? 5.____

    A. Heredity
    B. Brain chemistry
    C. Metabolism
    D. Race

6. In a recovery treatment center, which of the following behaviors or characteristics gives the STRONGEST indication that a subject is still addicted? 6.____

    A. Feeling caged or jailed
    B. Mood swings
    C. Nervousness
    D. Depression

7. Which of the following is NOT true of *leverages* used by members of an intervention team to induce an addicted person to voluntarily submit to treatment? 7.____
They should

    A. only be used as a last resort
    B. not be carried out if they will result in isolating the addicted person
    C. be agreed upon and supported by every member of the intervention team
    D. not be threatened unless they will definitely be implemented

8. What percentage of untreated alcoholics will eventually experience seizures?

    A. 5-15% B. 20-30% C. 40-50% D. 55-75%

9. Which of the following is a sign that an adolescent has entered the late stages of addiction?

    A. Impulsiveness
    B. Decrease in attention span
    C. Chronic depression
    D. Denial

10. The type of drug dependency requiring the longest treatment time is USUALLY caused by

    A. alcohol
    B. amphetamines
    C. opiates or cocaine
    D. hallucinogens

11. Which of the following is NOT one of the primary factors in the formula that results in addiction?

    A. Drug effect
    B. Social constraints
    C. Predisposition for abuse
    D. Enabling factors

12. Drugs sometimes used in detoxification and which occupy a person's opiate-receptor sites without creating an accompanying sense of euphoria or loss of consciousness are

    A. opioids
    B. opiates
    C. agonists
    D. placebos

13. The normalization process during the late recovery phase of treatment includes

    A. increasingly sobriety-centered lifestyle
    B. discussion of drug hunger
    C. personality growth
    D. stress reduction techniques

14. Which of the following unconscious defense mechanisms, used by an addicted person, is characterized by partial awareness of the severity of the addiction?

    A. Denial
    B. Minimization
    C. Rationalization
    D. Isolation

15. The characteristic of an addicted person's recovery illustrated by the person's attempt to repair the relationships damaged by his/her addiction is

    A. fellowship
    B. surrender
    C. admission
    D. restitution

16. Which of the following is a sign that a drinker has entered the late stages of alcoholism?

    A. Progressive increase in drinking
    B. Broken promises to friends and family
    C. Personality changes
    D. Malnutrition

17. An alcoholic subject is said to have entered stage four of the withdrawal process if he or she experiences

   A. seizures
   B. delirium tremens
   C. vomiting
   D. hallucinations

18. Which of the following unconscious defense mechanisms, used by an addicted person, is characterized by an avoidance of feelings through focusing on logic?

   A. Rationalization
   B. Intellectualization
   C. Repression
   D. Projection

19. Measuring from the starting point of detoxification, what is typically the amount of time required for a recovering person to regain the level of health and well-being associated with his/her pre-addiction lifestyle?

   A. 6 months   B. 1 year   C. 18 months   D. 3 years

20. A characteristic that typically differentiates teenage alcoholism from adult alcoholism is that teenagers

   A. are more likely to explain that they drink to celebrate or be sociable
   B. have a more difficult time with recovery
   C. claim drinking as an escape from life's problems
   D. sustain less physiological damage

21. Which type of recovery treatment is reserved for the most advanced cases of addiction?

   A. Day treatment
   B. Residential treatment
   C. Inpatient hospitalization
   D. Partial hospitalization

22. The use of which opiate drug typically carries the LOWEST risk for dependency or abuse?

   A. Percodan   B. Methadone   C. Codeine   D. Demerol

23. What is the APPROXIMATE mortality rate for alcoholic patients who suffer from delirium tremens?

   A. Zero   B. 1-10%   C. 10-20%   D. 20-30%

24. Addiction is a process influenced primarily by each of the following EXCEPT

   A. factors relating to the individual user
   B. various social factors
   C. factors relating to specific physiological health concerns
   D. factors relating to the drug being used

25. Which of the following statements about alcoholism is NOT true?

   A. Children of alcoholics often learn alcoholic behavior from their parents.
   B. Divorce, loss of a job, death of a loved one, and other life traumas can cause alcoholism.
   C. Alcoholism is often a symptom of larger psychological problems.
   D. An alcoholic in the throes of the disease drinks to avoid self-destruction.

KEY (CORRECT ANSWERS)

1.	B	11.	B
2.	A	12.	C
3.	B	13.	C
4.	B	14.	B
5.	D	15.	D
6.	A	16.	D
7.	B	17.	B
8.	A	18.	B
9.	C	19.	C
10.	C	20.	A

21. C
22. C
23. C
24. C
25. D

TEST 2

DIRECTIONS: Each question or incomplete statement is followed by several suggested answers or completions. Select the one that BEST answers the question or completes the statement. *PRINT THE LETTER OF THE CORRECT ANSWER IN THE SPACE AT THE RIGHT.*

1. Age, peers, and status are examples of _____ factors in an individual's predisposition to addiction. 1.____

    A. genetic   B. constitutional   C. psychological   D. sociocultural

2. How many days should an alcoholic subject's detoxification process typically last? 2.____

    A. 1-10   B. 10-20   C. 20-30   D. 30-40

3. Which of the following is NOT true of the confrontation that takes place between members of an intervention team and an addicted person? 3.____
It must

    A. be rehearsed by all team members together
    B. involve quick-thinking people who can formulate responses to unanticipated statements
    C. involve people from a variety of the addicted person's life experiences
    D. be rigidly planned and structured

4. What is the characteristic of an addicted person's recovery illustrated by the person's expression of willingness to accept the help of treatment staff in the recovery process? 4.____

    A. Surrender   B. Acceptance   C. Fellowship   D. Restitution

5. In the early stages of an addicted or alcoholic person's recovery, the process of nutritional repair should include each of the following EXCEPT 5.____

    A. three good meals a day
    B. total elimination of caffeine intake
    C. three nutritious snacks a day
    D. increasing the amount of sugars in the diet

6. Which of the following stages in the progression to freedom from addiction is considered to be the final stage, at which recovery is complete? 6.____

    A. Spiritual well-being   B. Mental well-being
    C. Total abstinence   D. Physical well-being

7. The FIRST goal of recovery treatment is to remedy _____ damage to the addicted person. 7.____

    A. social   B. psychological   C. physical   D. spiritual

8. Which of the following steps should be taken LAST by friends/family members who want to practice intervention in a person's addiction? 8.____

    A. Devising a treatment plan
    B. Confronting the addicted person
    C. Getting help for the person's family
    D. Asking others for help

9. Each of the following is a disadvantage associated with the use of sedatives during an alcoholic subject's withdrawal EXCEPT that it

   A. increases suspicion and paranoia
   B. conflicts with the *abstinence* goal of detoxification
   C. lengthens the detoxification period
   D. interferes with the subject's alertness and early participation in treatment

10. Which of the following symptoms does addiction MOST commonly share with other chronic, debilitating diseases?

    A. Central nervous system damage
    B. Seizures
    C. Denial
    D. Physiological damage

11. An addicted person who would require one of the more intense levels of recovery treatment and care would PROBABLY have

    A. minor withdrawal symptoms
    B. family members who attend Al-Anon
    C. already be resigned to treatment
    D. already attempted recovery at least once and failed

12. The enabling behavior MOST likely practiced by the addicted person's family members in the advanced stages of addiction is

    A. cooperation   B. protecting
    C. codependence   D. guilt

13. Which of the following is NOT a symptom associated with stage two in an alcoholic subject's withdrawal process?

    A. Rapid heartbeat   B. Hand tremors
    C. Insomnia   D. Seizures

14. During intervention, participants on the intervention team should avoid describing to the addicted person

    A. concerns for the addicted person's health
    B. observed examples of addiction-related incidents
    C. observed consequences of addiction-related incidents
    D. personal assessment of emotional damage inflicted upon the addicted person's relations

15. During recovery, a subject sometimes becomes dependent on a drug that has the same relative effects on the central nervous system as the drug for which the subject is being treated.
    This is known specifically as

    A. substitution   B. cross-addiction
    C. surrender   D. submission

16. During an intervention, which of the following types of statements should be offered to the addicted person by members of the intervention team? 16.____

    A. Generalized comments
    B. Judgments
    C. Observations
    D. Opinions

17. Past failures, emotional trauma, and personality defects are examples of _____ factors in an individual's predisposition to addiction. 17.____

    A. genetic
    B. constitutional
    C. psychological
    D. sociocultural

18. The normalization process during the restabilization phase of recovery treatment includes 18.____

    A. introducing external motivations for recovery
    B. personality restructuring
    C. personality growth
    D. stress reduction techniques

19. Which characteristic typically differs between female and male alcoholics? 19.____

    A. Age
    B. Rate of advancement through addictive stages
    C. Likelihood of concurrent addiction to prescription drugs
    D. Professional status

20. Each of the following is an important factor determining the overall effects of addiction on a family EXCEPT 20.____

    A. the type of substance used
    B. the sex of addicted parent
    C. existing feelings of nonaddicted family members toward the addicted
    D. where and when substances are used

21. The component of a comprehensive addiction treatment program that is included in the category of psychosocial rehabilitation is 21.____

    A. social assessment
    B. treating medical problems
    C. random drug screenings
    D. detoxification

22. Each of the following is considered a warning sign for the onset of alcoholism's early stages EXCEPT 22.____

    A. alcohol-related problems
    B. hiding bottles
    C. changes in drinking patterns
    D. preoccupation with alcohol

23. If sedatives are to be used by a subject during the alcoholic withdrawal period, APPROXIMATELY how long is the recommended period for their use? 23.____

    A. For the first overnight period
    B. For the first three or four days
    C. Until the subject does not appear to require sedation
    D. Throughout the entire period of detoxification

24. Which of the following is NOT one of the psychological factors influencing addiction? 24.___

    A. Coping mechanisms
    B. Denial
    C. Tolerance changes
    D. Reinforcing factors

25. The characteristic of an addicted person's recovery illustrated by the person's acknowledgement of his/her individual responsibility for recovery is termed 25.___

    A. surrender
    B. acceptance
    C. fellowship
    D. admission

KEY (CORRECT ANSWERS)

1. D
2. A
3. B
4. A
5. D

6. A
7. C
8. B
9. A
10. C

11. D
12. C
13. D
14. D
15. B

16. C
17. C
18. D
19. C
20. A

21. C
22. B
23. B
24. C
25. B

EXAMINATION SECTION
TEST 1

DIRECTIONS: Each question or incomplete statement is followed by several suggested answers or completions. Select the one that BEST answers the question or completes the statement. *PRINT THE LETTER OF THE CORRECT ANSWER IN THE SPACE AT THE RIGHT.*

1. Alcohol is absorbed

    A. through the stomach walls
    B. through the small intestine
    C. by the lungs
    D. all of the above

    1.____

2. Alcohol, when digested, is

    A. digested
    B. a stimulant
    C. absorbed directly into the bloodstream
    D. all of the above

    2.____

3. Most of the alcohol absorption takes place

    A. through the stomach walls
    B. through the small intestine
    C. through the lungs
    D. in the liver

    3.____

4. The absorption rate of alcohol is MOST greatly reduced if a person eats

    A. starches   B. fats
    C. proteins   D. carbohydrates

    4.____

5. The process of metabolism may BEST be defined as

    A. oxidation of alcohol
    B. stimulant to digestion
    C. conversion of alcohol into sugar
    D. entrance of alcohol into the bloodstream

    5.____

6. Alcohol is metabolized PRIMARILY in the

    A. stomach   B. small intestine
    C. liver   D. lungs

    6.____

7. Oxidation alters alcohol in that it _____ intoxication.

    A. increases the degree of
    B. decreases the degree of
    C. no longer causes
    D. causes

    7.____

8. Oxidation of alcohol can be sped up by

    8.____

A. drinking coffee
B. taking a brisk walk
C. acquiring more oxygen, deep breathing
D. none of the above

9. Some alcohol is eliminated from the body chemically unchanged   9.____

    A. by the kidneys   B. by the breathing process
    C. through perspiration   D. all of the above

10. The various physiological processes by which alcohol is handled by the body are   10.____

    A. neuromuscular, absorption, chemistetic
    B. absorption, metabolism, elimination
    C. metabolism, hereditary, psychological
    D. absorption, elimination, psychological

11. Four variables which affect the blood alcohol content are   11.____

    A. time, sex, weight, and stomach content
    B. profession, weight, time, and stomach content
    C. amount, age, time, and weight
    D. time, amount, weight, and stomach content

12. Tolerance to alcohol   12.____

    A. is a result of difference in alcohol metabolism
    B. is primarily dependent on age and sex
    C. occurs in an individual with previous exposure
    D. all of the above

13. The explanation for tolerance to alcohol is   13.____

    A. delayed absorption
    B. decreased penetration in nervous system
    C. increased tissue tolerance
    D. all of the above

14. Tolerance MOST frequently occurs at blood alcohol contents not exceeding   14.____

    A. .10%   B. .15%   C. .18%   D. .22%

15. The more drinking episodes a person has experienced, the   15.____

    A. more his blood alcohol content changes
    B. better he is able to compensate for the effects of alcohol
    C. lesser his drinking tolerance
    D. all of the above

16. Tolerance can be dependent upon   16.____

    A. sex   B. age
    C. experience   D. all of the above

17. Vision is substantially impaired in ALL subjects when the blood alcohol content exceeds 17.____

    A. .02%   B. .05%   C. .10%   D. .15%

18. Most experts agree that there is observable impairment of brain function when the blood alcohol content exceeds 18.____

    A. .02% B. .05% C. .10% D. .15%

19. The drinking and driving problem results from 19.____

    A. acceptable road use but deviant alcohol use
    B. acceptable alcohol use but deviant road use
    C. deviant use of both alcohol and roads
    D. all of the above

20. The approximate number of people killed on highways in the nation annually is 20.____

    A. 38,000 B. 45,000 C. 50,000 D. 60,000

21. What proportion of the fatal accidents are alcohol related? 21.____

    A. 1/4 B. 1/3 C. 1/2 D. 3/4

22. During his lifetime, the average drinker has what kind of chance of being involved in an accident with an alcohol impaired driver? 22.____
    1 chance in

    A. 10 B. 7 C. 4 D. 2

23. During his lifetime, the average drinker has what kind of a chance of being involved in a FATAL accident with an alcohol impaired driver? 23.____
    1 chance in

    A. 10 B. 7 C. 4 D. 2

24. Accident records serve as indicators in that 24.____

    A. all accidents are reported
    B. potential accidents are known
    C. drivers are prone to report driving and drinking drivers involved
    D. they provide guides for enforcement action

25. When a blood alcohol content of .10% is reached, the accident probability is_____ times as great. 25.____

    A. 3 B. 7 C. 14 D. 25

KEY (CORRECT ANSWERS)

1.	D	11.	D
2.	C	12.	C
3.	B	13.	D
4.	C	14.	A
5.	A	15.	B
6.	C	16.	D
7.	C	17.	C
8.	D	18.	C
9.	D	19.	C
10.	B	20.	C

21. C
22. D
23. A
24. D
25. B

EXAMINATION SECTION
TEST 1

DIRECTIONS: Each question or incomplete statement is followed by several suggested answers or completions. Select the one that BEST answers the question or completes the statement. *PRINT THE LETTER OF THE CORRECT ANSWER IN THE SPACE AT THE RIGHT.*

1. Methadone is a synthetic substitute for 1.____

    A. demerol
    C. laudanum
    B. morphine
    D. pentothal

2. A family of synthetic drugs made from coal tar is the 2.____

    A. opiates
    C. bromides
    B. cocaines
    D. barbiturates

3. A drug which does NOT cause physical addiction or withdrawal symptoms but is regulated by the government as a narcotic is 3.____

    A. codeine
    C. cocaine
    B. morphine
    D. heroin

4. The term *tracks* is associated with the users of 4.____

    A. L.S.D.
    C. methadone
    B. red devils
    D. heroin

5. Of the following drugs, the one that is a stimulant is 5.____

    A. alcohol
    C. barbiturates
    B. amphetamines
    D. opiates

6. Amytal, Seconal and Nembutal are prescription drugs classified as 6.____

    A. barbiturates
    C. opiates
    B. hallucinogens
    D. amphetamines

7. A drug which is classed legally as a narcotic while medically it is NOT is 7.____

    A. opium
    C. heroin
    B. cocaine
    D. codeine

8. Of the following regarding barbiturates, the INCORRECT statement is: 8.____

    A. More people die as a result of acute intoxication from barbiturates than from any other drug poisoning
    B. Taking barbiturates along with alcoholic beverages may prove to be fatal
    C. The medicinal use of barbiturates has been prescribed for sedation, sleep-producing, epilepsy, and high blood pressure
    D. Barbiturates are not depressants

9. The CORRECT association related to the special language of drug users is 9.____

    A. candy–hallucinogens
    B. cartwheels–tranquilizers
    C. bennies–barbiturates
    D. co-pilots–amphetamines

10. As related to treatment and rehabilitation of drug abuse, the CORRECT association is

    A. detoxification—substituting a less harmful drug
    B. maintenance—peer group support
    C. encounter therapy—in-patient hospitalization
    D. therapeutic community—halfway house using former addicts

11. Methaqualone is used medically as a

    A. safe substitute for barbiturates
    B. non-addicting anti-convulsant
    C. prescription for sleeplessness
    D. prevention of skeletal abnormalities in human fetuses

12. All of the following statements concerning the intake of alcohol in the body are correct EXCEPT:

    A. Although alcohol has a caloric content, it is expended instead of being stored in the body.
    B. A small percentage of the alcohol taken into the body is eliminated through the lungs.
    C. Alcohol produces a feeling of warmth with an actual lowering of body temperature.
    D. Digestive changes are necessary before alcohol can be absorbed from the stomach.

13. All of the following characteristics predispose a person to alcoholism EXCEPT having

    A. little tolerance for frustration
    B. low energy levels and strong impulse control
    C. strong feelings of alienation
    D. conflicts in family relationships

14. The MOST effective approach for a teacher to use in an alcohol education unit is to

    A. stress the evils of alcoholism
    B. emphasize the importance of the freedom of the individual to make responsible choices
    C. present facts about alcohol to the students
    D. use the scare approach to discourage students from using alcohol

15. In developing a program of treatment of the alcoholic, the LEAST important consideration is

    A. hospitalization until completion of the treatment
    B. detoxification
    C. physical rehabilitation including nutritional assistance
    D. maintenance of abstinence

16. One of the EARLIEST effects of alcohol on the body is

    A. reduced heart action
    B. loss of equilibrium
    C. decrease in judgment and self-control
    D. blurred and double vision

17. It is CORRECT to state that the *immediate* effect of alcohol on the body is to   17.____

    A. constrict surface blood vessels
    B. decrease the rate of the heartbeat
    C. increase blood pressure
    D. decrease body temperature

18. Of the following concerning alcohol, the CORRECT statement is: 18.____

    A. Alcohol acts principally on the central nervous system
    B. As a rule, black coffee will do away with intoxication
    C. There are no individual differences among people which relate to alcoholism
    D. About 50% of the alcohol consumed is eliminated unchanged through the kidneys and lungs

19. As alcohol is oxidized in the body tissues, the energy it contains is   19.____

    A. used up in muscular activity
    B. used in accelerated activity of the nervous system
    C. stored in the body
    D. given off as heat

20. Of the following, the substance with addicting properties would be   20.____

    A. mescaline   B. phenobarbital
    C. librium   D. cocaine

21. When considered as a drug, the MOST accurate classification which describes alcohol is that it is a   21.____

    A. stimulant   B. depressant
    C. hallucinogen   D. tranquilizer

22. The MOST common signs and symptoms associated with the use of marijuana are   22.____

    A. thirst, drowsiness, and passiveness
    B. pink eyes, increased pulse rate, and hunger
    C. discomfort, anxiety, and general ataxia
    D. increased libido, decreased blood pressure, and pupil dilation

23. While under the influence of morphine, an addict will *usually*   23.____

    A. experience an abnormal dryness of the nose
    B. have contracted, pinpoint pupils of the eyes
    C. feel strong and superior and experience loss of fatigue
    D. be very talkative and will not listen to others

24. Of the following statements concerning drugs, the CORRECT one is: 24.____

    A. As a person's tolerance to barbiturates increases, his tolerance level to other drugs also increases.
    B. Many heroin addicts will use amphetamines when they cannot obtain heroin.
    C. Most experts consider barbiturate addiction more dangerous than heroin addiction.
    D. When skin popping, the user will most often inject directly into a vein.

25. The time between the consuming of alcohol and its beginning to be absorbed into the bloodstream may be *as little as* _____ minutes.

    A. 2   B. 5   C. 8   D. 10

26. All of the following statements concerning alcohol and its effect on the body are correct EXCEPT:

    A. The constant presence of alcohol impairs the liver cells in their ability to store glycogen
    B. At high concentrations, alcohol causes the lessening of gastric juice secretion
    C. Beriberi is one of the commonest deficiency diseases associated with alcoholism
    D. Alcohol increases the enzyme action in the stomach

27. The MOST severe withdrawal reactions result from addiction to

    A. cocaine   B. heroin
    C. barbiturates   D. mescaline

28. The difference between marijuana and heroin is that

    A. marijuana has no proven medical use
    B. heroin is more addictive
    C. pure heroin is better to use than pure marijuana
    D. the emotions are more directly affected by marijuana than by heroin

29. With regard to marijuana, the CORRECT statement is:

    A. More severe penalties will decrease the problem.
    B. Marijuana use usually leads to heroin use.
    C. Marijuana is harmless.
    D. Driving under the influence of marijuana is hazardous.

30. Of the following statements, it is TRUE to say that marijuana

    A. is an aphrodisiac
    B. is addictive
    C. interferes with the thought processes
    D. causes violence and crime

31. The MOST widely misused of all drugs is

    A. alcohol   B. marijuana
    C. heroin   D. cocaine

32. All of the following concerning heroin are correct EXCEPT it

    A. is an antispasmodic
    B. is a derivative of opium
    C. is considered a hypnotic rather than a narcotic
    D. has mild, pain relieving powers

33. All of the following associations are correct EXCEPT

    A. narcotic–novocaine
    B. barbiturate–luminal
    C. stimulant–amphetamine
    D. sedative–benzedrine

34. Alcohol supplies to the body

    A. minerals
    B. protein
    C. calories
    D. none of these

35. All of the following statements concerning alcohol are correct EXCEPT:

    A. The effects of alcohol upon the brain are not felt until the alcohol begins to get into the bloodstream.
    B. While alcohol is absorbed quickly by the body, it is eliminated slowly.
    C. The metabolism of alcohol in the body is speeded up by increased activity.
    D. The stomach cannot change alcohol.

KEY (CORRECT ANSWERS)

1.	B	11.	C	21.	B
2.	C	12.	D	22.	B
3.	C	13.	B	23.	B
4.	D	14.	B	24.	C
5.	B	15.	A	25.	A
6.	A	16.	C	26.	B
7.	B	17.	D	27.	C
8.	D	18.	A	28.	B
9.	D	19.	D	29.	D
10.	B	20.	C	30.	C
		31.	A		
		32.	C		
		33.	D		
		34.	C		
		35.	C		

EXAMINATION SECTION
TEST 1

DIRECTIONS: Each question or incomplete statement is followed by several suggested answers or completions. Select the one that BEST answers the question or completes the statement. *PRINT THE LETTER OF THE CORRECT ANSWER IN THE SPACE AT THE RIGHT.*

1. The fact is that alcohol

    A. stimulates driving alertness when sleep is needed
    B. is a depressant
    C. has no caloric value
    D. affects all persons in the same degree

    1.____

2. The fallacy is that alcohol

    A. slows reaction time
    B. has no mineral value
    C. is an anesthetic
    D. cures a cold

    2.____

3. The CORRECT regimen for an alcoholic is to

    A. drink less gradually
    B. drink just before meals
    C. stop drinking alcohol beverages completely
    D. drink only at home

    3.____

4. In the brain, excessive alcohol acts as a(n)

    A. stimulant
    B. anaesthetic
    C. readily available fuel
    D. vitamin-carrier

    4.____

5. The trend toward alcoholism is MOST often

    A. a symptom of personality maladjustment
    B. caused by heredity
    C. associated with the sex of the individual
    D. associated with the individual's occupation

    5.____

6. Excessive intake of alcoholic beverages over a period of time

    A. hampers the production of gastric juice
    B. reduces nervous anxiety
    C. increases mental alertness
    D. dilates the blood vessels

    6.____

7. Today, the nature of general clinical treatment of alcoholism is   7.___

   A. group psychotherapy
   B. incarceration
   C. tapering off and substitution
   D. physiotherapy

8. An ounce of alcohol (95%) has an APPROXIMATE caloric value of   8.___

   A. 200   B. 300   C. 400   D. 500

9. *Alcoholics Anonymous* was organized by   9.___

   A. alcoholic addicts
   B. the federal government
   C. private organizations
   D. the American Medical Association

10. It is believed that atabuse   10.___

    A. sensitizes humans against alcohol
    B. forms an unstable compound with alcohol
    C. stimulates the gag reflex
    D. promotes elimination of alcohol from the body

11. Excessive alcohol intake ultimately   11.___

    A. stimulates body reactions
    B. accelerates mental alertness
    C. depresses
    D. lowers body resistance to infections

12. The malnutrition associated with alcoholism USUALLY results from   12.___

    A. impaired digestion
    B. disturbed metabolism
    C. excessive craving for proteins
    D. reduction in diet essentials

13. Excessive use of alcohol is indulged in because it is believed to   13.___

    A. quiet the nerves
    B. stimulate brain action
    C. relieve emotional tension
    D. overcome social inadequacy

14. Alcohol FIRST affects   14.___

    A. judgment   B. memory
    C. muscular coordination   D. control of speech

15. To the nervous system, alcohol acts as a

    A. stimulant B. depressant
    C. gratifier D. agitator

16. Characteristic symptoms of chronic alcoholism include

    A. damage to brain tissue
    B. increase in weight
    C. exsiccosis
    D. periods of depression

17. The anesthetizing action of alcohol FIRST affects the exercise of

    A. muscular coordination B. control of speech
    C. judgment D. memory

18. Acute intoxication may properly be labeled a psychosis because it involves

    A. severe loss of contact with reality
    B. emotional inadequacies
    C. intellectual limitations
    D. bodily as well as mental disease

19. The treatment of alcoholic pellagra is a balanced diet AND

    A. penicillin injections
    B. oral antibiotics
    C. thiamin injections
    D. amytal injections

20. *Cured* alcoholics

    A. can control the amount they drink
    B. cannot ever *drink normally*
    C. need moral help to drink within *normal limits*
    D. can drink some alcohol as long as they eat with it

21. Alcohol is MOST often used excessively in order to

    A. induce sleep
    B. stimulate brain action
    C. overcome social inadequacy
    D. furnish temporary release from tensions

22. To cure drug addiction, the A.M.A. believes that the BEST procedure is to

    A. maintain stable dosages in addicts
    B. furnish narcotics at no cost
    C. establish withdrawal clinics
    D. give constant control in a drug–free environment

23. Of the following, the MOST dangerous of the narcotic poisons is   23.___

    A. codeine   B. opium   C. heroin   D. marijuana

24. Statistics indicate that MOST youngsters start the drug habit with   24.___

    A. marijuana   B. heroin   C. cocaine   D. morphine

25. Alcohol is a   25.___

    A. stimulant   B. narcotic   C. depressant   D. none of these

KEY (CORRECT ANSWERS)

1. B		11. C	
2. D		12. D	
3. C		13. C	
4. B		14. A	
5. A		15. B	
6. A		16. D	
7. A		17. C	
8. A		18. A	
9. A		19. C	
10. A		20. B	

21. D
22. D
23. C
24. A
25. C

TEST 2

DIRECTIONS: Each question or incomplete statement is followed by several suggested answers or completions. Select the one that BEST answers the question or completes the statement. *PRINT THE LETTER OF THE CORRECT ANSWER IN THE SPACE AT THE RIGHT.*

1. In general, of the following, the MOST effective cure of addiction to drugs is   1.____

   A. sustained medical treatment
   B. change of occupation
   C. voluntary tapering off of the use of drugs
   D. conquering the habit by will power

2. The method used to train teenagers in the control of narcotic habits in a school on Ward's Island is the   2.____

   A. penal colony
   B. strict regulatory
   C. clinical examination control
   D. permissive

3. A drug which is a substitute for morphine in the treatment of drug addiction is   3.____

   A. codeine   B. demerol   C. pantapon   D. methadone

4. An hypnotic drug which does NOT initiate drug addiction is   4.____

   A. dormison   B. sodium amytal
   C. sodium phenobarbital   D. seconal

5. The MOST harmful drug derived from opium is   5.____

   A. heroin   B. morphine   C. cocaine   D. codeine

6. The MOST recent statistics indicate that, of the following, the leading cause of accidental deaths from poisoning is   6.____

   A. morphine   B. narcotine
   C. barbituates   D. lead

7. Marijuana is made from   7.____

   A. opium   B. codeine
   C. hemp leaves   D. cocoa

8. To a drug addict, reefer or joint mean   8.____

   A. cigarettes   B. powders
   C. capsules   D. pills

9. *Goofballs* used by drug addicts contained   9.____

   A. chloral   B. hyposcyamine
   C. stramonium   D. barbituric acid

10. Recent statistics indicate that MOST youngsters start the drug habit with   10.____

    A. marijuana   B. heroin   C. cocaine   D. morphine

11. Recent information regarding cocaine indicates that it

    A. is purely recreational
    B. is highly addictive
    C. is helpful in reducing stress and hypertension
    D. should be used only prescribed by a physician

12. A habit-forming drug is

    A. sulfathiozole   B. quinidine
    C. demerol   D. potassium acetate

13. Usually, the FIRST step to drugs by a youngster is a

    A. deck   B. snort   C. reefer   D. cap

14. Preventing unlawful trade in narcotics is assigned to

    A. Drug Authority
    B. Bureau of Narcotics
    C. Bureau of Customs
    D. United Nations Commission on Narcotic Drugs

15. *Tolerance* in drug addiction means the amount that

    A. quiets the nerves
    B. produces unconsciousness
    C. can be taken without character changes
    D. produces the desired effect

16. Marijuana is obtained from the

    A. hemp plant   B. thorn apple
    C. cocoa shrub   D. nightshade plant

17. According to the authorities, relationship between the incidence of cancer and smoking is

    A. controversial   B. negative
    C. positive   D. incidental

18. The responsibility for preventing unlawful domestic trade in narcotics rests with the

    A. United Nations Commission on Narcotics
    B. Bureau of Customs, U.S. Treasury Department
    C. Drug Enforcement Agency (DEA), U.S. Treasury Department
    D. United States Drug Authority, Legal Division

19. In addicts, drug withdrawal symptoms include vomiting and changes in

    A. A. pupils of the eyes
    B. muscular control
    C. color of the skin
    D. color of the whites of the eyeballs

20. If a teacher discovers a pupil who is taking drugs, she should report it to the

 A. dean or assistant principal
 B. police
 C. principal of the school
 D. pupil's parents

21. In addicts, a moderate drug abstinence syndrome is characterized by

 A. fever, increased blood pressure, insominia, acute restlessness, and rapid breathing
 B. depression, excessive perspiration, and yawning
 C. inertia, body tremors, and fits of sneezing
 D. diarrhea, chills, and depression

22. Opium is derived from

 A. hemp fiber B. nightshade plant
 C. poppy D. ragweed

23. A *mainliner* is a drug addict who uses the drug for

 A. intra-muscular injection
 B. snorting
 C. smoking
 D. intra-venal injection

24. Prolonged administration of narcotics is MOST likely to result in

 A. addiction
 B. reduced physical resistance
 C. increased aggressiveness
 D. need for a change in prescription

25. A plant from which peyote is obtained is the

 A. nightshade plant B. fox glove
 C. gentian D. mescal catcus

26. *Half-way house* is the name of a(n)

 A. dual purpose house providing facilities for living as well as conducting a business
 B. nursing home for terminal care of cancer patients
 C. rehabilitation center for ex-drug addicts and patients released from mental hospitals
 D. nursing home for senile aged persons

27. To avoid detection, the heroin addict injects the 27.___

    A. nasal mucosa and the gums
    B. gums and the vagina
    C. nasal mucosa and the vagina
    D. conjunctiva

28. A highly dangerous and addictive synthetic narcotic is 28.___

    A. amidol
    B. amidone
    C. cobalamine
    D. pyridoxine

29. During the 1993-1997 term of President Clinton, drug use by young people 29.___

    A. remained steady
    B. increased by one million
    C. declined
    D. cannot be statistically determined

30. A POSITIVE effect of decriminalizing drug use by medical administration would be 30.___

    A. fewer addicts
    B. increased medical costs
    C. less drug-related crime
    D. making drug use more acceptable

KEY (CORRECT ANSWERS)

1.	A	11.	B	21.	A
2.	D	12.	C	22.	C
3.	D	13.	C	23.	D
4.	A	14.	B	24.	A
5.	A	15.	D	25.	D
6.	C	16.	A	26.	C
7.	C	17.	C	27.	B
8.	A	18.	C	28.	B
9.	D	19.	A	29.	B
10.	A	20.	C	30.	C

EXAMINATION SECTION
TEST 1

DIRECTIONS: Each question or incomplete statement is followed by several suggested answers or completions. Select the one that BEST answers the question or completes the statement. *PRINT THE LETTER OF THE CORRECT ANSWER IN THE SPACE AT THE RIGHT.*

1. Research indicates that among the following psychological factors, the one most likely to increase an individual's potential for substance dependence is a(n) 1.____

   A. internal locus of control
   B. *Type A* personality
   C. high feeling of self-worth
   D. tendency toward risk-seeking behavior

2. Of the following substances, the use of_____ is most clearly linked to violent crime. 2.____

   A. marijuana
   B. alcohol
   C. LSD
   D. heroin

3. The neurotransmitter that is inhibited by sedative hypnotics is 3.____

   A. GABA
   B. dopamine
   C. acetylcholine
   D. serotonin

4. At moderate doses, stimulants can produce 4.____

   A. paranoia
   B. a sense of well-being
   C. a dreamy/sleepy state
   D. a loss of inhibitions

5. *Chipping* is a term that refers to the attempt to distribute lower doses of_____ at intervals that will avoid addiction. 5.____

   A. heroin
   B. marijuana
   C. cocaine
   D. alcohol

6. Amphetamines 6.____

   A. can cause panic, agitation, hallucinations, and paranoid delusions
   B. generally increase appetite and decrease fatigue
   C. block the reception of dopamine in the nervous system
   D. cause a period of depression and fatigue that is usually followed by feelings of euphoria

7. A person who is designated as a *Type 2* alcoholic has

   A. comorbid diabetes
   B. developed the disease early in life
   C. limited mobility
   D. a pronounced serotonin deficit in the brain

8. A common model of substance abuse has the person beginning with beer, wine, or cigarettes, and then moving on to hard liquor and marijuana, and subsequently to other illicit drugs. This progression is known as

   A. the tolerance curve
   B. situational use
   C. staging
   D. compulsion

9. The most appropriate goal of drug education programs is to

   A. relay information
   B. screen for likely drug users
   C. modify pre-addictive behaviors
   D. gather information from attendants

10. The primary factor in the decline in alcohol use among high school students from 1980 to the first decade of the 21st century was

    A. a trickle-down effect from the decline in alcohol use among college students
    B. a decline in binge drinking
    C. an increase in the use of illicit drugs
    D. less accessibility to alcohol

11. The most widely prescribed class of drugs in the United States is

    A. steroids
    B. barbiturates
    C. opiates
    D. benzodiazepines

12. The most likely cause of death among heavy users of alcohol is

    A. cardiovascular disease
    B. cirrhosis of the liver
    C. digestive disorders
    D. vehicular accidents

13. Cocaethylene, a dangerous drug metabolite, is produced by the combination of cocaine and

    A. alcohol
    B. heroin
    C. marijuana
    D. LSD

14. _____ is a central nervous system depressant.

   A. Heroin
   B. Marijuana
   C. Cocaine
   D. Alcohol

15. The main reason for the lengthy amount of time it takes to metabolize and excrete marijuana is that it is

   A. excreted only by the lungs
   B. stored in fat cells for up to several weeks after each use
   C. an inhaled particulate, rather than a liquid or solid
   D. one of the main components in renal calculi (kidney stones)

16. Among problem drinkers, the personality characteristic that is MOST likely to be shared is

   A. personal maladjustment
   B. depression
   C. emotional immaturity
   D. sexual dysfunction or deviance

17. Which of the following is a prominent SSRI (selective serotonin reuptake inhibitor) drug?

   A. Miltown
   B. Valium
   C. Darvon
   D. Prozac

18. Alcohol begins to influence the brain, vision, and decision-making at a blood alcohol concentration (BAC) of about

   A. 0.01
   B. 0.02
   C. 0.04
   D. 0.08

19. _____ is a term that refers to the violent behavior that results from the conflict inherent in the drug trade.

   A. Transferred intent
   B. Global wave
   C. Systemic link
   D. Collateral damage

20. The _____ theory of substance dependence holds that eventually, the vicious cycle develops in which the motivation for drug taking shifts from a desire for the euphoric high to the need to relive an increasingly intense *down* feeling that follows drug use.

   A. moral weakness
   B. circular reasoning
   C. gateway
   D. opponent-process

21. When compared to other routes of administration, drugs administered _____ are generally absorbed more slowly.

    A. by intravenous injection
    B. by intramuscular injection
    C. orally
    D. by inhalation

22. The substance _____ is used to treat overdose from heroin and other opioids by blocking the receptors that normally bind with the drug.

    A. naloxone
    B. clonidine
    C. disulfiram
    D. methadone

23. The antipsychotic drug chlorpromazine (Thorazine) is sometimes used to block the effects of each of the following, EXCEPT

    A. psilocybin
    B. mescaline
    C. PCP
    D. LSD

24. The neurotransmitter _____ is a primary agent in the *pleasure pathway* in the brain, which is believed to be involved in substance dependence.

    A. dopamine
    B. norepinephrine
    C. serotonin
    D. acetylcholine

25. Alcohol withdrawal symptoms can include
    I. convulsions
    II. insomnia
    III. tremors
    IV. hallucinations

    A. I, II and III
    B. II only
    C. II and III
    D. I, II, III and IV

KEY (CORRECT ANSWERS)

1.	D	11.	D
2.	B	12.	D
3.	A	13.	A
4.	A	14.	D
5.	A	15.	B
6.	A	16.	A
7.	B	17.	D
8.	C	18.	B
9.	A	19.	C
10.	D	20.	D

21. C
22. A
23. C
24. A
25. D

TEST 2

DIRECTIONS: Each question or incomplete statement is followed by several suggested answers or completions. Select the one that BEST answers the question or completes the statement. *PRINT THE LETTER OF THE CORRECT ANSWER IN THE SPACE AT THE RIGHT.*

1. The medical approach to alcoholism, which views it as a disease, also holds that the only acceptable goal is

    A. a lifetime prescription of Antabuse
    B. total abstinence
    C. controlled social drinking with trusted friends and family members
    D. inpatient confinement

2. Which of the following is NOT a typical symptom of alcohol withdrawal?

    A. Sweating
    B. Irritability
    C. Flushed skin
    D. Depression

3. In the human brain, a respiratory center necessary for breathing is located in the

    A. hindbrain
    B. cerebellum
    C. medulla
    D. thalamus

4. _____ prevention programs are designed to prevent substance dependence before it begins.

    A. Primary
    B. Secondary
    C. Tertiary
    D. Quaternary

5. Which of the following is NOT a synthetic opiate?

    A. Fentanyl
    B. Morphine
    C. Methadone
    D. Meperidine

6. Benzodiazepines are prescribed primarily to treat

    A. substance dependence
    B. depression
    C. anxiety
    D. pain

7. The area of the brain most effected by tetrahydrocannabinol (THC) is the

    A. hippocampus
    B. hypothalamus
    C. cerebrum
    D. medulla

8. The primary feature of substance abuse is the

    A. usage of increasing amounts to achieve the same high
    B. feeling of a need for the substance
    C. use of the substance in order to prevent withdrawal
    D. continued use of a substance despite risks or problems in living

8.____

9. Currently, methaqualone is a Schedule _____ drug.

    A. I
    B. II
    C. III
    D. IV

9.____

10. Among the elderly, the most common trigger event for excessive drinking is

    A. crime victimization
    B. retirement
    C. the death of a spouse
    D. the death of a child

10.____

11. Which of the following is a benzodiazepine?

    A. Placidyl
    B. Nembutal
    C. Valium
    D. Miltown

11.____

12. Clinically, opioids

    A. stimulate awareness
    B. have no medically recognized use
    C. increase appetite
    D. relieve pain

12.____

13. Alcoholic dementia is associated with

    A. an enlargement of the brain ventricles
    B. liver damage
    C. a permanent reduction in acetylcholine receptors
    D. a damaged hypothalamus

13.____

14. Which of the following factors is LEAST likely to result in a decrease in the intoxicating effect of a drug?

    A. concurrent intake of food
    B. increase in body fat stores
    C. greater body mass
    D. fewer body fat stores

14.____

15. Generally, the most dangerous combination of substances occurs with 15.___

    A. alcohol and marijuana
    B. alcohol and sedative hypnotics
    C. hallucinogens and narcotics
    D. amphetamines and sedative hypnotics

16. Which of the following is a risk factor for alcoholism? 16.___

    A. Not completing high school
    B. Being male
    C. Being African-American
    D. Being married

17. The route of administration that puts a drug into the layer of fat directly beneath the skin is 17.___

    A. inunction
    B. transdermal injection
    C. intramuscular injection
    D. subcutaneous injection

18. Which of the following is NOT an immediate effect of nitrous oxide? 18.___

    A. Euphoria
    B. Dehydration
    C. Cardiac arrhythmia
    D. Spontaneous laughter

19. LSD research has demonstrated that 19.___

    A. it is physiologically addictive
    B. tolerance is acquired rapidly
    C. it is absorbed slowly through the GI tract
    D. it is taken up selectively by the brain

20. In adulthood, the factor that is most closely linked to the onset of alcoholism is 20.___

    A. peer relations
    B. ethnic identity
    C. family history of alcoholism
    D. socioeconomic status

21. A primary duty of the federal Drug Enforcement Agency (DEA) is to 21.___

    A. enforce federal laws related to illicit narcotic drugs and cooperating with state and local agencies in the enforcement of state narcotics laws
    B. conduct drug abuse prevention programs
    C. gather intelligence on traffickers in illicit drugs
    D. regulate the flow and manufacture of legal but controlled drugs

22. At moderate doses, opiates can produce

    A. hypertension
    B. hypothermia
    C. respiratory depression
    D. constricted pupils

23. For most alcoholics, the first step in treatment is

    A. the first of the Twelve Steps
    B. detoxification
    C. individual therapy
    D. inpatient admission

24. *Club drugs* often used by young adults at all-night dance parties or at dance clubs and bars, include each of the following, EXCEPT

    A. ketamine
    B. GHB (gamma hydroxybutyrate)
    C. marijuana
    D. MDMA (ecstasy)

25. The most widely used opiate antagonist in withdrawal treatment is

    A. methadone
    B. clonidine
    C. chlorpromazine
    D. naltrexone

KEY (CORRECT ANSWERS)

1.	B	11.	C
2.	C	12.	D
3.	C	13.	A
4.	A	14.	D
5.	B	15.	B
6.	C	16.	B
7.	A	17.	D
8.	D	18.	B
9.	A	19.	B
10.	C	20.	C

21. D
22. B
23. B
24. C
25. D

TEST 3

DIRECTIONS: Each question or incomplete statement is followed by several suggested answers or completions. Select the one that BEST answers the question or completes the statement. *PRINT THE LETTER OF THE CORRECT ANSWER IN THE SPACE AT THE RIGHT.*

1. Which of the following sedative hypnotics is neither a barbiturate nor a benzodiazepine? 1.___

    A. Methaqualone
    B. Chlorazepate
    C. Diazepam
    D. Secobarbital

2. A substance that effectively increases the activity of a neurotransmitter by binding with a cell receptor and causing a response is known as a(n) 2.___

    A. barbiturate
    B. narcotic
    C. agonist
    D. analgesic

3. Which of the following is an opioid, developed for pharmaceutical use in the 1990s, which has proven to be addictive for many users? 3.___

    A. OxyContin
    B. Fen-Phen
    C. Tamgesic
    D. St. John's wort

4. Which of the following routes of administration greatly increases a drug user's risk for hepatitis and AIDS? 4.___

    A. Inhalation
    B. Ingestion (oral)
    C. Parenteral (injection)
    D. Topical (absorption through the skin)

5. The form of cannabis with the weakest concentration of tetrahydrocan-nabinol (THC) is 5.___

    A. marijuana
    B. sinsemilla
    C. hashish
    D. hashish oil

6. Each year, about 75 percent of the drug-related deaths in the United States are associated with 6.___

    A. alcohol
    B. polydrug episodes
    C. narcotics
    D. cocaine

7. The drug most often abused by adolescents is marijuana, followed by

   A. cocaine
   B. MDMA (ecstasy)
   C. barbiturates
   D. inhalants

8. What is the term for the interaction that takes place when two drugs are mixed together to produce a greater effect than that of either drug taken separately?

   A. Antagonism
   B. Potentiation
   C. Pronunciation
   D. Agonism

9. The oxidative rate-the rate at which the body metabolizes a substance-for alcohol in adults is a little under

   A. one drink per hour
   B. two drinks per hour
   C. three drinks in two hours
   D. four drinks per day

10. Which of the following is a common side effect associated with the use of antidepressant drugs, especially tricyclics (Elavil) and Serotonin and norepinephrine reuptake inhibitors (SNRIs)?

    A. Sweating
    B. Blotchy skin
    C. Constipation
    D. Ruid retention

11. _____ programs are designed to minimize the physiological changes associated with withdrawal from a substance.

    A. Withdrawal
    B. Therapeutic community
    C. 12-step
    D. Milieu

12. The most widely used sedative hypnotic drug is

    A. Seconal
    B. alcohol
    C. diazepam
    D. methaqualone

13. Of all Americans who complete a drug treatment program, the percentage who remain drug-free for at least a year afterward is about

    A. 5-10
    B. 15-35
    C. 30-50
    D. 60-80

14. *Speedball* is a street term that refers to the combination of   14.____

    A. methamphetamine and heroin
    B. cocaine and heroin
    C. cocaine and methamphetamine
    D. methamphetamine and LSD

15. Neurotransmitters are synthesized and metabolized in the body by   15.____

    A. enzymes
    B. amino acids
    C. axons
    D. metabolites

16. A substance that produces vivid sensory awareness or feelings of increased insight is said to have_____ properties.   16.____

    A. hallucinogenic
    B. psychedelic
    C. barbiturate
    D. narcotic

17. Which of the following is NOT a fundamental process associated with the concept of addiction?   17.____

    A. Reinforcement
    B. Tolerance
    C. Physical dependence
    D. Affective disorder

18. Blood alcohol concentration (BAC) becomes lethal at about   18.____

    A. 0.2
    B. 0.4
    C. 0.8
    D. 1.0

19. Which of the following is a common side effect of antipsychotic drugs?   19.____

    A. Photosensitivity
    B. Excitability
    C. Alzheimer's disease
    D. Constipation

20. Nembutal and Seconal are   20.____

    A. opiates
    B. barbiturates
    C. benzodiazepines
    D. stimulants

21. Of the following, the substance that causes the greatest overall damage to human tissue is

    A. marijuana
    B. LSD
    C. cocaine
    D. alcohol

22. Which of the following is NOT used as an alternative to anabolic steroids?

    A. Clonidine
    B. Clenbuterol
    C. GHB (gamma hydroxybutyrate)
    D. Androstenedione

23. The most likely result of drinking excessively before bedtime in order to relax is _____, which may produce anxiety and restlessness.

    A. nightmares
    B. hypertension
    C. dream deficit
    D. sleep deficit

24. Which of the following was originally used as a nasal decongestant?

    A. Cocaine
    B. Amphetamine
    C. Opium
    D. Morphine

25. The phenomenon that most clearly demonstrates that there is a cognitive as well as physiological factor involved in drug reaction and dependence is the

    A. disease model
    B. opponent-process theory
    C. expectancy effect
    D. contingency management

KEY (CORRECT ANSWERS)

1.	A	11.	A
2.	C	12.	B
3.	A	13.	C
4.	C	14.	B
5.	A	15.	A
6.	B	16.	A
7.	D	17.	D
8.	B	18.	B
9.	A	19.	A
10.	C	20.	B

21. D
22. A
23. C
24. B
25. C

TEST 4

DIRECTIONS: Each question or incomplete statement is followed by several suggested answers or completions. Select the one that BEST answers the question or completes the statement. *PRINT THE LETTER OF THE CORRECT ANSWER IN THE SPACE AT THE RIGHT.*

1. The *amotivational syndrome* is a controversial theory that refers to an indifference to long-range plans among habitual users of

    A. alcohol
    B. cocaine
    C. heroin
    D. marijuana

    1.____

2. Which of the following hallucinogens is derived from the peyote cactus?

    A. Mescaline
    B. Psilocybin
    C. Atropine
    D. Harmaline

    2.____

3. Which of the following is NOT an effect associated with the use of anabolic steroids in men?

    A. Increased sex drive
    B. Gynecomastia (breast development)
    C. Hair loss
    D. Increased blood cholesterol

    3.____

4. The most extensively used illicit drug in the United States today is

    A. marijuana
    B. amphetamine
    C. cocaine
    D. anabolic steroids

    4.____

5. The primary area of the brain that is inhibited by alcohol intoxication is the

    A. hippocampus
    B. medulla
    C. cerebrum
    D. hypothalamus

    5.____

6. Generally, the most difficult time in the process of withdrawal from heroin addiction occurs from_____ hours after the last use.

    A. 6 to 12
    B. 12 to 24
    C. 24 to 72
    D. 72 to 96

    6.____

7. Physical dependence on a drug is most closely associated with

    A. escalating use
    B. withdrawal symptoms
    C. missing days of work or school
    D. a strong compulsion to use the drug

8. Which of the following neurotransmitters is released at the somatic neuromuscular junctions?

    A. Dopamine
    B. Epinephrine
    C. Acetylcholine
    D. Serotonin

9. Alcohol's most significant health-related impact occurs in the _____ system.

    A. respiratory
    B. digestive
    C. endocrine
    D. central nervous

10. An effect common to the use of most inhalants is

    A. spontaneous laughter
    B. dizziness
    C. headache
    D. a loss of inhibition

11. Compared to cocaine, the stimulating effects of amphetamines are

    A. about the same in duration and intensity
    B. longer-lasting and more intense
    C. shorter-lasting and more intense
    D. longer-lasting and less intense

12. Drugs that are classified as *psychedelics* because they enhancing perceptive and thought processes of the brain include each of the following, EXCEPT

    A. LSD
    B. psilocybin
    C. mescaline
    D. ketamine

13. A disorder common among alcoholics, caused by vitamin B_1 deficiency and characterized by disorientation, confusion, abnormal eye movements, and amnesia, is _____ syndrome

    A. Ackerman's
    B. Korsakoff's
    C. Tourette's
    D. Reye's

14. The use of which of the following drugs is MOST likely to lead to tolerance or physical dependence?

    A. PCP (phencyclidine)
    B. Marijuana
    C. Amphetamine
    D. LSD

15. Common symptoms of cocaine abuse include each of the following, EXCEPT

    A. insomnia
    B. runny nose
    C. constricted pupils
    D. talkativeness

16. Available statistics on drugs and crime in the United States suggest that most narcotic addicts who commit crimes

    A. commit mostly *victimless* crimes
    B. are under the influence when they commit crimes
    C. began criminal activity after they became addicted
    D. were engaged in criminal activity before they became addicted

17. Most drugs and metabolites are excreted

    A. in the form of perspiration, saliva, and tears
    B. in the form of air expired by the lungs
    C. by the gallbladder
    D. by the kidneys

18. Which of the following drugs is used to reduce the severity of narcotic withdrawal symptoms?

    A. Clonidine
    B. Fentanyl
    C. Naltrexone
    D. Hydrocodone

19. Each of the following is a risk factor for alcohol abuse, EXCEPT

    A. peer relations
    B. a high tolerance for alcohol
    C. family relations
    D. heredity

20. By using alcohol, a person can induce an increased tolerance for Seconal, despite the fact that the user has never taken Seconal before. This is an example of

    A. distributive effect
    B. a breach in the blood-brain barrier
    C. cross-tolerance
    D. agonism

21. The class of drugs to which Ritalin belongs, and which are now the drugs of choice for treating attention-deficit/hyperactivity disorder, are   21.___

    A. stimulants
    B. depressants
    C. narcotics
    D. sedative hypnotics

22. Of the following substances, which is a narcotic?   22.___

    A. Heroin
    B. Amphetamine
    C. Alcohol
    D. LSD

23. Dexedrine and Benzedrine are commonly abused   23.___

    A. benzodiazepines
    B. amphetamines
    C. narcotics
    D. barbiturates

24. Nationwide, the primary purpose of the Drug Abuse Warning Network (DAWN) is to   24.___

    A. monitor drug-related hospital emergency department (ED) visits and drug-related deaths
    B. establish in-school programs that teach children about the consequences of drug abuse
    C. establish a network of drug treatment centers
    D. monitor the international trade in illicit drugs

25. The third stage of alcoholism, in which there is a loss of control of drinking and occasional binges of heavy drinking, is the _____ stage.   25.___

    A. pre-alcoholic
    B. chronic
    C. prodromal
    D. crucial

KEY (CORRECT ANSWERS)

1. D
2. A
3. A
4. A
5. C

6. C
7. B
8. C
9. D
10. D

11. D
12. D
13. B
14. C
15. C

16. D
17. D
18. A
19. B
20. C

21. A
22. A
23. B
24. A
25. D

EXAMINATION SECTION
TEST 1

DIRECTIONS: Each question or incomplete statement is followed by several suggested answers or completions. Select the one that BEST answers the question or completes the statement. *PRINT THE LETTER OF THE CORRECT ANSWER IN THE SPACE AT THE RIGHT.*

1. Research indicates that among all users of illicit drugs in the United States, about _____ percent use marijuana.

    A. 35
    B. 50
    C. 65
    D. 80

2. A drug's "anxiolytic" effect refers to its ability to

    A. relieve pain
    B. relieve anxiety
    C. metabolize rapidly
    D. produce a euphoric feeling

3. The mandrake and datura plants contain each of the following hallucinogens, EXCEPT

    A. scopolamine
    B. mescaline
    C. hyoscyamine
    D. atropine

4. A drug dependence that results from a physician's treatment for a recognized medical condition is known as _____ addiction.

    A. nosocomial
    B. incidental
    C. iatrogenic
    D. clinical

5. The subjective effects of barbiturates are practically indistinguishable from those of

    A. amphetamine
    B. alcohol
    C. hallucinogens
    D. benzodiazepines

6. Home drug testing kits are typically sensitive to evidence of each of the following, EXCEPT

    A. LSD
    B. alcohol
    C. amphetamine
    D. cocaine

7. The major portion of an alcoholic drink is metabolized by the

    A. liver
    B. stomach
    C. pancreas
    D. brain

8. The family and friends of a person suffering from substance dependence decide to stage an intervention. Which of the following is generally believed to be a component in an effective intervention?

    A. Convincing the substance abuser that dependence is a problem that is easily overcome.
    B. Making a specific list of the substance abuser's transgressions over the past several months.
    C. Focusing on all the ways in which the substance abuser is still able to function in family and society, despite his or her dependence.
    D. Emphasizing care and concern for the substance abuser.

9. Approximately what percentage of the antidepressants prescribed in the United States today are prescribed by physicians who are not psychiatrists?

   A. 10
   B. 33
   C. 50
   D. 75

10. Among older teenagers and young adults, one of the most powerful and consistent predictors for drug abuse is

    A. school problems
    B. personal/family crisis
    C. failed or failing relationships
    D. peer pressure

11. The greatest amount of direct societal costs, in terms of the "behavioral toxicity" of a substance, is associated in the United States with the abuse of

    A. cocaine
    B. marijuana
    C. heroin
    D. alcohol

12. Which of the following is NOT one of the classic signs of opiate overdose?

    A. Constricted pupils
    B. Coma
    C. Nausea
    D. Respiratory depression

13. The rate at which alcohol is absorbed into the bloodstream is affected by each of the following, EXCEPT the

    A. person's metabolic rate
    B. mixing of a drink with a carbonated beverage
    C. alcoholic concentration of the beverage
    D. time of day the drink is consumed

14. The rate of drug absorption is greatest in the

    A. large intestine
    B. small intestine
    C. stomach
    D. liver

15. In the human nervous system, information is transmitted outward from the nerve cell body by the

    A. mitochondrion
    B. synapse
    C. dendrite
    D. axon

16. Which of the following is NOT typically used as a "date rape" drug?

    A. Rohypnol
    B. Ketamine
    C. Ecstasy (MDMA)
    D. GHB (gamma hydroxybutyrate)

17. Which of the following is a street term for a smokeable form of amphetamine?

    A. Eight-ball
    B. Smack
    C. Ice
    D. Rock

18. The highest rate of adolescent drug use is found in

    A. the United States
    B. Thailand
    C. Russia
    D. France

19. Which of the following is a naturally occurring chemical in the brain hat has an effect similar to THC?

    A. Enkephalin
    B. Disulfiram
    C. GABA
    D. Anandamide

20. Which of the following is a synthetic opiate that is used to treat heroin withdrawal by satisfying cravings?

    A. Naloxone
    B. Morphine
    C. Methadone
    D. Disulfiram

21. Which of the following is an inhibitory neurotransmitter?

    A. GABA
    B. Serotonin
    C. Acetylcholine
    D. Norepinephrine

22. Death due to accidental overdose is MOST likely to be associated with the use of

    A. LSD
    B. stimulants
    C. barbiturates
    D. alcohol

23. Common symptoms of marijuana use include each of the following, EXCEPT

    A. talkativeness
    B. reddened eyes
    C. voracious appetite
    D. slurred speech

24. Women tend to metabolize alcohol more slowly than men because they

    A. are generally smaller in size
    B. generally have a higher percentage of body fat
    C. tend to drink more slowly
    D. usually eat more while drinking

25. Disulfiram is used as a treatment for alcoholism. It acts by

    A. blocking the reception of alcohol by brain receptors
    B. immediately breaking down alcohol into its harmless component molecules
    C. producing an immediate and severe negative reaction to alcohol intake
    D. alleviating physical withdrawal symptoms

KEY (CORRECT ANSWERS)

1. D
2. B
3. B
4. C
5. B

6. A
7. A
8. D
9. C
10. D

11. D
12. C
13. D
14. B
15. D

16. C
17. C
18. A
19. D
20. C

21. A
22. C
23. D
24. B
25. C

TEST 2

DIRECTIONS: Each question or incomplete statement is followed by several suggested answers or completions. Select the one that BEST answers the question or completes the statement. *PRINT THE LETTER OF THE CORRECT ANSWER IN THE SPACE AT THE RIGHT.*

1. The fastest growing cause of deaths related to illegal drug use today is

    A. alcohol/barbiturates overdose
    B. vehicular accidents among the intoxicated
    C. AIDS
    D. amphetamine overdose

2. During the acute phase of a person's detoxification from substance dependence, the primary focus for those who are with him/her should be to

    A. monitor physiological withdrawal symptoms and vital signs
    B. monitor for emotional outbreaks
    C. maintain wariness against manipulative or deceptive behavior
    D. arrange rehabilitation counseling

3. Among Americans, the highest rates of illicit drug use occur in the _____ age group.

    A. 11 to 18
    B. 18 to 25
    C. 26 to 33
    D. 34 to 41

4. For most people, signs of intoxication such as staggering, slurring of speech, or belligerence are likely to appear after about _____ alcoholic drinks.

    A. 1 or 2
    B. 3 or 4
    C. 5 or 6
    D. 9 or 10

5. The first federal Schedule of Controlled Substances was released in

    A. 1906
    B. 1933
    C. 1970
    D. 1984

6. Which of the following is a hallucinogen that is chemically similar to acetylcholine?

    A. Atropine
    B. Mescaline
    C. Psilocybin
    D. LSD

7. The "gateway theory" of drug use generally holds that a person's use of more dangerous illicit drugs is a predictable progression from his or her use of

    A. prescription opiates
    B. marijuana
    C. inhalants
    D. cocaine

8. Which of the following drugs has NOT been associated with significant physical withdrawal symptoms in users?

    A. Alcohol
    B. Caffeine
    C. LSD
    D. Amphetamines

9. Most drug screening programs are set up to test for

    A. the presence of drugs or metabolites in urine
    B. the presence of drugs or metabolites in blood

C. altered brain wave activity
D. heart arrhythmias or other irregularities

10. Common symptoms of alcohol use include each of the following, EXCEPT

   A. incoherent speech
   B. bloodshot eyes
   C. irregular walking or muscle movements
   D. heightened perception

11. In the late 20th century, federal jurisdiction for the regulation of anabolic steroids was transferred from the

   A. Drug Enforcement Agency (DEA) to the National Institutes of Health (NIH)
   B. NIH to the DEA
   C. Food and Drug Administration (FDA) to the DEA
   D. U.S. Department of Agriculture (USDA) to the FDA

12. Delirium tremens is most likely to occur in the _____ phase of alcoholism.

   A. crucial or acute
   B. chronic
   C. pre-alcoholic
   D. warning

13. The difference between the effective dose level of a drug and the lowest toxic dose is expressed as the

   A. Orange Book value
   B. margin of safety
   C. therapeutic index
   D. therapeutic equivalence

14. Generally, "moderate" drinking is defined as no more than _____ drink(s) a day for women and _____ drink(s) a day for men.

   A. 1/2; 1   B. 1; 2
   C. 2; 3   D. 2; 4

15. Studies have demonstrated a cross-tolerance between LSD and

   A. mescaline   B. MDMA (ecstasy)
   C. scopolamine   D. harmaline

16. Which of the following opiates is the most potent?

   A. Heroin   B. Morphine
   C. Fentanyl   D. Codeine

17. Naltrexone, a drug used in the treatment of alcoholism, acts by

   A. breaking alcohol down into separate molecules before it enters the bloodstream
   B. decreasing the pleasure associated with alcohol use
   C. mimicking the effects of alcohol in the brain, but with a lower intensity and duration
   D. causing the user to become ill if alcohol is ingested

18. Drug use is proportionately more common among   18.____

    A. ethnic minorities
    B. the upper class
    C. the lower classes
    D. middle-class males

19. Which of the following is an appropriate "exit result" for an abuse prevention program?   19.____

    A. A short-term effect
    B. A long-term effect
    C. A strategy for insuring and measuring success
    D. Evidence that the program is working

20. The determination of whether a person's use of a substance become "abuse" is most clearly linked to   20.____

    A. the number of times a person uses drugs in any given time period
    B. a pattern in which repeated use becomes connected to undesirable consequences
    C. the amount of the substance the user takes at any given time
    D. whether the person moves on to use illicit drugs

21. Kaposi's sarcoma is a form of cancer that has been linked to the habitual inhalation of   21.____

    A. ether
    B. nitrites
    C. petroleum distillates
    D. toluene

22. A child with one alcoholic parent has about a _____ percent chance of becoming an alcoholic him/herself.   22.____

    A. 33
    B. 50
    C. 65
    D. 80

23. The likelihood of alcohol use _____ is most likely to be determined by cultural factors.   23.____

    A. resulting in aggressive behavior
    B. reducing stress
    C. affecting the liver
    D. acting on the "pleasure pathway" of the brain

24. The substances known as endorphins, which are produced naturally in the brain and pituitary gland, are most like _____ their composition and effect.   24.____

    A. opiates
    B. stimulants
    C. barbiturates
    D. benzodiazepines

25. Schedule III drugs include   25.____
    I. anabolic steroids
    II. benzodiazepines
    III. Vicodin
    IV. morphine

    A. I only
    B. I and III
    C. II only
    D. II and IV

KEY (CORRECT ANSWERS)

1.	C	11.	C
2.	A	12.	B
3.	B	13.	B
4.	C	14.	B
5.	C	15.	A
6.	A	16.	C
7.	B	17.	B
8.	C	18.	C
9.	A	19.	A
10.	D	20.	B

21. B
22. B
23. A
24. A
25. B

TEST 3

DIRECTIONS: Each question or incomplete statement is followed by several suggested answers or completions. Select the one that BEST answers the question or completes the statement. *PRINT THE LETTER OF THE CORRECT ANSWER IN THE SPACE AT THE RIGHT.*

1. Alcohol breaks down in the body at a fairly constant rate of _____ ounce(s) per hour. 1.____

    A. 0.5 to 1.0
    B. 1.0 to 1.5
    C. 2 to 3
    D. 3 to 5

2. When the repeated intake of a substance leads to more enhanced effects, the phenomenon of sensitization, or _____, has occurred. 2.____

    A. reverse tolerance
    B. distributive effect
    C. cascading effect
    D. tolerance

3. A beverage that is "100 proof" contains _____ % alcohol 3.____

    A. 10
    B. 30
    C. 50
    D. 100

4. Marijuana is sometimes used medicinally to 4.____

    A. suppress appetite
    B. relieve intraocular (eye) pressure
    C. decrease heart rate
    D. dilate blood vessels

5. Of the following routes of administration, _____ results in the fastest delivery of a drug to the brain. 5.____

    A. ingestion
    B. inhalation
    C. topically, on the skin
    D. topically, in the eye

6. Of the following drugs, the use of _____ most commonly results in addiction. 6.____

    A. heroin
    B. methamphetamine
    C. cocaine
    D. LSD

7. The most likely reaction to the ingestion of amphetamine is 7.____

    A. loss of appetite
    B. hallucination
    C. sedation
    D. increased alertness

8. The most notorious of the "designer drugs," originally created to get around existing drug laws by modifying their molecular structures, is 8.____

    A. rohypnol
    B. ketamine
    C. psilocybin
    D. ecstasy (MDMA)

9. Naltrexone is sometimes used to treat alcoholism by 9.____

   A. reducing the craving for alcohol
   B. blocking the reception of alcohol by brain receptors
   C. reversing the effects of alcohol intoxication
   D. producing an immediate and severe negative reaction to alcohol intake

10. Of the following, which is a hallucinogen that is extremely dangerous in high doses? 10.____

    A. Phencyclidine (PCP)
    B. Mescaline
    C. Psilocybin
    D. LSD

11. "Crack" is a purified form of _____ that produces a rapid and intense reaction in the user. 11.____

    A. methamphetamine   B. cocaine
    C. marijuana   D. heroin

12. Which of the following hallucinogens is taken by ingesting mushrooms in which it naturally occurs? 12.____

    A. Psilocybin   B. Mescaline
    C. LAA (lysergic acid amide)   D. Datura

13. Which of the following approaches to drug dependence treatment is based on the idea that dependence is best treated by intensive individual and group counseling, in either a residential or non-residential setting? 13.____

    A. Therapeutic community
    B. Structural/functional
    C. Aversion therapy
    D. Medical treatment

14. Which of the following is a danger that is specific to the abuse of ether? 14.____

    A. Long-term tissue retention
    B. Powerful hallucinations
    C. Ocular damage
    D. High flammability

15. "Black tar" is a street term for an inexpensive form of 15.____

    A. heroin   B. cocaine
    C. marijuana   D. MDMA (ecstasy)

16. Which of the following is most often classified by itself because it is technically more than one drug, with a wide range of effects? 16.____

    A. MDMA (ecstasy)   B. Marijuana
    C. GHB   D. LSD

17. Drugs that are classified as Schedule II by the DEA are said to have an accepted medi-   17.____
    cal use in the United States, and a high liability for abuse. Examples include each of the
    following, EXCEPT

    A. methadone   B. ketamine
    C. pentobarbital   D. diazepam

18. The Pure Food and Drug Act, which required that all drugs be accurately labeled, was   18.____
    passed in

    A. 1888   B. 1906
    C. 1934   D. 1970

19. Company-sponsored drug abuse prevention programs generally have the greatest   19.____
    impact on businesses in the _____ sector.

    A. transportation
    B. health care
    C. telecommunications
    D. textile

20. Which of the following is most clearly classified as a stimulant?   20.____

    A. Morphine   B. Cocaine
    C. Alcohol   D. Marijuana

21. The Fourth Edition of the Diagnostic and Statistical Manual of Mental Disorders-com-   21.____
    monly known as the DSM-IV and published by the American Psychiatric Association-lists
    each of the following as a possible psychiatric diagnosis, EXCEPT

    A. substance dependence   B. substance abuse
    C. alcoholism   D. cannabis delirium

22. The primary risk associated with the medical model for managing alcohol withdrawal is   22.____

    A. the development of a dependence on a new substance
    B. seizure
    C. abnormal heart rhythm
    D. a de-emphasis on the psychological factors that led to abuse

23. _____ prevention programs are aimed at people who have tried a certain drug or other 23.____
    drugs, but have not been treated for dependence

    A. Primary   B. Secondary
    C. Tertiary   D. Quaternary

24. Most of the money-from all sources-used in the United States to fight the problem of sub- 24.____
    stance abuse is allocated to

    A. reducing the supply
    B. treatment programs
    C. law enforcement
    D. prevention programs

25. Alcohol contains
    I. vitamins
    II. calories
    III. minerals
    IV. proteins

    A. I and II
    B. II only
    C. I and III
    D. I, II, III and IV

25. ____

KEY (CORRECT ANSWERS)

1. A
2. A
3. C
4. B
5. B

6. A
7. D
8. D
9. A
10. A

11. B
12. A
13. A
14. D
15. A

16. B
17. D
18. B
19. A
20. B

21. C
22. A
23. B
24. C
25. B

TEST 4

DIRECTIONS: Each question or incomplete statement is followed by several suggested answers or completions. Select the one that BEST answers the question or completes the statement. *PRINT THE LETTER OF THE CORRECT ANSWER IN THE SPACE AT THE RIGHT.*

1. E.M. Jellinek's theory of alcoholism was that it was a(n)

    A. form of neurosis
    B. progressive disease that moved through several predictable stages
    C. form of deviance similar to other forms of insanity
    D. condition that arose directly as a result of one's home environment

2. The lifetime prevalence of alcohol dependence (the percentage of people who are alcoholics at any point in their lives) in the United States is about _____ percent.

    A. 6   B. 12
    C. 18   D. 25

3. Which of the following is NOT likely to be caused by chronic marijuana use?

    A. Impaired ability to learn
    B. Diminished motivation to work
    C. Aggressive behavior
    D. Decreased testosterone levels in men

4. "Hallucinogenic persisting perceptive disorder" is a clinical term for

    A. Formication   B. Eye twitches
    C. Flashback   D. Euphoria

5. Cocaine works by increasing the availability of _____ in the brain.

    A. acetylcholine   B. serotonin
    C. epinephrine   D. dopamine

6. Another term by which the opioid drugs are known is

    A. sedatives   B. barbiturates
    C. hypnotics   D. narcotics

7. Of the following substances, which is classified as both a hallucinogen and a stimulant?

    A. Cocaine   B. Ecstasy (MDMA)
    C. Heroin   D. Mescaline

8. In the year _____, the federal Food and Drug Administration began to require that new drugs had to be demonstrated to be effective before they could be marketed.

    A. 1906   B. 1912
    C. 1962   D. 1970

9. Accepted therapeutic uses of opiates include each of the following, EXCEPT

    A. cough suppression
    B. treatment of liver insufficiency
    C. treatment of severe diarrhea
    D. pain relief

10. Symptoms associated with heroin withdrawal include each of the following, EXCEPT

    A. muscle and bone pain
    B. vomiting
    C. cold sweats
    D. abdominal cramps

11. A drug introduced through IM injection will be absorbed most rapidly if injected into the

    A. deltoid
    B. abdominals
    C. quadriceps
    D. gluteals

12. When two drugs are present in the system at one time, but the effect of one reduces or blocks the effect of the other, it is said to have a(n) _____ effect.

    A. potentiating
    B. withdrawal
    C. inhibiting
    D. synergistic

13. A(n) _____ prevention program is oriented to those who have already been treated for substance abuse.

    A. primary
    B. secondary
    C. tertiary
    D. outpatient

14. Increased heart rate and blood pressure as the result of taking a drug are examples of _____ activation.

    A. somatic
    B. peripheral
    C. parasympathetic
    D. sympathetic

15. Mescaline and psilocybin belong to the _____ class of drugs.

    A. hallucinogen
    B. narcotic
    C. stimulant
    D. depressant

16. The primary behavioral consequences of marijuana use are associated with

    A. problem-solving
    B. impulse control
    C. memory and attention
    D. sleep and dreams

17. The "flushing syndrome" associated with alcohol use typically involves each of the following symptoms, EXCEPT

    A. memory problems
    B. hives
    C. headache
    D. rapid heart rate

18. Deliriant, or anticholinergic, drugs include

    A. ketamine
    B. nitrous oxide
    C. datura
    D. psilocybin

19. "Distilled spirits" or "hard liquor" generally has an alcohol content of about _____ percent

    A. 3.2 to 12.0
    B. 15 to 30
    C. 40 to 50
    D. 60 to 80

20. Which of the following is generally NOT an effect of chronic marijuana use?

    A. Lower infant birth weight
    B. Lower fertility for women
    C. Damage to the respiratory system
    D. Lowered sperm count in men

21. Currently, the preferred confirmatory test for the presence of alcohol and drugs is

    A. spectrophotometry
    B. radioimmunoassay
    C. gas chromatography/mass spectrometry (GC/MS)
    D. thin layer chromatography

22. Which of the following is a term for the state arising from alcohol abuse in which a person has difficulties in problem-solving, organizing facts about one's identity and environment, and remembering information?

    A. Alcoholic dementia
    B. Potentiation
    C. Alcoholic cirrhosis
    D. Alcoholic aphasia

23. Feelings of euphoria associated with the use of most inhalants tend to last about

    A. 40 seconds
    B. 10 minutes
    C. one hour
    D. 4 hours

24. A habitual marijuana user has discovered that he needs to smoke three times as much to achieve the level of intoxication he achieved a year ago.
    This phenomenon is known as

    A. withdrawal
    B. potentiation
    C. reversion
    D. tolerance

25. Drugs that are classified as Schedule I by the DEA are said to have no accepted medical use in the United States, and have a high liability for abuse. Examples of Schedule I drugs include each of the following, EXCEPT

    A. marijuana
    B. mescaline
    C. morphine
    D. heroin

KEY (CORRECT ANSWERS)

1.	B	11.	A
2.	B	12.	C
3.	C	13.	C
4.	C	14.	D
5.	D	15.	A
6.	D	16.	C
7.	B	17.	A
8.	C	18.	C
9.	B	19.	C
10.	D	20.	B

21. C
22. A
23. C
24. D
25. C

EXAMINATION SECTION
TEST 1

DIRECTIONS: Each question or incomplete statement is followed by several suggested answers or completions. Select the one that BEST answers the question or completes the statement. *PRINT THE LETTER OF THE CORRECT ANSWER IN THE SPACE AT THE RIGHT*

1. According to the federal government, the estimated annual economic cost of drug abuse in the United States is closest to

    A. $500 million
    B. $4 billion
    C. $180 billion
    D. $1.2 trillion

1.____

2. Which of the following is an anesthetic inhalant?

    A. Xylene
    B. Nitrous oxide
    C. Amyl nitrite
    D. Toluene

2.____

3. Short-term effects of marijuana use include

    A. reduced heart rate
    B. increased blood pressure
    C. bronchitis
    D. increased appetite

3.____

4. The first alkaloid ever isolated from the opium poppy was

    A. morphine
    B. codeine
    C. heroin
    D. methadone

4.____

5. In the United States, the most effective drug abuse prevention efforts have typically focused on

    A. peer and social influences
    B. real-life case studies
    C. worst-case scenarios
    D. legal rationales

5.____

6. Fatal consequences, although rare, are possible for those who suddenly stop their chronic use of _____ without medical supervision.
    I. barbiturates
    II. alcohol
    III. cocaine
    IV. heroin

6.____

A. I or II
B. II only
C. I, II or IV
D. I, II, III or IV

7. The use of drugs or alcohol to avoid withdrawal symptoms is an example of 7.____

   A. potentiation
   B. positive reinforcement
   C. negative tolerance
   D. negative reinforcement

8. The barbiturates are typically classified according to their 8.____

   A. duration of action
   B. potential for interaction with alcohol
   C. method of metabolism
   D. chemical structure

9. Which of the following is a club drag that stimulates the release of human growth hormone, and whose main ingredient is an industrial solvent? 9.____

   A. GHB (gamma hydroxybutyrate)
   B. GABA (ganima-aminobutyric acid)
   C. MDMA (ecstasy)
   D. Ketamine

10. Typically, heroin is about_____times stronger than morphine. 10.____

    A. 1-2
    B. 3-10
    C. 5-20
    D. 40

11. Among the following groups, the highest rates of illicit drug use are reported among 11.____

    A. construction workers
    B. physicians and nurses
    C. law enforcement officers
    D. social sendee professionals

12. It is estimated that about _____ percent of patients who suffer from a form of mental illness also have a substance abuse disorder. 12.____

    A. 10-20
    B. 25-35
    C. 40-75
    D. 70-85

13. The indirect effects of alcohol consumption are illustrated by the 13.____

    A. decrease in thiamin absorption
    B. increased risk of fetal alcohol syndrome among pregnant women

C. relationship between drinking and motor vehicle crashes
D. relationship between drinking and liver cancer

14. Which of the following is classified as a deliriant?

    A. Psilocybin
    B. Mescaline
    C. Datura
    D. LSD

15. Most first-time drinkers would likely be passed out by the time their blood alcohol content reaches _____ %.

    A. .05
    B. .08
    C. .15
    D. .20

16. Each of the following neurotransmitters is thought to play a role in a person's biological predisposition toward alcoholism, EXCEPT

    A. GABA
    B. norepinephrine
    C. serotonin
    D. dopamine

17. Typically, the alcohol in a drink will reach the bloodstream in about _____ minutes.

    A. 15
    B. 30
    C. 45
    D. 60

18. Which of the following drugs is used to treat manic symptoms?

    A. Lithium
    B. Methadone
    C. Paxil
    D. Librium

19. _____ drugs typically act by blocking the brain's dopamine receptors.

    A. Antipsychotic
    B. Steroidal
    C. Analgesic
    D. Opioid

20. For U.S. adolescents in a substance treatment program, the primary drug of abuse is most likely to be

    A. marijuana
    B. an inhalant
    C. alcohol
    D. cocaine

21. In 1988 the Anti-Drug Abuse Act created the government agency known as the

    A. White House Office of National Drug Control Policy (ONDCP)
    B. Substance Abuse and Mental Health Services Administration (SAMH-SA)
    C. Drug Enforcement Agency (DEA)
    D. National Institute on Drag Abuse (NIDA)

22. Babies whose mothers have used cocaine during pregnancy are likely to have a higher rate of
    I. low birth weight
    II. sudden infant death syndrome (SIDS)
    III. genito-urinary malformations
    IV. congenital heart delects

    A. I and II
    B. II and III
    C. II and IV
    D. I, II, III and IV

23. A "Type I" alcoholic generally has each of the following personality traits, EXCEPT

    A. optimism
    B. rigidity in behaviors and beliefs
    C. shyness
    D. sentimentality

24. Each of the following is a commonly occurring effect of chronic opiate dosing, EXCEPT

    A. weightless
    B. increased urination
    C. constricted pupils
    D. elevated body temperature

25. The late stages of alcoholism are often characterized by

    A. reverse tolerance
    B. synergism
    C. pharmacological tolerance
    D. cross-tolerance

KEY (CORRECT ANSWERS)

1. C
2. B
3. D
4. A
5. A

6. C
7. D
8. A
9. A
10. B

11. A
12. C
13. C
14. C
15. C

16. B
17. A
18. A
19. A
20. A

21. A
22. D
23. A
24. C
25. A

TEST 2

DIRECTIONS: Each question or incomplete statement is followed by several suggested answers or completions. Select the one that BEST answers the question or completes the statement. *PRINT THE LETTER OF THE CORRECT ANSWER IN THE SPACE AT THE RIGHT.*

1. Alcohol withdrawal differs significantly from withdrawal from other drugs in that it 1.____

    A. can result in hallucinations
    B. is purely psychological
    C. can be directly fatal
    D. is treatable with synthetic opioids

2. Although the terms "opioid" and "opiate" are often used interchangeably, "opiate" more properly refers only to 2.____

    A. opioids that are produced naturally by an organism
    B. natural opium alkaloids and the semi-synthetics derived from them.
    C. an opioid that is used only as prescribed
    D. fully synthetic opioids

3. Ingesting/injecting several anabolic steroids at once is referred to as 3.____

    A. stacking
    B. cycling
    C. chipping
    D. raging

4. Over the years, research has suggested that women who drink heavily die an average of _____ years earlier than women who do not drink at all. 4.____

    A. 5
    B. 10
    C. 15
    D. 25

5. The first stage of barbiturate withdrawal, the "delirium" stage, lasts for about 5.____

    A. 12 hours
    B. 48 hours
    C. 5 days
    D. 10 days

6. NMDA receptor antagonists include 6.____
    I. PCP
    II. ketamine
    III. psilocybin
    IV. LSD

    A. I only
    B. I and II
    C. II and III
    D. LSD

7. Rebound insomnia, in which a person has greater difficulty falling asleep, is often associated with the use of

    A. stimulants
    B. sedative hypnotics
    C. hallucinogens
    D. narcotics

8. A single marijuana cigarette is associated with about _____ the bronchial damage associated with a regular tobacco cigarette.

    A. half
    B. the same
    C. 4 times
    D. 20 times

9. A drug that is described as "diuretic"

    A. softens the stool and makes defecation easier
    B. is used to treat heart arrhythmias
    C. accelerates the elimination of fluid
    D. slows the elimination of fluid

10. As of 2007, Rohypnol is a Schedule _____ substance.

    A. I
    B. II
    C. III
    D. IV

11. If a drug is said to have a therapeutic index of 1:4, that means that

    A. the effective dose is 1/4 of the lethal dose.
    B. only 1 person in 4 can safely use the drug.
    C. the drug remains effective for 1-4 hours.
    D. only 1/4 of the effective dose is biotransformed every hour.

12. Between a third and two-thirds of all child-welfare cases in the United States involve

    A. child substance abuse
    B. parental substance abuse
    C. prenatal substance exposure
    D. parental tobacco use

13. Methamphetanine is sometimes prescribed today for the treatment of

    A. atrial fibrillation
    B. insomnia
    C. depression
    D. attention deficit/hyperactivity disorder (ADHD)

14. Which of the following drug abuse prevention methods teaches students to recognize, manage, and avoid situations that might involve drug abuse?

A. Resistance skills training
B. Values clarification
C. Negative reinforcement
D. Self-efficacy training

15. In the United States, about _____ percent of all primary care and hospitalized patients suffer from alcohol dependence.

    A. 5 to 7
    B. 15 to 20
    C. 25 to 40
    D. 35 to 50

16. Which of the following is NOT a common sign of barbiturate use?

    A. Constricted pupils
    B. Cyanosis
    C. Cold, clammy skin
    D. Muscle twitches

17. In a given day, about _____ Americans receive treatment for alcoholism.

    A. 700,000
    B. 1.2 million
    C. 3.4 million
    D. 6 million

18. Drugs that are known for their relatively narrow therapeutic window, or margin of safety, include
    I. digoxin
    II. lithium carbonate
    III. opioids
    IV. acetaminophen

    A. I and II
    B. I, II and IV
    C. III only
    D. I, II and III

19. The class of drugs with the fewest accepted medical uses are the

    A. hallucinogens
    B. stimulants
    C. anabolic steroids
    D. opioids

20. Which of the following is most commonly associated with stroke, lung and liver damage, and sudden death due to cardiac arrest?

    A. Ketamine
    B. Ecstasy
    C. Marijuana
    D. Cocaine

21. Quaalude, a barbiturate alternative, is a brand name for the drug   21. ____

    A. mefloquine
    B. quinine
    C. methaqualone
    D. quazepam

22. The median lethal dose for alcohol is a blood alcohol content (BAC) of about _____   22. ____
    percent.

    A. .20
    B. .40
    C. .60
    D. .80

23. Which of the following is a powerful opiate known by the slang term "China White"?   23. ____

    A. Morphine
    B. Darvon
    C. Percocet
    D. Fentanyl

24. When a person's average number of drinks per day are plotted on the horizontal axis of a   24. ____
    graph, beginning with "zero" in the lower left corner, and the risk of death is plotted
    upward on the vertical axis, the result is a(n)

    A. J-shaped curve
    B. straight diagonal line traveling to the upper right
    C. M-shaped curve
    D. bell curve , "

25. An example of a "harm reduction" policy approach to drug abuse is   25. ____

    A. mandatory diversions
    B. needle-exchange programs
    C. education programs
    D. decriminalization

KEY (CORRECT ANSWERS)

1.	C	11.	A
2.	B	12.	B
3.	A	13.	D
4.	C	14.	A
5.	C	15.	B
6.	B	16.	A
7.	B	17.	A
8.	D	18.	B
9.	C	19.	A
10.	D	20.	D

21. C
22. B
23. D
24. A
25. B

TEST 3

DIRECTIONS: Each question or incomplete statement is followed by several suggested answers or completions. Select the one that BEST answers the question or completes the statement. *PRINT THE LETTER OF THE CORRECT ANSWER IN THE SPACE AT THE RIGHT.*

1. In the United States, illicit drag use is most prevalent in

    A. inner city areas
    B. the suburbs
    C. rural areas
    D. the Midwest

2. The goal of the intervention process is to

    A. convince the person that he or she needs treatment
    B. identify the person's primary defense mechanism
    C. isolate the client to make him or her feel the consequences of behavior
    D. establish a working relationship with the physician or substance abuse counselor

3. Typically, about _____ percent of alcohol-dependent people seek treatment for their disorder.

    A. 10
    B. 25
    C. 35
    D. 50

4. The word "flip," in varying forms, is often used to describe a combination of the drug _____ with another recreational drug.

    A. ecstasy (MDMA)
    B. cocaine
    C. LSD
    D. marijuana

5. Which of the following does NOT bind with the brain's serotonin receptors?

    A. LSD
    B. Haloperidol
    C. Psilocybin
    D. DMT

6. The Fourth Edition of the Diagnostic and Statistical Manual of Mental Disorderscommonly known as the DSM-IV and published by the American Psychiatric Associationincludes each of the following in its criteria for a diagnosis of drug or alcohol dependency, EXCEPT

    A. developing a tolerance for the substance
    B. preoccupation with further use of the substance
    C. using the substance solely in moments of peak stress
    D. using the substance at inappropriate times

7. Neurotransmitters is involved in the voluntary movement of muscles include

    I. epinephrine
    II. dopamine
    III. acetylcholine
    IV. GABA

    A. I and II
    B. II and III
    C. II, III and IV
    D. I, II, III and IV

8. The psychoactive agent in permanent markers that are sniffed or inhaled is

    A. acetone
    B. xylene
    C. ether
    D. butane

9. Minor tranquilizers, nonbarbiturate sedatives, and barbiturates are classified as

    A. sedative hypnotics
    B. psychedelics
    C. benzodiazepines
    D. inhalants

10. Other than methadone, which of the following is a synthetic drug approved for treating narcotic withdrawal?

    A. GHB
    B. Fentanyl
    C. LAAM
    D. Thiamine

11. The psychological trait most often linked with drug use is

    A. antisocial personality disorder
    B. low self-esteem
    C. impulsiveness
    D. denial

12. The smallest amount of a drug required to produce an effect is called the _____ dose.

    A. therapeutic
    B. standard
    C. threshold
    D. marginal

13. As a group, the ethnicity that typically records the lowest alcohol consumption in the United States is

    A. Asian Americans
    B. Hispanic Americans
    C. Euro-Americans
    D. African Americans

14. Injecting cocaine provides the highest blood levels of the drug in the shortest amount of time, but is generally avoided by users because it

    A. tends to cause immediate unconsciousness
    B. is very dangerous
    C. results in a loss of motor control
    D. tends to cause uncontrollable vomiting

14.____

15. Physiological symptoms associated with heroin use include
    I. vomiting
    II. sleepiness
    III. constipation
    IV. reduced sex drive

    A. I and II
    B. II only
    C. II and III
    D. I, II, III and IV

15.____

16. Each of the following has been classified as a psychedelic drug, EXCEPT

    A. Ketamine
    B. LSD
    C. marijuana
    D. ecstasy (MDMA)

16.____

17. During the hour after cocaine is used, the risk of heart attack increases by a factor of about

    A. 5
    B. 10
    C. 25
    D. 50

17.____

18. Tricyclic drags, when combined with _____ , may produce a fatal reaction.

    A. LSD
    B. benzodiazepines
    C. alcohol
    D. narcotics

18.____

19. Which of the following is NOT a health risk associated with alcoholism?

    A. Bladder cancer
    B. Pancreatitis
    C. Hypertension
    D. Breast cancer

19.____

20. Statistics show that most people in drug or alcohol treatment programs throughout the United States

    A. use primarily one drug of choice
    B. are unlikely to use again after completing the program

20.____

C. use more than one substance
D. are between the ages of 35 and 44

21. The age group most likely to abuse inhalants is 21.____

    A. 12-17
    B. 18-25
    C. 25-44
    D. 45-60

22. Under the Controlled Substances Act, benzodiazepines are Schedule _____. 22.____

    A. I
    B. II
    C. III
    D. IV

23. A single drink containing one ounce (28 grams) of alcohol will increase the average person's BAC by roughly _____ percent. 23.____

    A. .01
    B. .03
    C. .05
    D. .07

24. Withdrawal from THC is commonly associated with each of the following, EXCEPT 24.____

    A. nausea
    B. paranoia
    C. insomnia
    D. loss of appetite

25. When a pregnant woman drinks alcohol, the fetal blood alcohol will equal the mother's in about 25.____

    A. 15 minutes
    B. 1 hour
    C. 3 hours
    D. 6 hours

KEY (CORRECT ANSWERS)

1.	A	11.	D
2.	A	12.	C
3.	A	13.	A
4.	A	14.	D
5.	B	15.	D
6.	C	16.	A
7.	C	17.	C
8.	B	18.	C
9.	A	19.	A
10.	C	20.	C

21. A
22. D
23. B
24. B
25. A

TEST 4

DIRECTIONS: Each question or incomplete statement is followed by several suggested answers or completions. Select the one that BEST answers the question or completes the statement. *PRINT THE LETTER OF THE CORRECT ANSWER IN THE SPACE AT THE RIGHT.*

1. In the United States, about _____ percent of the convicts housed in federal prisons are there because of drug-related crimes.　　1.____

    A. 10
    B. 30
    C. 50
    D. 70

2. Which of the following is NOT an opioid?　　2.____

    A. Codeine
    B. Oxycodone
    C. Heroin
    D. Cocaine

3. Marijuana is most likely to be used medically as a(n)　　3.____

    A. anti-emetic
    B. laxative
    C. anti-inflammatory
    D. diuretic

4. The brain's center of arousal and motivation, and attention is known as the　　4.____

    A. reticular activating system
    B. limbic system
    C. frontal cortex
    D. basal ganglia

5. Which of the following is a brand name for a benzodiazepine most commonly used to induce sleep?　　5.____

    A. Xanax
    B. Valium
    C. Librium
    D. Halcion

6. The class of drugs known as hypnotics typically includes　　6.____
    I. GHB
    II. benzodiazepines
    III. opiates
    IV. barbiturates

    A. I and II
    B. I, III and IV
    C. II and IV
    D. I, II, III and IV

7. It usually takes about _____ for inhaled drugs to reach the brain.

    A. less than a second
    B. 5-8 seconds
    C. 20-30 seconds
    D. 1-3 minutes

8. What is the term for a chemical substance that crosses a synapse to a receptor site?

    A. Hormone
    B. Dendrite
    C. Neurotransmitter
    D. Agonist

9. Which of the following is NOT classified as a dissociative anesthetic drug?

    A. Psilocybin
    B. Ketamine
    C. Phencyclidine (PCP)
    D. Dextromethorphan

10. For at-risk students in the United States, the most effective drug abuse prevention programs are usually _____ in their approach.

    A. confrontational
    B. alternative
    C. highly structured
    D. peer-led

11. Heavy consumption of alcohol reduces the production of the neuroinhibito

    A. GABA
    B. glutamate
    C. glycine
    D. NDMA

12. In the United States of the early 21st century, the drug of abuse most likely to be administered intravenously was

    A. cocaine
    B. Flunitrazepam (Rohypnol)
    C. methamphetamine
    D. heroin

13. Of the following physical effects of narcotics, the LEAST common is

    A. dry mouth
    B. nausea
    C. respiratory depression
    D. constipation

14. The "controlled drinking" approach to treating alcoholism is not recommended for people with

A. little or no social support
B. functional problems related to alcoholism
C. liver disease
D. cancer

15. The route of administration for anabolic steroids that showed the largest growth in popularity during the early 21st century was

    A. intravenous injection
    B. intramuscular injection
    C. creams, gels, and transdermal patches
    D. oral ingestion

15.___

16. Of the following routes of administration, which is LEAST likely to lead to overdose?

    A. Injecting
    B. Smoking
    C. Swallowing
    D. Snorting

16.___

17. In the United States, a blood alcohol concentration reported as .20% means specifically that

    A. every 100 milliliters of a person's blood contains .02 grams of alcohol
    B. every 1000 grams of a person's blood contains 2 grams of alcohol
    C. every 200 grams of a person's blood contains a milliliter of alcohol
    D. every 1000 milliliters of a person's blood contains .02 milliliters of blood

17.___

18. The increasing use of inhalants by American teenagers has been largely attributed to

    A. the low cost and availability of inhalants
    B. a lack of clear regulation regarding their use
    C. a celebrity culture that glorifies the use of inhalants
    D. the increasing refinement of inhalants that produce euphoria

18.___

19. When abused, methamphetamines are especially harmful to the _____ system.

    A. gastrointestinal
    B. dental
    C. autonomic nervous
    D. cardiovascular

19.___

20. At the beginning of the 21st century, the world's largest producer of illegal opium was

    A. Myanmar
    B. Colombia
    C. Afghanistan
    D. China

20.___

21. Another term for antipsychotic drugs is

    A. minor tranquilizers
    B. benzodiazepines

21.___

C. major tranquilizers
D. hypnotics

22. Chronic alcohol use affects the body's immune system in each of the following ways, EXCEPT by   22._____

    A. increasing the susceptibility to infection
    B. inhibiting white blood cells
    C. interfering with recovery from colds and flu
    D. increasing red blood cell counts

23. Each of the following has been linked to steroid use, EXCEPT   23._____

    A. Liver and kidney cancer
    B. Pancreatitis
    C. Low sperm count
    D. Abrupt mood swings

24. In the last half-century, the medical community has been most significantly influenced by the _____ model as the explanation for why people abuse alcohol.   24._____

    A. social learning
    B. disease
    C. stress-response-dampening
    D. tension reduction

25. The Drug Abuse Warning Network (DAWN) is a system that   25._____

    A. seeks to discourage interest in illegal drugs, gangs, and violence through education
    B. improves the quality and availability of prevention, treatment, and rehabilitative services in order to reduce illness, death, disability, and cost to society resulting from substance abuse and mental illness
    C. monitors drug-related visits to hospital emergency departments and drug-related deaths investigated by medical examiners and coroners
    D. establishes policies, priorities, and objectives to eradicate illicit drug use, manufacturing, and trafficking, drug-related crime and violence, and drug-related health consequences in the United States

KEY (CORRECT ANSWERS)

1. C
2. D
3. A
4. A
5. D

6. C
7. B
8. C
9. A
10. B

11. A
12. C
13. C
14. C
15. C

16. C
17. A
18. A
19. D
20. C

21. C
22. D
23. B
24. B
25. C

EXAMINATION SECTION
TEST 1

DIRECTIONS: Each question or incomplete statement is followed by several suggested answers or completions. Select the one that BEST answers the question or completes the statement. *PRINT THE LETTER OF THE CORRECT ANSWER IN THE SPACE AT THE RIGHT.*

1. Which of the following benzodiazepines is treated most strictly by the federal government?

    A. Flunitrazepam (Rohypnol)
    B. Diazepam (Valium)
    C. Chlordiazepoxide (Librium)
    D. Alprazolam (Xanax)

2. Which of the following neurotransmitters generally governs a person's wakefulness and arousal, and is involved in the "fight or flight" response?

    A. Acetylcholine
    B. Norepinephrine
    C. Dopamine
    D. Serotonin

3. Another name for anticholinergic substances is

    A. dissociatives
    B. deliriants
    C. cannabinoids
    D. hormones

4. Which of the following terms is used to denote efforts to halt the import, sale, and manufacture of illicit drugs?

    A. Narcoterrorism
    B. Diversion
    C. Customs
    D. Interdiction

5. The psychoactive substance found in the peyote cactus is

    A. ketamine
    B. mescaline
    C. phencyclidine
    D. psilocybin

6. Drugs that are used to treat the symptoms of alcoholic withdrawal include
    I. Librium
    II. phenobarbital
    III. methadone
    IV. disulfiram

    A. I and II   B. II only   C. II, III and IV   D. I, II, III and IV

7. Which of the following drugs is used to stabilize the chemical balance of the brain, which would otherwise be disrupted by alcoholism?

    A. Acaraprosate (Campral)
    B. Naltrexone
    C. Baclofen
    D. Disulfiram (Antabuse)

8. Marijuana is known to affect the _____, or the part of the brain that controls memory.

    A. cerebellum
    B. hippocampus
    C. pons
    D. hypothalamus

9. The most common cause of impotence among middle-aged men is

    A. overuse of stimulants
    B. nicotine addiction
    C. high blood pressure
    D. alcohol overuse

10. In medicine, narcotic analgesics are favored over other types of painkillers because they involve fewer adverse affects on

    A. the synaptic response
    B. the gastrointestinal system
    C. memory
    D. intellectual and motor function

11. A person's perception and judgement can be affected by moderate amounts of alcohol in each of the following ways, EXCEPT

    A. impaired sexual performance
    B. enhanced olfactory perception
    C. a diminished sensation of cold
    D. motor skill impairment

12. Which of the following effects is MOST likely to be associated with anabolic steroid abuse?

    A. loss of appetite
    B. elevated sperm count
    C. decreased blood pressure
    D. increased levels of low-density lipoproteins (LDL) in the blood

13. "Poppers" is a slang term used to denote the inhalant

    A. amyl nitrite
    B. butane
    C. diethyl ether
    D. nitrous oxide

14. A person finds that she needs larger and larger doses of a drug to achieve intoxication or other desired effects. This person has developed

    A. psychological dependence
    B. a potentiating response
    C. a physical dependence
    D. hypersensitivity to the drug

15. Which of the following is NOT a common side effect of antipsychotics?

    A. Dystonia
    B. Parkinsonism
    C. Impotence
    D. Cardiac arrhythmia

16. Which of the following terms is used to denote an enhanced, unpredictable effect caused by ingesting two or more substances?

    A. Covariance
    B. Synergism
    C. Stacking
    D. Tolerance

17. Insufflation is a technical term for the introduction of a drug by

    A. smoking
    B. suppository
    C. snorting
    D. using a skin patch

18. One criticism of the disease model for diagnosing and treating alcoholism is that

    A. it tends to stigmatize the individual who suffers from it
    B. it is too limited and should apply to other forms of behavioral intervention
    C. it calls upon the use of public resources to treat what is essentially an individual disorder
    D. the terminology seems to discount the individual's role in the process of addiction and treatment

19. Which of the following substances are naturally released by the brain when a person feels stress or pain?

    A. Endorphins
    B. GABA
    C. Carbon monoxide
    D. Morphine

20. Which of the following has been identified as a factor that may significantly reduce the likelihood of drug abuse?

    A. Strong family ties
    B. High socioeconomic status
    C. Race
    D. Higher level of education completed

21. When marijuana is smoked, it generally takes _____ for its psychoactive substance to reach the brain. 21.___

    A. a few seconds
    B. 30-45 seconds
    C. 2-3 minutes
    D. 5-8 minutes

22. Of the following processes, which produces the highest alcohol content? 22.___

    A. cold-filtering
    B. fermentation
    C. distillation
    D. brewing

23. Which of the following is a sympathomimetic effect? 23.___

    A. Constricted bronchial passages
    B. Constricted blood vessels
    C. Nausea
    D. Reduced cardiac output

24. Which of the following is an irreversible consequence of chronic alcohol abuse? 24.___

    A. Hepatitis
    B. Cirrhosis
    C. Pancreatitis
    D. Fatty liver

25. Historically, about _____ percent of heroin addicts have been able to break their addiction. 25.___

    A. 10
    B. 25
    C. 40
    D. 55

KEY (CORRECT ANSWERS)

1.	A	11.	B
2.	B	12.	D
3.	B	13.	A
4.	D	14.	C
5.	B	15.	D
6.	A	16.	B
7.	A	17.	C
8.	B	18.	D
9.	D	19.	A
10.	D	20.	A

21. A
22. C
23. B
24. B
25. A

TEST 2

DIRECTIONS: Each question or incomplete statement is followed by several suggested answers or completions. Select the one that BEST answers the question or completes the statement. *PRINT THE LETTER OF THE CORRECT ANSWER IN THE SPACE AT THE RIGHT.*

1. Typically, alcohol first produces noticeable cognitive changes at a blood alcohol concentration (BAC) of   1.___

   A. .02% to .03%
   B. .05% to .08%
   C. .10% to .15%
   D. .16% to .20%

2. The most common class of drugs used to treat the symptoms of those undergoing alcohol detoxification are the   2.___

   A. analgesics
   B. benzodiazepines
   C. amphetamines
   D. opiates

3. The most common reason for young people to try illegal drugs is   3.___

   A. emotional turmoil
   B. negative reinforcement
   C. curiosity
   D. peer pressure

4. About _____ percent of those who are classified as "heavy" marijuana users go on to use cocaine.   4.___

   A. 10
   B. 35
   C. 50
   D. 75

5. The slang term "chronic" is used to denote a potent form of marijuana, or marijuana laced with   5.___

   A. heroin
   B. ecstasy (MDMA)
   C. cocaine
   D. LSD

6. The ingestion of alcohol is followed by the release of _____ in the brain.   6.___
       I. dopamme
       II. serotonin
       III. norephinephrine
       IV. endorphins

   A. I and II
   B. I, II and III
   C. III and IV
   D. I, II, III and IV

7. _____ drinking is classified as drinking up to three or four standard alcoholic drinks in a day, no more than three days a week.

   A. Social
   B. Moderate
   C. Problem
   D. Binge

8. Widespread methamphetamine abuse in the United States is generally thought to have begun in

   A. the Midwest
   B. the South
   C. the West
   D. New England

9. The term _____ is used to describe people who have both a drug problem and a psychiatric disorder.

   A. dual diagnosis
   B. compound disorder
   C. bipolar
   D. differential diagnosis

10. Which of the following common household substances can—in massive doses—cause visual and auditory hallucinations?

    A. Banana peels
    B. Nutmeg
    C. Tomatoes
    D. Ginger

11. The use of cocaine in the United States peaked between the years

    A. 1920 and 1925
    B. 1940 and 1945
    C. 1960 and 1970
    D. 1980 and 1990

12. By definition, an analgesic is a drug that is designed to

    A. relieve pain by inducing unconsciousness
    B. stimulate the central nervous system
    C. relieve pain by stimulating a natural release of endorphins
    D. relieve pain without causing a loss of consciousness

13. Creatine is most accurately classified as a(n)

    A. vitamin
    B. drug
    C. nutritional supplement
    D. steroid

14. Substances commonly considered to be "gateway" drugs include each of the following, EXCEPT   14.___

    A. nicotine
    B. caffeine
    C. marijuana
    D. alcohol

15. Which of the following inhalants are typically inhaled out of paper or plastic bags?   15.___

    A. Oxides
    B. Solvents
    C. Nitrites
    D. Ether

16. Research based on the lives of twins has suggested that the heritability of alcohol abuse is about _____ percent,   16.___

    A. 10-25
    B. 30-40
    C. 50-60
    D. 70-85

17. Each of the following drugs causes withdrawal symptoms, EXCEPT   17.___

    A. marijuana
    B. alcohol
    C. caffeine
    D. ibuprofen

18. For nearly all of the drags of abuse, the "site of action" is the   18.___

    A. central nervous system
    B. physical location where the drug enters the body
    C. particular receptor where the substance prevents or accelerates the uptake of a certain neurotransmitter
    D. peripheral nervous system

19. Which of the following neurotransmitters plays an important role in emotional, mental, and motor functions?   19.___

    A. Endorphin
    B. Glutamate
    C. Serotonin
    D. Dopamine

20. Most hallucinogenic drugs are   20.___

    A. found in the natural environment
    B. Schedule III drugs
    C. synthetics
    D. legal

21. A teenager takes some of her mother's anti-anxiety medication to contend with the stress of final examinations. This is an example of _____ use.

    A. socio-recreational
    B. experimental
    C. circumstantial-situational
    D. intensified

22. When methadone is administered to avoid the withdrawal symptoms associated with heroin, it is administered

    A. hourly
    B. twice a day
    C. daily
    D. three times a week

23. The route of administration that introduces drugs into the bloodstream the fastest is

    A. intramuscular injection
    B. snorting
    C. smoking or inhaling into lungs
    D. intravenous injection

24. A common feature of fetal alcohol syndrome is _____ deformities.

    A. digital
    B. intestinal
    C. facial
    D. cardiac

25. The part of the brain that controls the emotional response is the

    A. pons
    B. limbic system
    C. hypothalamus
    D. reticular activating system

5 (#2)

KEY (CORRECT ANSWERS)

1.	A	11.	B
2.	B	12.	D
3.	D	13.	C
4.	D	14.	B
5.	C	15.	B
6.	B	16.	C
7.	B	17.	D
8.	C	18.	A
9.	A	19.	D
10.	B	20.	A

21. C
22. C
23. D
24. C
25. B

———

TEST 3

DIRECTIONS: Each question or incomplete statement is followed by several suggested answers or completions. Select the one that BEST answers the question or completes the statement. *PRINT THE LETTER OF THE CORRECT ANSWER IN THE SPACE AT THE RIGHT.*

1. Treatment for substance abuse is often considered to be a form of _____ prevention. 1.____

    A. primary
    B. secondary
    C. tertiary
    D. compound

2. Which of the following substances generally involves the LOWEST degree of physical dependence? 2.____

    A. LSD
    B. Valium
    C. Alcohol
    D. Methadone

3. Each of the following is a Schedule I drug, EXCEPT 3.____

    A. MDMA (ecstasy)
    B. GHB
    C. Cocaine
    D. LSD

4. Which of the following substances is known by the slang term "knockout drops"? 4.____

    A. Ketamine
    B. Ether
    C. Flunitrazepam (Rohypnol)
    D. Chloral hydrate

5. The most frequently committed crime in the United States is 5.____

    A. drinking underage
    B. underage purchase of alcohol
    C. driving while intoxicated
    D. illegal drug use

6. The word "psychotropic" is most accurately defined as 6.____

    A. addictive
    B. mind-altering
    C. hallucinatory
    D. mind-affecting

7. Which of the following causes of death is LEAST likely to be associated with the use of inhalants? 7.____

    A. respiratory depression   B. hypoxia
    C. cardiac arrest   D. aspiration of vomit

8. Physical dependence on a substance is indicated by the presence of

   A. denial
   B. withdrawal symptoms
   C. agonists
   D. psychological symptoms

9. Which of the following terms is used to denote the condition of a loss of contact with reality?

   A. Sociopathy
   B. Psychosis
   C. Personality disorder
   D. Neurosis

10. Which of the following is LEAST likely to be a condition that accompanies cocaine dependence?

    A. Heart failure
    B. Stroke
    C. Paranoia
    D. Irrepressible sex drive

11. More than any other drug, _____ is known for being taken in common with other recreational drugs.

    A. marijuana
    B. amphetamine
    C. ecstasy (MDMA)
    D. cocaine

12. Stage II of alcoholic withdrawal is characterized by

    A. convulsions
    B. rapid heartbeat
    C. hallucinations
    D. delirium

13. One of the earliest proponents of the therapeutic properties of cocaine was

    A. Sigmund Freud
    B. Everett Koop
    C. Timothy Leary
    D. King James I of England

14. Phencyclidine (PCP) tends to accumulate in

    A. the pancreas
    B. the liver
    C. extracellular fluid
    D. body fat

15. Which of the following neurotransmitters plays a significant role in regulating pain, eating, perception, and sleep?   15.____

    A. Dopamine
    B. Epinephrine
    C. Serotonin
    D. GABA

16. Common symptoms of marijuana use include each of the following, EXCEPT   16.____

    A. bloodshot eyes
    B. dry mouth
    C. increased intracranial pressure
    D. increased heart rate

17. Which of the following is NOT a sub-category of the class of drugs known as hallucinogens?   17.____

    A. Deliriants
    B. Psychedelics
    C. Hypnotics
    D. Dissociatives

18. Research has indicated that women who are problem drinkers   18.____

    A. have less risk for liver damage than men who are problem drinkers
    B. are at a much higher risk for osteoporosis than women who are not heavy drinkers
    C. are less likely to have an alcoholic parent than male problem drinkers
    D. are usually smokers as well

19. Of all the cases of pancreatitis that develop in the United States in a given year, about _____ % are thought to be caused by the use of alcohol.   19.____

    A. 16-25
    B. 26-35
    C. 46-55
    D. 66-75

20. Today, the most acceptable and available treatment for heroin addicts is   20.____

    A. the methadone maintenance program
    B. electroshock therapy
    C. group therapy
    D. a 12-step program similar to Alcoholics Anonymous

21. A person who is described as a compulsive drug user is likely to use drugs in order to   21.____

    A. achieve pleasure
    B. avoid discomfort
    C. satisfy curiosity
    D. fit in with peers

22. The primary ingredient in most over-the-counter stimulants is

    A. nicotine
    B. caffeine
    C. diphenhydramine
    D. amphetamine

23. The peripheral nervous system is composed of the _____ and the _____ nervous systems.

    A. somatic; autonomic
    B. limbic; spinal
    C. sympathetic; parasympathetic
    D. central; enteric

24. When snorted, cocaine takes about _____ to reach the brain.

    A. 10-15 seconds
    B. 1-5 minutes
    C. 10-15 minutes
    D. 30-45 minutes

25. Of the following, the best predictor of alcoholism is

    A. genetic predisposition
    B. level of education achieved
    C. peer pressure
    D. socioeconomic status

KEY (CORRECT ANSWERS)

1.	C	11.	C
2.	A	12.	C
3.	C	13.	A
4.	D	14.	D
5.	C	15.	C
6.	D	16.	C
7.	C	17.	C
8.	B	18.	B
9.	B	19.	D
10.	D	20.	A

21. B
22. B
23. A
24. C
25. A

TEST 4

DIRECTIONS: Each question or incomplete statement is followed by several suggested answers or completions. Select the one that BEST answers the question or completes the statement. *PRINT THE LETTER OF THE CORRECT ANSWER IN THE SPACE AT THE RIGHT.*

1. Each of the following is a risk factor that makes drug use more likely, EXCEPT   1.____

    A. a caregiver who abuses drugs
    B. poor family relations
    C. poor classroom behavior
    D. low socioeconomic status

2. The key characteristic that distinguishes hypnotic drugs from sedatives is that hypnotics are   2.____

    A. sometimes prescribed to relieve anxiety
    B. used to induce sleep
    C. prescribed to relieve pain
    D. controlled substances

3. Which of the following is NOT one of the four characteristic symptoms of addiction?   3.____

    A. Loss of control
    B. Negative consequences
    C. Compulsion to use the substance
    D. Recognition of the problem

4. The second dose or drink often does not have as great an effect as the first—an illustration of _____ tolerance.   4.____

    A. psychological   B. acute   C. behavior   D. reverse

5. One of the risks of amyl nitrite abuse is   5.____

    A. memory problems   B. flashbacks
    C. stroke   D. angina pectoris

6. The first barbiturate to be synthesized and commercially marketed was   6.____

    A. barbital   B. pento barbital
    C. secobarbital   D. methohexital

7. Which of the following drugs, first synthesized in 1874, was considered a wonder drug for the relief of pain?   7.____

    A. Aspirin   B. Laudanum   C. Cocaine   D. Heroin

8. Of the following, the class of drugs most often associated with anxiolytic (anxiety-reducing) properties is   8.____

    A. narcotics
    B. benzodiazepines
    C. hallucinogens
    D. barbiturates

9. In the United States, illicit drug use has a high correlation with 9.__

   A. depression
   B. race
   C. antisocial behavior
   D. socioeconomic status

10. A person's vital functions are regulated by the 10.__

    A. thalamus
    B. pituitary gland
    C. brain stem
    D. hippocampus

11. What is the term for a drug that is used to block the effects of narcotics? 11.__

    A. Agonist   B. Inhibitor   C. Antagonist   D. Methadone

12. A substance that reduces the effects mediated by acetylcholine in the central nervous 12.__
    system and the peripheral nervous system is a(n)

    A. hallucinogen
    B. benzodi azepi ne
    C. agonist
    D. anticholinergic

13. The first state to eliminate penalties for the medical use of marijuana was 13.__

    A. Alaska   B. California   C. Massachusetts   D. Oregon

14. In its effect on the central nervous system, amphetamine is very similar to 14.__

    A. marijuana   B. nicotine   C. cocaine   D. heroin

15. The psychoactive agent in glue that is sniffed or inhaled is 15.__

    A. toluene
    B. alkyl nitrite
    C. acetone
    D. xylene

16. Which of the following is a Schedule II drag? 16.__

    A. Heroin
    B. Benzodiazepines
    C. Phenobarbital
    D. Ritalin

17. At the beginning of the 21st century, alcohol was a factor in about _____ percent of traf- 17.__
    fic deaths in the United States.

    A. 20
    B. 40
    C. 60
    D. 80

18. Of the following, the stimulant most likely to be used illegally by college students in the early 21st century was

    A. cocaine
    B. methamphetamine
    C. ecstasy (MDMA)
    D. Ritalin

19. The type of drinking most often practiced by college students is _____ drinking.

    A. social
    B. binge
    C. moderate
    D. light

20. For many alcoholics, the first sign of alcohol-induced liver problems is

    A. hypertension
    B. fatty liver
    C. cirrhosis
    D. cellular edema

21. Drug addiction is typically distinguished from misuse or abuse by _____ factors.

    A. psychological
    B. criminal
    C. spiritual
    D. physical

22. Which of the following substances generally involves the HIGHEST degree of psychological dependence?

    A. Seconal
    B. Methadone
    C. LSD
    D. Methamphetamine

23. The highest rate of alcohol consumption in the United States is among

    A. adolescents
    B. young and middle-aged adults
    C. women
    D. the elderly

24. Which of the following has both hallucinogenic and anesthetic properties?

    A. Phencyclidine (PCP)
    B. Mescaline
    C. LSD
    D. Marijuana

25. At the beginning of the 21st century, the largest cocaine-producing country in the world was

    A. Colombia
    B. Bolivia
    C. Mexico
    D. Afghanistan

KEY (CORRECT ANSWERS)

1. D
2. B
3. D
4. B
5. C

6. A
7. D
8. B
9. C
10. C

11. C
12. D
13. B
14. C
15. A

16. D
17. B
18. D
19. B
20. B

21. D
22. D
23. B
24. A
25. A

EXAMINATION SECTION
TEST 1

DIRECTIONS: Each question or incomplete statement is followed by several suggested answers or completions. Select the one that BEST answers the question or completes the statement. *PRINT THE LETTER OF THE CORRECT ANSWER IN THE SPACE AT THE RIGHT.*

1. An addict who uses the same amount of narcotics each day over a period of time is said to be

    A. systemized B. protracted
    C. stabilized D. temporized

2. The final phase of the addiction rehabilitation process is USUALLY known as

    A. spin off B. re-entry
    C. out straight D. wake up

3. If a drug addict says that he *scored,* he MOST likely means that he

    A. bribed a policeman B. obtained and used drugs
    C. was detoxified D. was arrested and beaten

4. The *synthesis* of a drug refers to its

    A. action B. composition
    C. cost D. popularity

5. An addict's feeling of well-being from taking drugs is known as feeling

    A. satch B. skagg
    C. straight D. strung out

6. An addict who is *boosting* is MOST likely engaged in

    A. informing B. overdosing
    C. quarreling D. stealing

7. A mixture of horse and high C is known as a

    A. flip out B. panic C. rainbow D. speedball

8. *Acapulco gold* is a type of

    A. heroin B. marijuana C. cocaine D. milk sugar

9. *Lebanese Blond* and *Moroccan Black* are slang terms for types of

    A. cocaine B. hashish C. morphine D. peyote

10. The presence of quinine in urine is MOST likely to reveal the use of

    A. glue B. hashish C. heroin D. LSD

11. The percentage of heroin addicts being treated by all existing addiction treatment programs is generally believed to be MOST NEARLY

    A. 5% B. 15% C. 25% D. 35%

12. The BASIC purpose of a referral unit for drug addiction programs is to direct the addict to a treatment program which

    A. applies a conventional form of treatment
    B. employs former addicts in its program
    C. meets his needs in terms of his personality
    D. will adjust him to its program

12.____

13. The MAJOR purpose of therapeutic communities is to

    A. change a resident's drug-related behavior, but not his attitudes
    B. enforce outward conformity to acceptable behavior
    C. resocialize a resident to a better lifestyle
    D. get people jobs in the outside world

13.____

14. The AVERAGE length of stay for a resident in a therapeutic community is

    A. less than one year
    B. 12 to 18 months
    C. two years
    D. two to three years

14.____

15. The one of the following which would MOST quickly increase tension in a therapeutic community is to

    A. prevent new residents from getting mail
    B. stop visits from neighbors
    C. allow new residents to talk with one another
    D. ban coffee and cigarettes

15.____

16. MOST persons who have been graduated from therapeutic communities are, in effect, trained for employment in

    A. drug-free programs
    B. youth work agencies
    C. social work agencies
    D. methadone programs

16.____

17. In a therapeutic community, the job of knowing everything that is taking place in the facility, particularly the attitudes of individuals, is assigned to the

    A. dingbat
    B. assistant director
    C. expeditor
    D. re-entry leader

17.____

18. The Daytop orientation places MAJOR emphasis on

    A. intensive psychoanalysis
    B. the addict's self-responsibility
    C. *polite* forms of group therapy
    D. meditation and isolation

18.____

19. Synanon, the California-based therapeutic community, has sought to recruit addicts in New York City for residency in its California facility. The requirements stated by Synanon's local representative are that an applicant must

    A. have a multiple addiction and have failed in a similar program
    B. be over 25 years of age and not be on probation or parole
    C. pay his own plane fare to California and have a sincere desire to *kick* drugs
    D. submit to short-term detoxification and have a stable personality

19.____

20. Studies of drug addiction suggest that people are introduced to drugs PRIMARILY through

    A. the activities of drug wholesalers
    B. the seeking after drugs by people for the purpose of experimentation
    C. intimate association with addicts
    D. accidental circumstances

21. When administered in regulated doses, methadone produces

    A. a desire to give up drugs
    B. an anti-alcohol reaction
    C. a stabilized *blockade* phenomenon
    D. changes in basic personality structure

22. In the field of drug addiction treatment, the MAJOR purpose of an induction center is to

    A. provide short-term therapy mainly for *soft* drug abusers
    B. motivate heroin addicts toward long-term treatment
    C. provide a non-threatening residential setting for those who are unwilling to enter a hospital
    D. provide out-patient treatment through chemotherapy

23. Methadone is used in the detoxification of ambulatory heroin users PRIMARILY to

    A. serve as a long-range substitute for heroin
    B. ease the pain of withdrawal
    C. make other therapy unnecessary
    D. overcome multiple addiction

24. Detoxification units usually attempt to do all of the following EXCEPT to

    A. deal with the underlying causes of addiction
    B. direct the patient to an appropriate program after detoxification
    C. free the heroin addict of his physiological habit
    D. administer short-term doses of an opiate antagonist

25. The Food and Drug Administration's proposed regulations on methadone are PRIMARILY intended to

    A. end its diversion for illicit use
    B. ease take-home rules in clinics
    C. make it easier for private doctors to treat addicts
    D. discontinue liquid dosages in clinics

KEY (CORRECT ANSWERS)

1.	C	11.	A
2.	B	12.	C
3.	B	13.	C
4.	B	14.	B
5.	C	15.	D
6.	D	16.	A
7.	D	17.	C
8.	B	18.	B
9.	B	19.	C
10.	C	20.	C

21.	C
22.	B
23.	B
24.	A
25.	A

TEST 2

DIRECTIONS: Each question or incomplete statement is followed by several suggested answers or completions. Select the one that BEST answers the question or completes the statement. *PRINT THE LETTER OF THE CORRECT ANSWER IN THE SPACE AT THE RIGHT.*

1. One proposal that has been suggested to eliminate the profit motive from the sale of heroin is that drugs be distributed free of charge. However, according to its critics, a MAJOR risk in this approach is that

    A. the total number of addicts may increase
    B. some physicians may become illicit drug sellers
    C. public opinion may cause complete legalization
    D. the potency may be too low for most addicts

2. The increase in drug abuse has brought with it an increase in infectious diseases caused by contaminated needles and syringes used for drug injections. Aside from AIDS, one other such disease often fatal is bacterial or fungal endocarditis, which affects the

    A. brain   B. lungs   C. heart   D. liver

3. Which of the following is PRIMARILY a chemotherapy technique?

    A. Ambulatory detoxification
    B. Community outreach
    C. Methadone maintenance
    D. Multi-modal therapy

4. The mental state brought about by the use of LSD by a normal person is MOST similar to that experienced by

    A. hysterics   B. neurotics
    C. the feeble-minded   D. schizophrenics

5. The one of the following statements which is accurate according to a study sponsored by the National Commission on Marijuana and Drug Abuse is that heavy use of marijuana

    A. impairs performance on tests of cognitive or motor function
    B. does not interfere with the perception of the rate at which time passes
    C. improves the ability to recall recent events
    D. does not decrease the motivation to work

6. The MOST serious withdrawal symptoms are USUALLY produced by the discontinuance of

    A. barbiturates   B. cocaine
    C. heroin   D. *ice*

7. A characteristic of a methedrine user who regularly injects the drug directly into his bloodstream is that he

    A. becomes addicted
    B. usually becomes depressed during his *high*
    C. often exhausts his mental and physical reserves
    D. seldom becomes violent

8. The initial observable effects following glue-sniffing are MOST likely to be

    A. loss of memory, headaches, and slowness in response
    B. spasms of the muscles of the neck and the lower extremities
    C. sneezing, coughing, and drooling
    D. similar to drunken behavior and a vague joyousness of manner

9. As the user's dosage of a psychoactive agent is increased, his response is MOST likely to be influenced by factors which are

    A. environmental   B. pharmacological
    C. psychological   D. social

10. In the treatment of heroin addicts, the use of cyclazocine is considered by some medical experts to be preferable to methadone PRIMARILY because, in general, the use of cyclazocine

    A. cuts the cost of treatment by approximately 40%, compared to the use of methadone
    B. does not produce the allergic side effects sometimes associated with methadone
    C. shortens the period of time necessary for treatment
    D. significantly reduces the need for auxiliary supportive services

11. The mixture which addicts inject into their companions who have taken an overdose of heroin is composed of

    A. sugar and coffee   B. nutmeg and alcohol
    C. salt and water   D. sugar and peroxide

12. MOST of the estimated 300,000 alcoholics residing in the city are

    A. employed   B. skid row types
    C. under treatment   D. under 27 years of age

13. Employee alcoholism programs are usually more effective than community programs MAINLY because

    A. most alcoholics are more cooperative in a friendly setting
    B. continued employment usually depends upon a successful recovery
    C. employers spend more funds for their programs because of the high standards set by the Industrial Conference Board
    D. penalties generally imposed against employers for alcohol-precipitated accidents are severe

14. Which of the following is an addiction treatment program operated DIRECTLY by the Addiction Services Agency?

    A. Addicts Rehabilitation Center   B. Horizon Project
    C. Odyssey House   D. Reality House

15. The Vera Institute's Heroin Treatment Plan is PRIMARILY intended to reach those who   15.____

    A. acquired a serious addiction in the U.S. Armed Forces
    B. are over age 35 and have used heroin for 15 years
    C. have failed on methadone and refuse treatment not involving heroin
    D. have been convicted of a drug-related felony

16. The State Narcotics Addiction Control Commission is PRIMARILY concerned with treating   16.____

    A. addicted war veterans
    B. criminal addicts
    C. youthful drug experimenters
    D. non-opiate substance abusers

17. Under the State Youthful Drug Abuser Act, a number of programs are conducted in the schools. The basic principle upon which all of these programs are founded is that drug addiction is GENERALLY attributed to   17.____

    A. frustration with school
    B. individual pathology
    C. adult group pressures
    D. political and environmental forces

18. Out-patient units using the youth center approach USUALLY concentrate on young people who   18.____

    A. are at a low level of drug abuse
    B. are likely to become habitual users of marijuana
    C. experiment with substances that are not considered dangerous
    D. are addicted to the use of common hard drugs

19. In order to determine the degree to which participants in youth-oriented addiction programs successfully manage to pursue positive life goals, *before* and *after* studies should be made of all such participants. Which of the following would be the LEAST useful measure in such studies?   19.____

    A. School attendance
    B. Non-delinquent behavior
    C. Salary earned after treatment
    D. Withdrawal from the drug culture

20. Those who conduct drug education programs in the urban school setting USUALLY find that younger children are   20.____

    A. particularly knowledgeable about the costs of drugs
    B. indifferent to drug education as currently presented
    C. highly motivated to learn about drug abuse
    D. mainly interested in the history of drug traffic

21. Federal law enforcement officials sometimes ignore street addicts and general drug abusers mainly because the MAJOR concern of federal officials in fighting drug abuse is to

    A. concentrate on interstate criminal activities since they are federal offenses
    B. encourage local officials to develop appropriate law enforcement capabilities
    C. gather information for technical studies and schedules of controlled substances
    D. stop organized drug traffic by prosecuting high-level importers, dealers, and distributors

22. The Narcotics Register is maintained by the

    A. Addiction Services Agency
    B. Bureau of Mental Health
    C. Department of Health
    D. Health and Hospitals Corporation

23. In a recent poll, it was found that, compared to the sixties, college students today

    A. confine their use of drugs and other substances to a small circle of friends
    B. have almost entirely abandoned substance abuse in favor of various religious and mystical practices
    C. use amphetamines about as often as they use alcohol
    D. were more likely to use marijuana and cocaine

24. Crimes committed by drug addicts MOST often victimize the

    A. middle class in outlying sections
    B. poor in slum areas
    C. wealthy in exclusive sections
    D. foreign-born in ethnic enclaves

25. The National Commission on Marijuana and Drug Abuse unanimously recommended, with regard to marijuana,

    A. eliminating all criminal penalties for its private use and possession
    B. increasing civil penalties for anti-social acts committed under its influence
    C. classifying its use by adults as a misdemeanor
    D. encouraging its use as a substitute for alcohol

KEY (CORRECT ANSWERS)

1.	A	11.	C
2.	C	12.	A
3.	C	13.	B
4.	D	14.	B
5.	A	15.	C
6.	A	16.	B
7.	C	17.	B
8.	D	18.	A
9.	B	19.	C
10.	C	20.	C

21. D
22. C
23. D
24. B
25. A

TEST 3

DIRECTIONS: Each question or incomplete statement is followed by several suggested answers or completions. Select the one that BEST answers the question or completes the statement. *PRINT THE LETTER OF THE CORRECT ANSWER IN THE SPACE AT THE RIGHT.*

Questions 1-3.

DIRECTIONS: Questions 1 through 3 are to be answered SOLELY on the basis of the following paragraph.

A substantial source of opposition to legalising heroin is those people who are convinced that this idea is simply another form of social and economic injustice. Instead of getting at the fundamental causes of addiction, they say, the result will be to turn hundreds of young addicts into the living dead.

1. According to the above paragraph, opposition to legalizing heroin is based, in part, on the belief that

   A. some addicts will become walking dead people
   B. the problem is entirely one of educating individuals
   C. the pushers will simply turn to other criminal activities
   D. the root causes of addiction are still mysterious

1.___

2. Which of the following treatment approaches would the author of the above paragraph be MOST likely to oppose?

   A. Ambulatory detoxification
   B. Methadone maintenance
   C. Drug-free therapeutic community
   D. Youth intervention program

2.___

3. As used in the paragraph, the underlined word *substantial* means MOST NEARLY

   A. known   B. large   C. strange   D. unanimous

3.___

Questions 4-8.

DIRECTIONS: Questions 4 through 8 are to be answered SOLELY on the basis of the following paragraph.

In the past dozen years or so, there has emerged an argument which obviously has a certain persuasiveness among young people: that drugs are being used not as an expression of antisocial behavior or for escape, but to define a different, anti-establishment culture. Drugs can, of course, be used that way; it's very possible to have a youth culture that uses drugs as a norm. But it's also possible to have a youth culture that is opposed to using drugs as a norm. For example, in China, around 1910, a very effective campaign against opium was led largely by students who felt that the use of drugs was the reason China had suffered so much at the hands of the Western powers.

4. According to the above paragraph, the Chinese students opposed the use of opium because

   A. it contradicted Chinese religious values
   B. it interfered with their studies
   C. they believed it weakened their country
   D. the Western powers encouraged addiction

5. The writer of the above paragraph seems to believe that there is no necessary connection between

   A. escapism and culture
   B. norms and values
   C. students and politics
   D. youth and drugs

6. According to the above paragraph, it is possible to have a youth culture that considers the use of drugs

   A. completely acceptable
   B. legally defensible
   C. morally uplifting
   D. physically beneficial

7. The underlined word *emerged* means MOST NEARLY

   A. come into view
   B. gone through
   C. required to be
   D. responded quickly

8. As used in the above paragraph, the underlined word *norm* means MOST NEARLY

   A. argument or explanation
   B. error or mistake
   C. pleasure or reward
   D. rule or average

Questions 9-11.

DIRECTIONS: Questions 9 through 11 are to be answered SOLELY on the basis of the following paragraph.

Drug abuse prevention efforts are only in their beginning stages. Far less is known about how to design programs that successfully counter the seductive effects which drugs have upon the young than about how to build clinics and programs to treat those who have become addicts. The latter can be done with enough dollars, managerial competence, and qualified personnel. The former depends upon such intangibles as community leadership, personal attitudes, and, in the final analysis, individual choices. Given this void in our society's understanding of what it is that makes us so vulnerable to addiction, government must build upon its growing experience to invest wisely in those efforts that offer positive alternatives to drug abuse.

9. The one of the following which is probably the BEST title for the above paragraph is

   A. The Youthful Drug Abuser
   B. Government's Management of Drug Programs
   C. A Scientific Analysis of Drug Cures
   D. The Difficulty of Drug Abuse Prevention

10. According to the above paragraph, treating drug addicts, as compared to preventing drug addiction among the young, is GENERALLY

   A. *easier,* mainly because there is more public interest in this method
   B. *harder,* mainly because qualified personnel are not readily available
   C. *easier,* mainly because there is more known about how to accomplish this objective
   D. *harder,* mainly because confirmed drug addicts do not give up the habit readily

11. According to the above paragraph, the role of government in dealing with the problem of drug addiction and youth should be to

   A. build larger clinics and develop additional programs for treatment of offenders
   B. help attract youth to behavior which is more desirable than that provided by the drug culture
   C. provide the funds and personnel essential to successful enforcement programs
   D. establish centers for the study and analysis of those factors that make our citizens vulnerable to addiction

Questions 12-15.

DIRECTIONS: Questions 12 through 15 are to be answered SOLELY on the basis of the following paragraph.

Alcoholics are to be found in both sexes, in every major religious and racial group, and at all socio-economic levels. What they share in common are psychiatric problems which they seek to ease or dull through alcohol. Ideally, every heavy drinker should be subjected to <u>intensive</u> psychiatric therapy. Unfortunately, even psychiatric treatment is not always successful, and in any case the nation has <u>allocated</u> neither the funds nor the personnel nor the facilities that would be required for such a massive therapeutic effort.

12. According to the above paragraph, national priorities in connection with psychiatric treatment for alcoholism do NOT provide for

   A. fair and impartial treatment
   B. large-scale programs
   C. proper religious values
   D. strict laws against alcoholism

13. According to the above paragraph, alcoholics are MOST likely to be

   A. emotionally disturbed   B. ultimately curable
   C. unable to function   D. under medical care

14. As used in the above paragraph, the underlined word *intensive* means MOST NEARLY

   A. concentrated   B. modern
   C. prompt   D. specialized

15. As used in the above paragraph, the underlined word *allocated* means MOST NEARLY

   A. assigned   B. conserved   C. desired   D. recognized

KEY (CORRECT ANSWERS)

1. A
2. B
3. B
4. C
5. D

6. A
7. A
8. D
9. D
10. C

11. B
12. B
13. A
14. A
15. A

EXAMINATION SECTION
TEST 1

DIRECTIONS: Each question or incomplete statement is followed by several suggested answers or completions. Select the one that BEST answers the question or completes the statement. *PRINT THE LETTER OF THE CORRECT ANSWER IN THE SPACE AT THE RIGHT.*

1. Making an illegal purchase of drugs is known as 1.____
   A. popping   B. rushing   C. scagging   D. scoring

2. A narcotics detective is known as a 2.____
   A. narc   B. red bull   C. mule   D. schmeck

3. *Speed* is a street term for an often-abused drug which is sometimes used in the treatment of 3.____
   A. allergies   B. epilepsy   C. insomnia   D. obesity

4. An addict who is *copping* would MOST likely be 4.____
   A. attempting detoxification
   B. engaged in crime
   C. undergoing therapy
   D. under emotional stress

5. An inert or neutral substance given to a person who requests unneeded medication, or used in an experiment where it is necessary to secretly substitute an inactive substance for an active substance, is known as a 5.____
   A. cross-over   B. placebo
   C. response   D. sedative

6. The *generic* name of a drug is the name that is 6.____
   A. a popular street term in general usage
   B. an abbreviation of the hospital name
   C. chemically, pharmacologically, or technically descriptive
   D. used as a trademark by its manufacturer

7. The physiological effect that the abuse of a specific substance will have on an individual person is LEAST likely to be influenced by the substance's 7.____
   A. dosage   B. frequency of use
   C. potency   D. street cost

8. Two kinds of patients in need of detoxification are heroin addicts and serious abusers of 8.____
   A. barbiturates   B. cocaine
   C. volatile substances   D. mescaline

9. An amphetamine abuser's prolonged sleep, lasting a day or two, is known as 9.____
   A. bugging   B. flaking   C. crashing   D. zonking

10. Chemical solvents are substances subject to abuse USUALLY by means of

 A. ingestion
 B. inhalation
 C. subcutaneous injection
 D. skin absorption

11. Of the following, it is LEAST desirable for a drug-free day care center to

 A. be situated in a low drug abuse area
 B. have kitchen facilities on the premises
 C. be located near public transportation
 D. provide treatment on weekends

12. Of the following, the MAIN justification for minimal security measures at a drug-free day care center is that

 A. the people on the premises are trustworthy
 B. the clients might otherwise be insulted
 C. there are no unauthorized visitors on the premises
 D. there are no drugs on the premises

13. No applicant may be processed for admission to a methadone treatment program unless it has been verified that he meets all Federal criteria for admission and

 A. an exact dosage has been determined and prescribed for him by the attending physician for daily administration in liquid form
 B. the applicant properly signs a waiver giving his informal consent to forego drug-free types of treatment
 C. the methadone treatment program is not serving more than 150 rehabilitants at any one time
 D. the sources and methods of such verification have been recorded as specific documentation in the applicant's case folder

14. The following statements refer to abuse of amphetamine:
 I. Contrary to popular belief, amphetamine abuse rarely kills
 II. Long-term high-dose intravenous injection of amphetamine will usually induce paranoid psychosis symptoms
 III. Sleep deprivation worsens and complicates the direct pharmacological effects of amphetamine

 Which of the following choices lists all of the above statements that are CORRECT?

 A. I only
 B. I and III *only*
 C. II and III *only*
 D. I, II, and III

15. In a methadone treatment program, unless another method has been approved, urine specimens must be collected

 A. *before* the patient has eaten breakfast
 B. *in* containers which are provided in sterile condition
 C. *under* the visual supervision of a staff member
 D. *within* one hour after the patient has eaten breakfast

16. In a methadone treatment program, urine specimens must be acquired in accordance with a randomized schedule. A schedule which is *randomized* provides for specimens to be collected from individual patients

    A. carefully
    B. intensely
    C. irregularly
    D. privately

17. In a methadone treatment program, a problem patient should be removed from the program if his misbehavior results from

    A. a temporary phase he is undergoing
    B. violent acting-out
    C. deterioration of personality
    D. pathological depression

18. According to the outpatient drug-free treatment manual, card-playing and pool should be de-emphasized in a drug-free day care program PRIMARILY because such activities

    A. appear as unbusinesslike to participants
    B. are usually of little interest to participants
    C. tend to be unfamiliar to participants
    D. relate to and reinforce participants' past negative lifestyle

19. To be selected for participation in the A.S.A. Court Referral Project, an individual must not be charged with certain crimes.
    Which of the following choices does NOT mention a crime that would probably bar participation in this project?

    A. Aggravated assault, embezzlement
    B. Forgery, larceny
    C. Reckless endangerment, armed robbery
    D. Felonious assault, theft of services

20. Federal regulations concerning the confidentiality of the records of drug abuse patients require that such records be disclosed only for certain purposes and under certain circumstances.
    Following are three possible reasons for disclosure:
    I. To medical personnel to the extent necessary to meet a genuine medical emergency
    II. To a qualified academic research person who affirms that his published report will contain only objective statements and only the names of former patients
    III. One authorized by an appropriate order of a court of competent jurisdiction granted after application showing good cause therefor
    Which of the following choices lists all of the above statements that describe PROPER reasons for disclosure?

    A. I and II *only*
    B. II and III *only*
    C. I and III *only*
    D. I, II, and III

21. Opinions vary as to whether caffeine is addicting, depending upon the definition of addiction. However, caffeine is a potent poison when taken in very large doses.
Which of the following over-the-counter preparations contains caffeine in concentrated form?

    A. Compoz B. NoDoz C. Nytol D. Sominex

22. A recent study showed that while many teenagers are convinced that cigarette smoking causes cancer and heart attacks, they still start to smoke cigarettes. One major reason for their starting to smoke, according to the study, is that they have not been told that nicotine is an addicting drug.
The DIRECT result of such lack of knowledge is that most of them who become smokers

    A. start smoking because their elders smoke
    B. imitate other teenagers and begin smoking
    C. lack knowledge of the Surgeon General's findings on the dangers of smoking
    D. expect to stop smoking at some future time

23. Researchers have asked young drug users why they first began to use drugs.
The MOST common answer is

    A. the influence of profit-motivated pushers
    B. peer-group pressures
    C. enjoyment of drug-taking
    D. a family member's example

24. Researchers have found that young drug users who had not sought treatment offered several different explanations for not doing so.
The MOST common reason given was that the individual

    A. believed that he did not need help
    B. never thought about treatment
    C. was discouraged by rumors of waiting lists
    D. was unfamiliar with the types of treatment available

25. Those who have had any success in treating drug addicts are certain of one thing. Without the willing cooperation of the addicts themselves in the treatment leading to a cure, you will get nowhere.
Based on this viewpoint, it is MOST reasonable to state that in order to treat addicts successfully it is necessary for workers to

    A. view the problem of addiction as the addicts themselves do
    B. realize that total drug abstinence is necessary for rehabilitation
    C. first attempt to alter the addict's lifestyle
    D. employ the *up-front* techniques of encounter groups and similar confrontation therapies

KEY (CORRECT ANSWERS)

1.	D	11.	A
2.	A	12.	D
3.	D	13.	D
4.	B	14.	D
5.	B	15.	C
6.	C	16.	C
7.	D	17.	B
8.	A	18.	D
9.	C	19.	B
10.	B	20.	C

21. B
22. D
23. B
24. A
25. A

TEST 2

DIRECTIONS: Each question or incomplete statement is followed by several suggested answers or completions. Select the one that BEST answers the question or completes the statement. *PRINT THE LETTER OF THE CORRECT ANSWER IN THE SPACE AT THE RIGHT.*

1. In many societies in which use or abuse of a substance has been largely restricted to the lowest social classes, it is often difficult to know to what extent ascribed characteristics of users represent alterations related to such use or the institutionalized prejudices of persons of higher social status.
Based on the foregoing statement *only,* it is MOST reasonable to state that substance abusers in such societies are

    A. indifferent to the legal rights of other people
    B. likely to be members of the least advantaged groups
    C. tradition-bound and therefore unwilling to alter their lifestyle
    D. ignorant of the long-term harmfulness of substance abuse

2. It is not really known whether substance abuse causes a loss of conventional competitive motivation among youth. The one of the following statements which BEST explains this lack of knowledge is:

    A. Drug users are found in all age groups and social classes, not merely among alienated youth
    B. Little evidence exists to support the theory that unmotivated youth could develop and establish a counterculture
    C. It is often difficult to distinguish a possible drug-related loss of motivation from that produced by the prevailing values found among youth
    D. Loss of motivation is the underlying cause of decreasing interest in traditional values, but there is little agreement on a definition of such values

3. The following three statements refer to marijuana use in the United States:
    I. Use is highly age-related and, to a lesser extent, to educational status
    II. Use is more common among rural residents than among urban residents
    III. A daily user is less likely to sell *(deal)* than is a monthly user
Which of the following choices CORRECTLY classifies the above statements into those which are correct and those which are not?

    A. I is correct, but II and III are not.
    B. I and II are correct, but III is not.
    C. III is correct, but I and II are not.
    D. II and III are correct, but I is not.

4. Clients referred to a methadone program are MOST likely to

    A. be willing to accept strongly interactive therapy
    B. benefit from a highly structured environment
    C. have little potential for self-support through legitimate employment
    D. have the social support of friends or family

5. Professional social workers have at times been criticized, by those who favor the ex-addict leadership mode, for taking erroneous approaches to the treatment of addiction. The MOST common erroneous approach of professional social workers is said to be the tendency to

   A. believe that addicts derive great pleasure in the release from psychic tension that drugs provide
   B. expect an ideal client and an ideal client-worker relationship
   C. give high priority to drugs and their use as the major concern of the abuser's life
   D. sacrifice the role of psychotherapist for one of a strong helping figure

6. Researchers have recommended several changes in drug treatment programs. Which of the following is NOT one of these recommendations?

   A. Sixteen- and seventeen-year-old drug abusers should be given special treatment.
   B. The age requirement for entering methadone maintenance programs should be lowered.
   C. The requirement of parental consent for a minor to enter a drug treatment program should be eliminated.
   D. The use of rehabilitated youthful drug abusers to educate others about the true conditions in treatment programs should be discouraged.

7. Following are three statements which may or may not be correct about drug users:
   I. An insignificant percentage of the drug users had begun their drug use by the age of 11.
   II. Most of the drug users use crack alone.
   III. Most of the drug users are regular users, using drugs at least once a week.

   Which of the following choices CORRECTLY classifies the above statements into those which are correct and those which are not?

   A. I is correct, but II and III are not.
   B. III is correct, but I and II are not.
   C. I and II are correct, but III is not.
   D. II and III are correct, but I is not.

8. Because of the fad-like aspects of marijuana use, it can be expected that rates of use at individual high schools and colleges will _____ the national averages.

   A. *be identical* to
   B. *lag behind*
   C. *remain stable* despite fluctuations in
   D. *vary widely* from

9. In developing staffing requirements for a new drug-free day care center, which of the following is LEAST important?
   The

   A. size of the planned program
   B. treatment philosophy to be followed at the center
   C. ages of potential staff members
   D. availability of ancillary community resources

10. In the recruitment of new staff for a drug-free day care center, emphasis should be placed PRIMARILY on an applicant's having

   A. therapeutic skills
   B. a knowledge of community resources
   C. no history of drug use
   D. the ability to teach vocational rehabilitation

11. In social research, the selection of a good test involves considering a number of criteria. The MOST important single criterion is the test's

   A. popularity   B. format
   C. simplicity   D. validity

12. Of the following substances, the one MOST often and closely associated with homicides and aggressive assaults is

   A. marijuana   B. crack
   C. alcohol   D. barbiturates

13. The phenomenon of _____ has caused an epidemic in drug use. The use of _____, which had declined, is on an upswing. _____ was part of an effective treatment program but the abuses of its administration and the subsequent increase in those addicted to it have rendered its future use in doubt.

   A. ice; marijuana; cocaine
   B. heroin; cocaine; methadone
   C. crack; marijuana; ice
   D. crack; heroin; methadone

14. Which of the following statements BEST characterizes the position of the Administration on marijuana use?

   A. Its illegality is a deterrent to large numbers of potential users.
   B. Its prohibition serves to clutter the courts, diverts the police from attending to serious crimes, and enriches the legal profession.
   C. Public policy regarding its use should be made analogous to current policy regarding alcohol and tobacco.
   D. The central issue stemming from its use is the erosion of the nation's moral fiber, not the narrow question of penalties or stigmatization.

15. A community's opinion about a new addiction treatment center located in the neighborhood is LEAST likely to be favorably affected by

   A. permitting visits by community residents
   B. press releases and advertisements
   C. the behavior and attitude of participants or clients
   D. discussions between the center's director and members of local organizations

16. Assume that you are assigned to give an informal talk, including a question-and-answer session, to a community group in order to tell them about a new program of the addiction services agency.
In order to carry out this assignment, you should consider doing each of the following EXCEPT

   A. preparing an outline of the speech
   B. beginning the speech with an attention-getting opening
   C. giving standard, memorized answers to questions without deviation
   D. closing the speech with a brief summary

17. Experienced public speakers sometimes attempt to gain rapport with the audience by leading the audience to identify themselves with the speaker or to identify him with something they find admirable. For example, the speaker may remark, *I was born and grew up in this neighborhood,* or *I, like many of you, am married and have children,* or whatever else he thinks will be meaningful to his audience.
Of the following, which is the GREATEST danger of this approach?
The

   A. basic feelings and cultural patterns of the audience may be ignored
   B. attempt to deceive the audience is doomed to failure
   C. audience will become interested in the speaker as a person
   D. link between the speaker's life and the audience's life may seem remote

18. Assume that you have planned a general public information program on drug addiction prevention which employs various techniques of presenting information. You have scheduled a presentation at a large community center, which you expect to be well-attended. Shortly before this meeting, several community leaders inform you that many people are interested in a problem which you know is not dealt with in your material. Which of the following materials which you have already prepared could you adapt MOST quickly to meet this changed situation?

   A. Booklet
   B. Film
   C. Speech outline
   D. Slide show with synchronized taped commentary

19. When a public agency conducts a public relations program, it is MOST likely to find that each recipient of its message will

   A. disagree with the basic purpose of the message if the officials are not well known to him
   B. accept the message if it is presented by someone perceived as having a definite intention to persuade
   C. ignore the message unless it is presented in a literate and clever manner
   D. give greater attention to certain portions of the message as a result of his individual and cultural differences

20. Following are three statements about public relations and communications:
    I. A person who seeks to influence public opinion can speed up a trend.
    II. Mass communications is the exposure of a mass audience to an idea.
    III. All media are equally effective in reaching opinion leaders.
    Which of the following choices CORRECTLY classifies the above statements into those which are correct and those which are not?

    A. I and II are correct, but III is not.
    B. II and III are correct, but I is not.
    C. I and III are correct, but II is not.
    D. III is correct, but I and II are not.

KEY (CORRECT ANSWERS)

1.	B	11.	D
2.	C	12.	C
3.	A	13.	D
4.	D	14.	A
5.	B	15.	B
6.	D	16.	C
7.	B	17.	D
8.	D	18.	C
9.	C	19.	D
10.	A	20.	A

EXAMINATION SECTION
TEST 1

DIRECTIONS: Each question or incomplete statement is followed by several suggested answers or completions. Select the one that BEST answers the question or completes the statement. *PRINT THE LETTER OF THE CORRECT ANSWER IN THE SPACE AT THE RIGHT.*

1. Which one of the following "suggestions to interviewers" should be AVOIDED? 1.____

    A. Encourage the client to verbalize his thoughts and feelings.
    B. Cover as much as possible in each interview.
    C. Don't hesitate to refer the client to someone else who might be more helpful in the situation.
    D. The problem which is presented initially, or the one which seems most obvious, often is not the real one.

2. If it seems clear that disturbance in parents' marital relationships is a major factor in causing a child to be emotionally disturbed, the counselor should 2.____

    A. point this out to the parents and tell them that for the welfare of their children, they should resolve their difficulties
    B. suggest that he will be willing to discuss their marital difficulties with them
    C. ignore this and concentrate on helping the child
    D. tactfully suggest that their marital difficulties may be playing a part in their child's disturbance and offer to refer the parents to a qualified marriage counseling service

3. The process of collecting, analyzing, synthesizing and interpreting information about the client should be 3.____

    A. completed prior to counseling
    B. completed early in the counseling process
    C. limited to counseling which is primarily diagnostic in purpose
    D. continuous throughout counseling

4. Catharsis, the "emotional unloading" of the client's feelings, has a value in the early stages of counseling because it accomplishes all BUT which one of the following goals? 4.____

    A. It relieves strong physiological tensions in the client.
    B. It increases the client's anxiety and therefore his motivation to continue counseling.
    C. It provides a verbal substitute for "acting out" the client's aggressive feelings.
    D. It releases emotional energy which the client has been using to maintain his defenses.

5. During the first interview, the counselor can expect the client to participate at his BEST when the counselor 5.____

    A. structures the nature of the counseling process
    B. attempts to summarize the client's problem for him
    C. allows the client to verbalize at his own pace
    D. tells the client that he understands the presenting problem

6. To obtain the most effective results in change of attitude and behavior through parent education, the leader should be

   A. thoroughly grounded in the whole field of psychology
   B. able to help members of the group look at their own attitudes and behavior in constructive ways
   C. completely confident as to the right solution to problems that may be brought up
   D. a warm, charming, friendly human being

7. A social worker's report about a client states that a mother has ambivalent feelings concerning her child. This means that the mother

   A. has contradictory emotional reactions concerning her child
   B. is overprotective of the child
   C. strongly rejects the child
   D. is unduly apprehensive about the child's welfare

8. A psychological report notes, "The client shows little effect." This means that the client

   A. did not take the test too seriously
   B. did not show emotional behavior in situations which normally call for such reactions
   C. did not show signs of fatigue as the testing progressed
   D. reacted to the test situation in a generally favorable manner

9. A psychologist's report states, in part, that a client exhibits some masochistic symptoms. This will be evident to the counselor through the client's persistent attempts at

   A. self-assertion
   B. self-effacement
   C. inflicting physical harm on others
   D. sexual molestation of others of the same sex

10. According to research studies, the type of counselor response that is MOST often followed by a client's expression of insight or illumination is

    A. clarification of feeling
    B. reflection of feeling
    C. simple acceptance
    D. exploratory question

11. Of the following, the BEST way to deal with a 12-year-old boy who feels inferior to his peers is to

    A. provide tasks which he can master with little difficulty
    B. show him how irrational his feelings are
    C. accept his declarations of lack of confidence sympathetically
    D. carefully arrange situations in which he will be obliged to show leadership

12. In counseling or psychotherapy, the factor which is the MOST important for success tends to be the

    A. counselor's theoretical orientation
    B. counselor's attitudes and feelings toward the client

C. techniques used by the counselor
D. amount of experience and training possessed by the counselor

13. Transference is an important aspect of 13.____

    A. test construction
    B. grade placement
    C. anecdotal record keeping
    D. therapy

14. The MOST desirable way of establishing rapport with a client who comes to the counselor with a problem is to 14.____

    A. demonstrate sincere interest in him
    B. offer to do everything possible to solve his problem for him
    C. use the language of the client
    D. promise to keep his problem confidential

15. Role playing has been used as a technique in parent education work. Of the following, the major value is that it 15.____

    A. permits parents to express unconscious feelings and thereby solve conflicts
    B. tells a story in a forceful and therefore lasting way
    C. provides an opportunity for the individual to view his problems by standing off and looking at them through the eyes of someone else
    D. brings to light problems people never knew they had

16. If during a counseling situation a client expressed anger about a particular situation, which of the following responses would a non-directive counselor MOST likely make? 16.____

    A. "Why are you so angry?"
    B. "Is there any need to get so upset about this?"
    C. "This has really made you very mad, hasn't it?"
    D. "Do you feel better now that you have expressed your anger?"

17. In a counseling process, the counselor should usually give information 17.____

    A. whenever it is needed
    B. at the end of the process
    C. in the introductory interview
    D. just before the client would ordinarily request it

18. "After having recognized and clarified feelings and conflicts, it is usually necessary to go beyond the stage of understanding and to elaborate a constructive plan for future action." Which of the following people would NOT go along with the above statement? 18.____

    A. Thorne
    B. Robinson
    C. Williamson
    D. Rogers

19. The counselor should focus his attention in the beginning upon 19.____

    A. the transference phenomenon
    B. evidences of hostility
    C. the unique characteristics of the particular relationship at hand
    D. indications of client aggressiveness

20. A recent guidance text that stresses the broad developments of our national heritage, our contemporary social setting, our value patterns, and also the integration into guidance of many disciplines-sociology, anthropology, philosophy, psychology-is

    A. FOUNDATIONS OF GUIDANCE - Miller
    B. GUIDANCE POLICY AND PRACTICE - Mathewson
    C. GUIDANCE IN TODAY'S SCHOOLS - Mortenson & Schmuller
    D. GUIDANCE SERVICES - Humphreys, Traxler & North

20.____

21. Which one of the following characteristics of counseling is inconsistent with the others?

    A. Counseling is more than advice-giving.
    B. Counseling involves something more than the solution to an immediate problem.
    C. Counseling concerns itself with attitudes rather than actions.
    D. Counseling involves intellectual rather than emotional attitudes as its basic raw material.

21.____

22. One approach to counseling has been labeled "non-directive". The word "non-directive" derives from the fact that, in this approach to counseling, the counselor

    A. does not tell the client what he should do
    B. makes the client responsible for the direction of the course of the interviews
    C. does not make judgments about the behavior of the client
    D. avoids possible areas of threat to the client

22.____

23. Of the following personality traits, which would be LEAST essential for an effective counselor to possess?

    A. Extroversion   B. Objectivity
    C. Security   D. Sensitivity

23.____

24. Interpretation as a therapeutic tool is considered a hindrance to therapy progress by

    A. orthodox Freudians   B. neo-analysts
    C. Rogerians   D. Adlerians

24.____

25. The current interpersonal behavior of the client is probably MOST important as a therapy topic to which two analytic theorists?

    A. Freud and Adler   B. Adler and Rank
    C. Freud and Rank   D. Horney and Sullivan

25.____

KEY (CORRECT ANSWERS)

1.	B	11.	A
2.	D	12.	B
3.	D	13.	D
4.	B	14.	A
5.	C	15.	C
6.	B	16.	C
7.	A	17.	A
8.	B	18.	D
9.	B	19.	C
10.	C	20.	A

21. D
22. B
23. A
24. C
25. D

TEST 2

DIRECTIONS: Each question or incomplete statement is followed by several suggested answers or completions. Select the one that BEST answers the question or completes the statement. *PRINT THE LETTER OF THE CORRECT ANSWER IN THE SPACE AT THE RIGHT.*

1. When a counselor is listening to a client, it is MOST important that he be able to

    A. show interest and agreement with what the client is saying
    B. paraphrase what the client is saying
    C. understand the significance of what the client is saying
    D. differentiate between fact and fiction in what the client is saying

2. On which one of the following is successful counseling LEAST likely to depend?

    A. The counselor's theoretical orientation
    B. The counselor's ability to bring the client's feelings and attitudes into the open
    C. The counselor's diagnostic ability
    D. The client's readiness for counseling

3. A client is referred to you for counseling against his will and is suspicious and uncooperative. You should

    A. explain to him that you cannot help him unless he is prepared to cooperate
    B. explain that you are not taking sides and that you will be impartial
    C. show him that you know how he feels and encourage him to talk about it
    D. explain that you are on his side and will listen sympathetically to anything that he might care to bring up

4. Which one of the following would NOT be considered a basic objective of the first interview between a client and a counselor?

    A. Beginning a sound counseling relationship
    B. Identifying the client's real problem
    C. Opening up the area of client feelings and attitudes
    D. Clarifying the nature of the counseling process for the client

5. All of the following counselor statements or actions are appropriate techniques for ending an interview EXCEPT

    A. "Our time is nearly up. Is there something else you have in mind for today?"
    B. "Let's see now. Suppose we go over what we've accomplished today."
    C. Counselor may glance at his watch and say, "When would you like to come in again?"
    D. Counselor may shuffle papers on desk and say, "Now, let's see; when is my next appointment?"

6. It has been recognized in recent literature that the value structure of the individual counselor has what kind of effect on the counseling process?

    A. Direct   B. Indirect
    C. Little   D. None

7. The intensive study of the same individuals over a fairly long period of time represents the

   A. cross-sectional approach
   B. longitudinal approach
   C. clinical approach
   D. biographical approach

8. Of the following techniques, the one which is MOST characteristic of non-directive or client-centered therapy is

   A. encouraging transference
   B. free association
   C. reflection of feeling
   D. permissive questioning

9. In making predictions about how a client will behave in a given situation, a counselor

   A. should limit himself to those situations for which "actuarial" data are available
   B. must rely on "clinical" judgment in many situations but use "actuarial" data wherever possible
   C. should rely on "clinical" judgment in all situations, since they are more valid than "actuarial" predictions
   D. always uses "actuarial" data, but modifies them in light of his "clinical" impression of the client

10. A research study that establishes an hypothesis, sets up control groups, collects data, and generalizes from the data is

    A. formulative
    B. diagnostic
    C. experimental
    D. exploratory

11. The MOST usable single index of the social and economic status of all the members of any family is

    A. occupation of the father
    B. religious affiliation of the family
    C. location of the home in the community
    D. socio-economic rating by neighbors

12. When a counselor does NOT understand the meaning of a response that a counselee has made, the counselor usually should

    A. proceed to another topic
    B. admit his lack of understanding and ask for clarification
    C. act as if he understands so that the counselee's confidence in him is not shaken
    D. ask the counselee to choose his words more carefully

13. When the counselor makes a response which touches off a high degree of resistance in the counselee, he should

    A. apologize and rephrase his remark in a less threatening manner
    B. accept the resistance
    C. ignore the counselee's resistance
    D. recognize that little more will be accomplished in the interview and offer another appointment

14. Directive and non-directive counseling are two emphases in counseling theory and practice. From the pairs of names listed below, indicate the two that are representative of the Directive school. 14.____

    A. Thorne and Williamson
    B. Rogers and Thorne
    C. Williamson and Sullivan
    D. Sullivan and Rogers

15. Rogerian counseling theory is based on the assumption that the potential and tendency for growth toward a fully functioning personality is present in 15.____

    A. a few "self-actualized" persons
    B. most people of above average intelligence
    C. people whose behavior can be considered as "normal" and socially effective
    D. all people

16. Anecdotal records should contain which type(s) of information? 16.____

    A. Evaluations
    B. Interpretations
    C. Factual reports
    D. Prognoses

17. RESISTANCE in relation to psychological counseling typically refers to the 17.____

    A. client's defenses against his inner conflicts
    B. counselor's unwillingness to deal with the client's emotional problems
    C. client's having enough ego strength so that he can face his problems
    D. counselor's having enough ego strength so that he can help the client face his problems

18. On which one of the following does the democratic leader specifically rely? His ability to 18.____

    A. listen and tactfully guide the discussion in the direction he has planned and the members' willingness to cooperate
    B. diagnose situations, to interpret and explain them to the members and their willingness to accept
    C. discern the issues which the members could profitably discuss and his willingness to allow them with his help to do so
    D. understand the meaning of the response from the member's frame of reference and his willingness for them to make decisions

19. Advisement in counseling is MOST effective when the counselee is in a state of 19.____

    A. perceiving his problem as related to a conflict with inner forces
    B. minimal conflict and of optimal readiness for action
    C. perceiving his problem as related to an external conflict
    D. feeling extremely ambivalent about his self-concept

20. Of the following, the MOST valid use of projective techniques is the study of the 20.____

    A. problems which an individual faces
    B. cultural effects upon an individual
    C. inner world of an individual
    D. human relationships of an individual

21. Diagnosis is NOT regarded as a helpful antecedent to counseling by

    A. Cottle
    B. Rogers
    C. Thorne
    D. Williamson

22. The beginning counselor must be alert to interferences to rapport. Which one of the following is NOT considered an intereference?

    A. Injecting the counselor's present mood
    B. Engaging in "small talk" at the start of the interview
    C. Registering surprise or dismay
    D. Emphasizing the counselor's ability

23. There is some evidence according to Rogers that counseling is more effective with

    A. younger adults or higher intelligence
    B. older adults of higher intelligence
    C. younger adults of lower intelligence
    D. older adults of lower intelligence

24. In assisting with the scheduling of interviews for educational planning, the counselor should suggest that group instruction

    A. follow the counseling interview
    B. is not necessary when individual interviews can be scheduled since each case is different
    C. precede the counseling
    D. may either precede or follow the counseling interview

25. A client has requested an interview with the counselor to discuss a personal problem. In general, the BEST way to begin the interview is to

    A. come directly to the point and encourage the client to talk about his problem
    B. assure him that everything discussed will be confidential
    C. offer to help him in every way possible
    D. inquire whether he has discussed the problem with anyone else

KEY (CORRECT ANSWERS)

1.	C	11.	A
2.	A	12.	B
3.	C	13.	B
4.	B	14.	A
5.	D	15.	D
6.	A	16.	C
7.	B	17.	A
8.	C	18.	C
9.	B	19.	B
10.	C	20.	C

21. B
22. B
23. A
24. C
25. A

EXAMINATION SECTION
TEST 1

DIRECTIONS: Each question or incomplete statement is followed by several suggested answers or completions. Select the one that BEST answers the question or completes the statement. PRINT THE LETTER OF THE CORRECT ANSWER IN THE SPACE AT THE RIGHT.

1. When a counselor is planning a future interview with a client, of the following, the MOST important consideration is the

    A. recommendations he will make to the client
    B. place where the client will be interviewed
    C. purpose for which the client will be interviewed
    D. personality of the client

    1._____

2. For a counselor to make a practice of reviewing the client's case record, if available, prior to the interview, is, usually,

    A. *inadvisable,* because knowledge of the client's past record will tend to influence the counselor's judgment
    B. *advisable,* because knowledge of the client's background will help the counselor to identify discrepancies in the client's responses
    C. *inadvisable,* because such review is time-consuming and of questionable value
    D. *advisable,* because knowledge of the client's background will help the counselor to understand the client's situation

    2._____

3. Assume that a counselor makes a practice of constantly reassuring clients with serious and complex problems by making such statements as: "I'm sure you'll soon be well;" "I know you'll get a job soon;" or "Everything will be all right."
Of the following, the MOST likely result of such a practice is to

    A. encourage the client and make him feel that the counselor understands what the client is going through
    B. make the client doubtful about the counselor's understanding of his difficulties and the counselor's ability to help
    C. confuse the client and cause him to hesitate to take any action on his own initiative
    D. help the client to be more realistic about his situation and the probability that it will improve

    3._____

4. In order to get the maximum amount of information from a client during an interview, of the following, it is MOST important for the counselor to communicate to the client the feeling that the counselor is

    A. interested in the client
    B. a figure of authority
    C. efficient in his work habits
    D. sympathetic to the client's lifestyle

    4._____

5. Of the following, the counselor who takes extremely detailed notes during an interview with a client is *most likely* to

    A. encourage the client to talk freely

    5._____

B. distract and antagonize the client
C. help the client feel at ease
D. understand the client's feelings

6. As a counselor, you find that many of the clients you interview are verbally abusive and unusually hostile to you.
Of the following, the MOST appropriate action for you to take *first* is to

   A. review your interviewing techniques and consider whether you may be provoking these clients
   B. act in a more authoritative manner when interviewing troublesome clients
   C. tell these clients that you will not process their applications unless their troublesome behavior ceases
   D. disregard the clients' troublesome behavior during the interview

7. During an interview, you did not completely understand several of your client's responses. In each instance, you rephrased the client's statement and asked the client if that was what he meant.
For you to use such a technique during interviews would be considered

   A. *inappropriate;* you may have distorted the client's meaning by rephrasing his statements
   B. *inappropriate;* you should have asked the same questioE until you received a comprehensible response
   C. *appropriate;* the client will have a chance to correct you if you have misinterpreted his responses
   D. *appropriate;* a counselor should rephrase clients' responses for the records

8. A counselor is interviewing a client who has just had a severe emotional shock because of an assault on her by a mugger.
Of the following, the approach which would generally be MOST helpful to the client is for the counselor to

   A. comfort the client and encourage her to talk about the assault
   B. sympathize with the client but refuse to discuss the assault with her
   C. tell the client to control her emotions and think positively about the future
   D. proceed with the interview in an impersonal and unemotional manner

9. A counselor finds that her questions are misinterpreted by many of the clients she interviews.
Of the following, the MOST likely reason for this problem is that the

   A. client is not listening attentively
   B. client wants to avoid the subject being discussed
   C. counselor has failed to express her meaning clearly
   D. counselor has failed to put the client at ease

10. For a counselor to look directly at the client and observe him during the interview is generally

   A. *inadvisable;* this will make the client nervous and uncomfortable
   B. *advisable;* the client will be more likely to refrain from lying
   C. *inadvisable;* the counselor will not be able to take notes for the case record
   D. *advisable;* this will encourage conversation and accelerate the progress of the interview

11. You are interviewing a client who is applying for social services for the first time. In order to encourage this client to freely give you the information needed for you to establish his eligibility, of the following, the BEST way to start the interview is by

    A. asking questions the client can easily answer
    B. conveying the impression that his responses to your questions will be checked
    C. asking two or three similar but important questions
    D. assuring the client that your sole responsibility is "getting the facts"

12. Counselors are encouraged to record significant information obtained from clients and services provided for clients. Of the following, the MOST important reason for this practice is that these case records will

    A. help to reduce the need for regular supervisory conferences
    B. indicate to counselors which clients are taking up the most time
    C. provide information which will help the agency to improve its services to clients
    D. make it easier to verify the complaints of clients

13. As a counselor you find that interviews can be completed in a shorter period of time if you ask questions which limit the client to a certain answer.
    For you to use such a technique would be considered

    A. *inappropriate*, because this type of question usually requires advance preparation
    B. *inappropriate*, because this type of question may inhibit the client from saying what he really means
    C. *appropriate*, because you know the areas into which the questions should be directed
    D. *appropriate*, because this type of question usually helps clients to express themselves clearly

14. Assume that, while you are interviewing an individual to obtain information, the individual pauses in the middle of an answer.
    The BEST of the following actions for you to take at this time is to

    A. correct any inaccuracies in what he has said
    B. remain silent until he continues
    C. explain your position on the matter being discussed
    D. explain that time is short and that he must complete his story quickly

15. You have been assigned to interview the mother of a five-year-old son in her home to get information useful in locating the child's absent father. During the interview, you notice many serious bruises on the child's arms and legs, which the mother explains are due to the child's clumsiness. Of the following, your BEST course of action is to

    A. accept the mother's explanation and concentrate on getting information which will help you to locate the father
    B. advise the mother to have the child examined for a medical condition that may be causing his clumsiness
    C. make a surprise visit to the mother later, to see if someone is beating the child
    D. complete your interview with the mother and report the case to your supervisor for investigation of possible child abuse

16. During an interview, the former landlord of an absent father offers to help you to locate the father if you will give the landlord confidential information you have on the financial situation of the father.
Of the following, you should

   A. immediately end the interview with the landlord
   B. urge the landlord to help you but explain that you are not permitted to give him confidential information
   C. freely give the landlord the confidential information he requests about the father
   D. give the landlord the information only if he promises to keep it confidential

17. You feel that your client, a released mental patient, is not adjusting well to living on his own in an apartment. To gather more information, you interview privately his next-door neighbor, who claims that the client is creating a "disturbance" and speaks of the client in an angry and insulting manner.
Of the following, the BEST action for you to take in this situation is to

   A. listen patiently to the neighbor to try to get the facts about your client's behavior
   B. inform the neighbor that he has no right to speak insultingly about a mentally ill person
   C. make an appointment to interview the neighbor some other time when he isn't so upset
   D. tell the neighbor that you were not aware of the client's behavior and that you will have the client moved

18. As a counselor, you are interviewing a client to determine his eligibility for a work program. Suddenly the client begins to shout that he is in no condition to work and that you are persecuting him for no reason.
Of the following, your BEST response to this client is to

   A. advise the client to stop shouting or you will call for the security guard
   B. wait until the client calms down, then order him to come back for another interview
   C. insist that you are not persecuting the client and that he must complete the interview
   D. wait until the client calms down, say that you understand how he feels, and try to continue the interview

19. You are interviewing a mother whose 17-year-old son has recently been returned home from a mental institution. Although she is willing to care for her son at home, she is frightened by his strange and sometimes violent behavior and does not know the best arrangement to make for his care.
Of the following, your MOST appropriate response to this mother's problem is to

   A. describe the supportive services and alternatives to home care which are available
   B. help her to accept her son's strange and violent behavior
   C. tell her that she will not be permitted to care for her son at home if she is frightened by his behavior
   D. convince her that she is not responsible for her son's mental condition

5 (#1)

20. Assume that you are interviewing an elderly man who comes to the center several times a month to discuss topics with you which are not related to social services. You realize that the man is lonely and enjoys these conversations.
Of the following, it would be MOST appropriate to

   A. politely discourage the man from coming in to pass the time with you
   B. avoid speaking to this man the next time he comes into the center
   C. explore with the client his feelings about joining a senior citizens' center
   D. continue to hold these conversations with the man

21. A client you are interviewing tends to ramble on after each response that he gives, so that many clients are kept waiting.
In this situation, of the following, it would be MOST advisable to

   A. try to direct the interview, in order to obtain the necessary information
   B. reduce the number of questions asked so that you can shorten the interview
   C. arrange a second interview for the client so that you can give him more time
   D. tell the client that he is wasting everybody's time

22. A non-minority counselor is about to interview a minority client on public assistance for job placement when the client says: "What does your kind know about my problems? You've never had to survive out on these streets."
Of the following, the counselor's MOST appropriate response in this situation is to

   A. postpone the interview until a minority counselor is available to interview the client
   B. tell the client that he must cooperate with the counselor if he wants to continue receiving public assistance
   C. explain to the client the function of the counselor in this unit and the services he provides
   D. assure the client that you do not have to be a member of a minority group to understand the effects of poverty

23. When you are interviewing someone to obtain information, the BEST of the following reasons for you to repeat certain of his exact words is to

   A. *assure* him that appropriate action will be taken
   B. *encourage* him to elaborate on a point he has made
   C. *assure* him that you agree with his point of view
   D. *encourage* him to switch to another topic of discussion

24. fou are interviewing a young client who seriously under-estimates the amount of education and training he will require for a certain occupation.
For you to tell the client that you think he is mistaken would generally be considered

   A. *inadvisable,* because counselors should not express their opinions to clients
   B. *inadvisable,* because clients have the right to self-determination
   C. *advisable,* because clients should generally be alerted to their misconceptions
   D. *advisable,* because counselors should convince clients to adopt a proper life style

25. Of the following, the MOST appropriate manner for a counselor to assume during an interview with a patient is

    A. authoritarian
    B. paternal
    C. casual
    D. businesslike

25.___

KEY (CORRECT ANSWERS)

1. C
2. D
3. B
4. A
5. B

6. A
7. C
8. A
9. C
10. D

11. A
12. C
13. B
14. B
15. D

16. B
17. A
18. D
19. A
20. C

21. A
22. C
23. B
24. C
25. D

TEST 2

DIRECTIONS: Each question or incomplete statement is followed by several suggested answers or completions. Select the one that *BEST* answers the question or completes the statement. *PRINT THE LETTER OF THE CORRECT ANSWER IN THE SPACE AT THE RIGHT.*

1. You are interviewing a legally responsible absent father who refuses to make child support payments because he claims the mother physically abuses the child.
   Of the following, the *BEST* way for you to handle this situation is to tell the father that you

   A. will report his complaint about the mother, but he is still responsible for making child support payments
   B. suspect that he is complaining about the mother in order to avoid his own responsibility for making child support payments
   C. are concerned with his responsibility to make child support payments, not with the mother's abuse of the child
   D. can not determine his responsibility for making child support payments until his complaint about the mother is investigated

   1.____

2. You are interviewing an elderly woman who lives alone to determine her eligibility for homemaker service at public expense. Though obviously frail and in need of this service, the woman is not completely cooperative, and during the interview, is often silent for a considerable period of time.
   Of the following, the *BEST* way for you to deal with these periods of silence is to

   A. realize that she may be embarrassed to have to apply for homemaker service at public expense, and emphasize her right to this service
   B. postpone the interview and make an appointment with her for a later date, when she may be better able to cooperate
   C. explain to the woman that you have many clients to interview and need her cooperation to complete the interview quickly
   D. recognize that she is probably hiding something and begin to ask questions to draw her out

   2.____

3. During a conference with an adolescent boy at a juvenile detention center, you find out for the first time that he would prefer to be placed in foster care rather than return to his natural parents.
   To uncover the reasons why the boy dislikes his own home, of the following, it would be *MOST* advisable for you to

   A. ask the boy a number of short, simple questions about his feelings
   B. encourage the boy to talk freely and express his feelings as best he can
   C. interview the parents and find out why the boy doesn't want to live at home
   D. administer a battery of psychological tests in order to make an assessment of the boy's problems

   3.____

4. You are interviewing a mother who is applying for Aid to Families with Dependent Children because the husband has deserted the family. The mother becomes annoyed at having to answer your questions and tells you to leave her apartment.
   Which one of the following actions would be *most appropriate* to take *FIRST* in this situation?

   4.____

A. Return to the office and close the case for lack of cooperation
B. Tell the mother that you will get the information from her neighbors if she does not cooperate
C. Tell the mother that you must stay until you get answers to your questions
D. Explain to the mother the reasons for the interview and the consequences of Her failure to cooperate

5. A counselor counseling juvenile clients finds that, although he can tolerate most of their behavior, he becomes infuriated when they lie to him.
Of the following, the counselor can *BEST* deal with his anger at his clients' lying by

A. recognizing his feelings of anger and learning to control expression of these feelings to his clients
B. warning his clients that he cannot be responsible for his anger when a client lies to him
C. using will power to suppress his feelings of anger when a client lies to him
D. realizing that lying is a common trait of juveniles and not directed against him personally

6. During an interview, one of your clients, a former drug addict, has expressed an interest in attending a community counseling center and resuming his education.
In this case, the *MOST* appropriate action that you should take *FIRST* is to

A. determine whether this ambition is realistic for a former drug addict
B. send the client's application to a community counseling center which provides services to former addicts
C. ask the client whether he is really motivated or is just seeking your approval
D. encourage and assist the client to take this step, since his interest is a positive sign

7. You are interviewing a client who, during previous appointments, has not responded to your requests for information required to determine his continued eligibility for services. On this occasion, the client again offers an excuse which you feel is not acceptable.
For you to advise the client of the probable loss of services because of his lack of cooperation is

A. *inappropriate,* because the threat to withhold services will harm the relationship between counselor and client
B. *inappropriate,* because counselors should not reveal to clients that they do not believe their statements
C. *appropriate,* because social services are a reward given to cooperative clients
D. *appropriate,* beca,us.e the counselor should Inform clients of the consequences of their lack of cooperation

8. Assume that you are counselling an adolescent boy in a juvenile detention center who has been a ringleader in smuggling "pot" into the center.
During your regular interview with this boy, of the following, it would be *advisable* to

A. tell him you know that he has been involved in smuggling pot and that you are trying to understand the reasons for his misbehavior
B. ignore his pot smuggling in order to reassure him that you understand and accept him, even though you do not agree with his standards of behavior
C. warn him that you have reported his pot smuggling and that he will be punished for his misbehavior
D. show him that you disapprove of his pot smuggling, but assure him that you will not report him for his misbehavior

9. Your unit has received several complaints about a homeless elderly woman living outdoors in various locations in the area. To help determine the need for protective services for this woman, you interview several persons in the neighborhood who are familiar with her, but all are uncooperative or reluctant to give information.
Of the following, your BEST approach to these persons is to explain to them that

   A. you will take legal steps against them if they do not cooperate with you
   B. their cooperation may enable you to help this homeless woman
   C. you need their cooperation to remove this homeless woman from their neighborhood
   D. they will be responsible for any harm that comes to this homeless woman

10. Assume that you are interviewing a client regarding an adjustment in budget. The client begins to scream at you that she holds you responsible for the decrease in her allowance.
Of the following, which is the BEST way for you to handle this situation?

    A. Attempt to discuss the matter calmly with the client and explain her right to a hearing
    B. Urge the client to appeal and assure her of your support
    C. Tell the client that her disorderly behavior will be held against her
    D. Tell the client that the reduction is "due to red tape" and is not your fault

11. As a counselor assigned to a juvenile detention center, you are having a counselling interview with a recently admitted boy who is having serious problems in adjusting to confinement in the center. During the interview, the boy frequently interrupts to ask you personal questions. Of the following, the BEST way for you to deal with these questions is to

    A. tell him in a friendly way that your job is to discuss his problems, not yours
    B. try to understand how the questions relate to the boy's own problems and reply with discretion
    C. take no notice of the questions and continue with the interview
    D. try to win the boy's confidence by answering his questions in detail

12. A counselor is interviewing an elderly woman who hesitates to provide necessary information about her finances to determine whether she is eligible for supplementary assistance. She fears that this information will be reported to others and that her neighbors will find out that she is destitute and applying for "welfare." Of the following, the counselor's MOST appropriate response is to

    A. tell her that, if she hesitates to give this information, the agency will get it from other sources
    B. assure her that this information is kept strictly confidential and will not be given to unauthorized persons
    C. convince her that her application will be turned down unless she provides this information as soon as possible
    D. ask for the name and address of her nearest relative and obtain the information from that person

13. You are counseling a couple whose children have been placed in a foster home because of the couple's quarreling and child neglect. When you interview the wife by herself, she tells you that she knows the husband often "cheats" on her with other women, but she is too afraid of the husband's temper to tell him how much this hurts her.
For you to immediately reveal to the husband the wife's unhappiness concerning his "cheating" is, generally,

    A. *good practice,* because it will help the husband to understand why his wife quarrels with him
    B. *poor practice,* because information received from the wife should not be given to the husband without her permission
    C. *good practice,* because the husband will direct his anger at you rather than at his wife
    D. poor *practice,* because the wife may have told you a false story about her husband in order to win your sympathy

14. A counselor is beginning a job placement interview with a tall, strongly built young man. As the man sits down, the counselor comments: "I know a big fellow like you wouldn't be interested in any clerical job."
For the counselor to make such a comment is, generally,

    A. *appropriate,* because it creates an air of familiarity which may put the man at ease
    B. *inappropriate,* because the man may be sensitive about his physical size
    C. *appropriate,* because, the counselor is using his judgment to help speed up the interview
    D. *inappropriate,* because the man may feel he is being pressured into agreeing with the counselor

15. A counselor in a men's shelter is counseling a middle-aged client for alcoholism. During counseling, the" client confesses that, many years ago, he had often enjoyed sexually abusing his ten-year-old daughter. The counselor tells the client that he personally finds the client's behavior "morally disgusting."
For the counselor to tell the client this is, generally,

    A. *acceptable counseling practice,* because it may encourage the client to feel guilty about his behavior
    B. un*acceptable* couse*ling practice* , because the client may try to shock the counselor by confessing other similar behavior
    C. *acceptable counseling practice,* because "letting off steam" in this manner may relieve tension between the counselor and the client
    D. *unacceptable counseling practice,* because the client may hesitate to discuss his behavior frankly with the counselor in the future

16. During an interview, your client, who wants to move to a larger apartment, asks you to decide on a suitable neighborhood for her.
    For you to make such a decision for the client would, generally, be considered

    A. *appropriate,* because you can save time and expense by sharing your knowledge of neighborhoods with the client
    B. *inappropriate,* because counselors should not help clients with this type of decision
    C. *appropriate,* because this will help the client to develop confidence in her ability to make decisions
    D. *inappropriate,* because the client should be encouraged to accept the responsibility of making this decision

17. A client tells you that he is extremely upset by the treatment that he received from Center personnel at the information desk.
    Which of the following is the *BEST* way to handle this complaint during the interview?

    A. Explain to the client that he probably misinterpreted what occurred at the information desk
    B. Let the client express his feelings and then proceed with the interview
    C. Tell the client that you are not concerned with the personnel at the information desk
    D. Escort the client to the information desk to find out what really happened

18. You are finishing an interview with a client in which you have explained to her the procedure she must go through to apply for income maintenance.
    Of the following, the *BEST* way for you to make sure that she has fully understood the procedure is to ask her

    A. whether she feels she has understood your explanation of the procedure
    B. whether she has any questions to ask you about the procedure
    C. to describe the procedure to you in her own words
    D. a few questions to test her understanding of the procedure

19. You are interviewing a client in his home as part of your investigation of an anonymous complaint that he has been receiving Medicaid fraudulently. During the interview, the client frequently interrupts your questions to discuss the hardships of his life and the bitterness he feels about his medical condition.
    Of the following, the *BEST* way for you to deal with these discussions is to

    A. cut them off abruptly, since the client is probably just trying to avoid answering your questions
    B. listen patiently, since these discussions may be helpful to the client and may give you information for your investigation
    C. remind the client that you are investigating a complaint against him and he must answer directly
    D. seek to gain the client's confidence by discussing any personal or medical problems which you yourself may have

20. While interviewing an absent father to determine his ability to pay child supprt, you realize that his answers to some of your questions contradict his answers to other questions. Of the following, the BEST way for you to try to get accurate information from the father is to

    A. confront him with his contradictory answers and demand an explanation from him
    B. use your best judgment as to which of his answers are accurate and question him accordingly
    C. tell him that he has misunderstood your questions and that he must clarify his answers
    D. ask him the same questions in different words and follow up his answers with related questions

21. The one of the following types of interviewees who presents the LEAST difficult problem to handle is the person who

    A. answers with a great many qualifications
    B. talks at length about unrelated subjects so that the counselor cannot ask questions
    C. has difficulty understanding the counselor's vocabulary
    D. breaks into the middle of sentences and completes them with a meaning of his own

22. A man being interviewed is entitled to Medicaid, but he refuses to sign up for it because he says he cannot accept any form of welfare.
    Of the following, the BEST course of action to take FIRST is to

    A. try to discover the reason for his feeling this way
    B. tell him that he should be glad financial help is available
    C. explain that others cannot help him if he will not help himself
    D. suggest that he speak to someone who is already on Medicaid

23. Of the following, the outcome of an interview by a counselor depends MOST heavily on the

    A. personality of the interviewee
    B. personality of the counselor
    C. subject matter of the questions asked
    D. interaction between counselor and interviewee.

24. Some clients being interviewed are primarily interested in making a favorable impression. The counselor should be aware of the fact that such clients are *more likely* than other clients to

    A. try to anticipate the answers the interviewer is looking for
    B. answer all questions openly and frankly
    C. try to assume the role of interviewer
    D. be anxious to get the interview over as quickly as possible

25. The type of interview which a counselor usually conducts is substantially different from most interviewing situations in all of the following aspects EXCEPT the

    A. setting   B. kinds of clients
    C. techniques employed D. kinds of problems

KEY (CORRECT ANSWERS)

1. A
2. A
3. B
4. D
5. A

6. D
7. D
8. A
9. B
10. A

11. B
12. B
13. B
14. D
15. D

16. D
17. B
18. C
19. B
20. D

21. C
22. A
23. D
24. A
25. C

26 WAYS TO RECOGNIZE DRUG ABUSE

CONTENTS

		Page
1.	Speech	1
2.	Vocabulary	1
3.	Change of Personality	1
4.	Eyes	1
5.	Sleep	1
6.	Stealing	1
7.	Excessive Smoking and Finger Burns	1
8.	Liquor	1
9.	Chemical Aromas	1
10.	Yawning	1
11.	Weight-Loss	2
12.	Eating Habits	2
13.	Irritability	2
14.	Mobility	2
15.	Medicine Bottles	2
16.	Pills	2
17.	Prescriptions Forms	2
18.	Truancy	2
19.	Companions	2
20.	Pin-Like Punctures	2
21.	Black N' Blue Veins	3
22.	Blood Stains	3
23.	Unexplainable Illness	3
24.	Hallucination	3
25.	Strange Paraphernalia	3
26.	Hepatitis Infection	3

26 WAYS TO RECOGNIZE DRUG ABUSE

1. SPEECH

   Does your child's speech pattern conform with his customary actions? Look for slurring, difficulty of speech, as if drunk.

2. VOCABULARY

   In his conversations, do you hear words like: Twisted, bent, high, acid, spike, decks, bags, hit, downs, ups, head, grass, speed, trip, turned-on ... etc.?

3. CHANGE OF PERSONALITY

   Is the child acting contrary to his known personality makeup? Is the child sleepy-looking? Is there unexplained elation? Is there erratic behavior?

4. EYES

   Is there a glassy look? Are the pupils pin-pointed? Do the eyes look strange to you?

5. SLEEP

   Is there evidence of restlessness? Are there signs of nightmares? Is there sign of night sweating?

6. STEALING

   Money buys drugs... Is your child stealing or pawning articles? Are household items strangely disappearing? Are pawn tickets found with his belongings? Is there an increased need for money?

7. EXCESSIVE SMOKING AND FINGER BURNS

   Is there a marked increase in smoking? Are there heavy nicotine stains, or burned fingers? Often under heavy stupor of drugs (Nodding) cigarettes can burn to the flesh of the fingers and pain is not felt immediately.

8. LIQUOR

   Very often youngsters experimenting with drugs use liquor to fool parents into thinking they have been drinking and not using drugs. Spilling liquor, beer, wine on clothing conceals the real cause of their "high".

9. CHEMICAL AROMAS

   Do you smell strange aromas like glue, carbona, magic markers? Have you found paper bags with tubes of airplane glue smashed in side the bag? Does your child's breath smell of any strange chemical odor?

10. YAWNING

    Despite a good night's sleep, is there evidence of excessive yawning? Is there marked tiredness? Is there evidence of general laziness?

11. WEIGHT-LOSS 11.____

   Drugs take a toll on a user's physique. Do you notice steady loss of weight, and general "rundown" look?

12. EATING HABITS 12.____

   Is there evidence of loss of appetite? Is there unusual use of sweets, soda, sugar, etc.?

13. IRRITABILITY 13.____

   Is there noticeable scratching? Is there more nervousness, restlessness, or general itching of the body?

14. MOBILITY 14.____

   Is there unusual trait in child's walking? Is there unstab-ility? Are there movements similar to those of an intoxicated person?

15. MEDICINE BOTTLES 15.____

   Are the prescription cough syrups disappearing from the cabinet? Are there unexplained numbers of medicinal bottles around? If a user is "high", a sweet breath may indicate child is using cough syrups.

16. PILLS 16.____

   Are your prescription pills disappearing? Are strange colored pills found on clothing, dressers, or on person?

17. PRESCRIPTION FORMS 17.____

   Are there blank or written prescriptions about, signed with unfamiliar doctors? Often pushers sell prescription blanks to youngsters who, in turn, use forms to secure drugs.

18. TRUANCY 18.____

   If a youngster is of school age, is there a history of truancy? Then check into the causes of the truancy.

19. COMPANIONS 19.____

   What do you know of your child's friends? What are their interests? What impressions do you have as to their behavior, appearance, and personal habits? If not in school, are they employed?

20. PIN-LIKE PUNCTURES 20.____

   Are there pin-like scabs about the body? "Skin-popping" (use of needle) is method used to inject drug into the body. Beginners and girls usually use this method of injecting drug.

21. BLACK N'BLUE VEINS   21._____

Pin-like punctures over the veins could indicate user is injecting drug through the vein (Main-lining). After long periods of injections, veins collapse, harden into blue looking "tracks", with the scabs sometime becoming ulcerated. The confirmed addict has "tracks" almost over every vein. "Mainliners" have tracts on inside of arms, along veins on back of hands.

22. BLOOD STAINS   22._____

Often after user injects drug he fails to wipe blood caused by the injection; blood then may appear on the sleeve of shirt, clothing. Blood-stains may also appear on bed sheets, causedby the injection scabs that fall off during sleep.

23. UNEXPLAINABLE ILLNESS   23._____

Cramps, nasal discharge, sweating, muscular twitching, vomiting, diarrhea ... These combined symptoms could indicate user need for "shot" and that the youngster is going through "withdrawal".

24. HALLUCINATION   24._____

User senses distortion, there may be intensification of sensory perception. There may be a loss of reality or unexplainable psychotic or antisocial behavior. User when on L.S.D. or other hallocinogenic drug might also want to destroy himself.

25. STRANGE PARAPHERNALIA   25._____

Have you found: Miniature pipes, strange loose tobacco, cigarette paper, sugar cubes, syringes, eye-droppers, hypodermic needles, glassine packets with strange white powder, burned metal bottle caps?

26. HEPATITIS INFECTION   26._____

This disease does not mean that infection was secured through infectious hypodermic needles. There are many other reasons for the infection. However, this is a very common infection suffered by addicts.

BASIC QUESTIONS AND ANSWERS ON ALCOHOL

TABLE OF CONTENTS

		Page
Introduction		1
I.	What is alcohol?	1
II.	How does alcohol work in the body?	1
III.	How fast does alcohol take effect?	2
IV.	Why do people drink?	2
V.	What is drunkenness?	3
VI.	What is a hangover?	3
VII.	What physical harm can heavy drinking cause?	3
VIII.	How can you tell if someone is alcoholic?	4
IX.	How can a person with an alcohol problem be helped?	4
X.	Can alcohol problems be prevented?	5

BASIC QUESTIONS AND ANSWERS ON ALCOHOL

HOW WIDELY ARE ALCOHOLIC BEVERAGES USED?

As far back as historical records go, beverages containing alcohol have been made and used by people. Such beverages are part of the cultures of peoples throughout the world.

In fact, two-thirds of the adult population in the United States do drink at least occasionally, while one-third do not drink at all. Among the youth of this country, a recent survey found that most American adolescents have had at least some experience with alcoholic beverages. Almost 80 percent have had at least one drink; about 74 percent have had at least two or three drinks; and over one-half of all adolescents drink at least once a month.

I. WHAT IS ALCOHOL?

Alcohol, the major active ingredient in wine, beer, and distilled liquor, is a natural substance formed by the reaction of fermenting sugar with yeast spores. There are many alcohols, but the kind in alcoholic beverages is ethyl alcohol -- a colorless, inflammable liquid with an intoxicating effect.

Ethyl alcohol is a drug which can produce feelings of well-being, sedation, intoxication, or unconsciousness--depending on the amount and the manner in which it is drunk. Technically, it can also be classified as a food, since it contains colories; however, it has no nutritional value.

Various alcoholic beverages are produced by using different sources of sugar for fermentation. For instance, beer is made from grapes or berries, whiskey from malted trains, and rum from molasses. Hard liquors--such as whiskey, gin, and vodka--are produced by distillation, which further concentrates the alcohol resulting from fermentation.

ALCOHOL CONTENT OF TYPICAL ALCOHOLIC BEVERAGES

Beer   - 4%
Dinner wine   - 10-12%
Fortified wine   - 17-20%
Distilled liquor - 40-50%

Each fluid ounce of 100 percent alcohol contains about 200 calories, although the alcoholic beverages and drinks derived from them vary widely. About the same alcoholic content, one-half ounce of pure alcohol, is found in:

        a 12-ounce can of beer
        a 5-ounce glass of dinner wine
        a cocktail containing 1 1/2 ounces of 86-proof liquor

II. HOW DOES ALCOHOL WORK IN THE BODY?

Unlike other "food," alcohol does not have to be digested. When you drink an alcoholic beverage, 20 percent of the alcohol in it is absorbed immediately into the bloodstream through the stomach walls. The other 80 percent of the alcohol enters the bloodstream almost as fast after being quickly processed through the gastrointestinal tract. Moments after it is consumed, alcohol can be found in all tissues, organs, and secretions of the body. The alcohol eventually acts on the brain's central control areas to slow down or depress brain activity

A low level of alcohol in the blood, such as would result from sipping one drink--for example, a 12-ounce can of beer--has a mild tranquilzing effect on most people. Although basically a sedative, alcohol seems to act temporarily as a stimulant for many after they first start drinking. This is due to the fact that alcohol's initial effects are on those parts of the brain affecting learned behavior patterns such as self-control. After a drink or two, this learned behavior may temporarily disappear, making you lose your inhibitions, talk more freely, or feel like the "life of the party." On the other hand, you may feel aggressive or depressed.

Higher blood alcohol levels depress brain activity to the point that memory, as well as muscle coordination and balance, may be temporarily impaired. Still larger alcohol intake within a relatively short period of time depresses deeper parts of the brain, severely affecting judgment and dulling the senses.

If steady heavy drinking continues, the alcohol anesthetizes the deepest levels of the brain and can cause coma or death by depressing heart functions and breathing.

III. HOW FAST DOES ALCOHOL TAKE EFFECT?

The rapidity with which alcohol enters the bloodstream and exerts its effects on the brain and body depends on several factors:

How fast you drink. The half-ounce of pure alcohol in an average highball, can of beer, or glass of wine can be burned up or metabolized in the body in about 2 hours. If you sip your drink slowly and do not have more than one drink every 2 hours, the alcohol will not have a chance to jolt your brain or build up significantly in your blood, and you will feel little unpleasant effect. On the other hand, gulping drinks produces immediate, intoxicating effects and depression of deeper brain centers.

Whether your stomach is empty or full. Eating, especially before you drink but also while you drink, will slow down alcohol's rate of absorption into your bloodstream and produce a more even response to the alcohol.

What you drink. The alcohol in wine and beer is more diluted and is, therefore, absorbed somewhat more slowly into the bloodstream than alcohol from hard liquor. Diluting distilled spirits with water also helps to slow down absorption, but mixing with carbonated beverages can increase the rate of absorption.

How much you weigh. The effect of alcohol on the body varies according to a person's weight. Alcohol is quickly distributed uniformly within the circulatory system. Therefore, if the same amount is drunk by a 120-pound person and a 180-pound person, the alcohol is more concentrated in the bloodstream of the lighter individual and therefore more intoxicating to that person.

The setting, your mood or expectations. If you are sitting down relaxed while having a drink with a friend, alcohol will not affect you as much as when you are standing and drinking at a cocktail party. If you are emotionally upset, under stress, or tired, alcohol may have a stronger impact on you than normal. Your expectations will also have an influence. If you think you are going to become drunk, you are likely to get that way more quickly.

IV. WHY DO PEOPLE DRINK?

People drink for a variety of social, cultural, religious, or medical reasons. They drink at parties and celebrations with friends and relatives. They drink in religious ceremonies. Some drink wine to complement the taste of their dinners. Some drink to relax. Some drink to increase their appetites.

The drinking of most people is "integrative" drinking; that is, the use of alcohol is an adjunct to other activities, such as meals, family and religious feasts, or an evening with friends.

Among Orthodox Jews, native Italians, and other groups where alcohol is part of religious or social traditions, there is a low incidence of problem drinking, though there is almost universal use of alcoholic beverages.

There are, however, large numbers of people who drink for reasons that are not social, cultural, religious, or medical. They use alcohol to forget their worries, to escape from reality, or to gather courage to face the stresses of life. They are using alcohol as a drug and are in danger of becoming dependent upon it.

V. WHAT IS DRUNKENNESS?

Drunkenness is characterized by a temporary loss of control over physical and mental powers caused by excessive alcohol intake. Symp-toms of drunkenness vary, but they can include impaired vision, distorted depth perception, thick speech, and bad coordination. The ability to solve problems is reduced, emotion and mood become unpredictable, memory is impaired, and judgment becomes poor.

In most States a person is considered legally drunk when he or she has a 0.10 percent blood alcohol level. This means that one part in every thousand parts of the person's blood is presently composed of pure alcohol. Such a situation generally results when a person weighing about 160 pounds has had about seven drinks within 2 hours after eating. A person will reach this stage with fewer drinks if body weight is less than 160 pounds, with more drinks if weight exceeds this fugure. In a few States, the legally drunk level is 0.15 percent. In either case, it is illegal to drive a car after the specified blood alcohol concentration is reached.

Contrary to a widespread impression, one cannot sober up by such devices as drinking black coffee, taking a cold shower, or breathing pure oxygen. It takes a specific amount of time for the body to burn up a quantity of alcohol, generally at the rate of 7 grams (about 1/4 ounce) of pure alcohol per hour. The effect of drinking alcohol can be varied only by controlling the rate and concentration with which it is drunk. Once alcohol is in the bloodstream, nothing can be done about its effects except to wait until it is metabolized by the body.

VI. WHAT IS A HANGOVER?

A hangover is the body's reaction to excessive drinking. The associated miseries of nausea, gastritis, anxiety, and headache vary from case to case, but there is always extreme fatigue. No scientific evidence supports the curative claims for coffee, raw eggs, oysters, chili peppers, steak sauce, vitamins or other drugs, or the "hair of the dog." Doctors ususally prescribe aspirin, rest, and solid food.

If you choose to drink, the best way to avoid a hangover is to avoid drunkenness. Sip slowly, with food in the stomach, under relaxed circumstances, and pay attention to your responses to the alcohol so you don't drink too much.

VII. WHAT PHYSICAL HARM CAN HEAVY DRINKING CAUSE?

Heavy drinking over time can cause severe physiological damage. Cirrhosis of the liver is closely linked to heavy, continuous consumption of alcohol, and there is also a link between this type of drinking and ulcers, heart disease, and diabetes. Heavy drinking over many years may also contribute to serious nervous or mental disorders, or may cause permanent brain damage. Alcohol, like many other drugs that affect the central nervous system, can be physiologically addictive, producing withdrawal symptoms when alcohol intake ceases.

Of course, drinking need not be long-term or addictive to cause accidental injury or death. Only two cans of beer or two drinks of 86-proof whiskey consumed by the average 160-pound person within an hour on an empty stomach generally result in a blood alcohol level of 0.05 percentone part of alcohol in every 2,000 parts of blood. Scientific studies have revealed that even these small amounts limit coordination and increase a person's risk of becoming involved in a traffic or household accident. This often comes as a surprise to people being tested, since many feel more capable and mentally alert than they did before drinking.

VIII. HOW CAN YOU TELL IF SOMEONE IS ALCOHOLIC?

Alcoholism is marked by dependence on alcohol and loss of control over one's drinking. This loss of control may develop almost imperceptibly over a long period, or it may manifest itself almost from the start of a person's drinking. When a person continues to drink despite the fact that it causes serious psychological, physical, or social problems, alcoholism is developing or is already present.

We tend to think of "typical" alcohol people as skid row inhabitants, but only about 3-5 percent of alcoholic Americans are in that category. Actually, alcoholic people represent a cross-section of America, embracing rich and poor, young and old, white-collar workers and blue-collar workers--in fact, every level of society. Most alcoholics are employed and most have families--much like their neighbors and fellow citizens.

Seldom can you spot alcoholic people by their appearance. However, for those close to a person who seems to be more and more dependent on alcohol in order to function, there are indicators that his or her drinking may be reaching the danger point. For example is there the immediate reaction to pour a drink when faced with any problem; has getting drunk become a regular occurrence; is there a record of missing work because of drinking or regular attendance at work with an ill-disguised odor of liquor on the breath; has the person's license been suspended for driving while drunk; has the person gotten into trouble with authorities for no "logical" reason; has the person been involved in several unexplainable accidents without evidence of physical impairment; has his or her home life become intolerable because of excessive drinking or arguments resulting from drinking?

When such signs are present, it means that a person's drinking pattern, if not already out of control, is heading that way.

IX. HOW CAN A PERSON WITH AN ALCOHOL PROBLEM BE HELPED?

In the past, most people believed that nothing could be done for a person with a drinking problem. It is now recognized that the overwhelming number can be helped at any stage so long as adequate treatment and rehabilitation resources are available, care is marked by acceptance and understanding, and the stigma of having an alcohol problem is not allowed to stand in the way of treatment.

Help can be provided by a doctor, a clergyman, a local welfare agency, a clinic, a social worker, a psychologist or psychiatrist, a general hospital or psychiatric hospital, an alcoholism treatment cen-ter, or the local chapter of Alcoholics Anonymous. Many large business or industrial firms and labor unions also have programs to help their alcoholic employees and members find treatment and rehabilitation.

Alcoholics Anonymous is probably the best known source of help for alcoholic persons. This organization is a self-help group in which members help each other in a type of group therapy setting that utilizes mutual experience for mutual support. Alcoholics Anonymous is listed in all local directories.

Other community and social agencies also offer referral services or direct help. Local affiliates of the National Council on Alcoholism exist in many communities, and every State and many communities have official alcoholism programs where help can be found or sources of treatment recommended. Again, the local telephone directory is the key to obtaining their services.

The treatment used for alcoholism is as varied as the reasons for alcoholic drinking, and programs which individualize the treatment approaches to the patient's needs offer the best results. Doctors may prescribe a drug, Antabuse, which makes an alcoholic person violently ill if he or she drinks alcohol. Psychotherapy and counseling may be used to provide long-range help. Although considerable success has been reported in nonmedical, social setting withdrawal from alcohol, in the case of acute alcoholism or acute intoxication, hospitalization may be required for a short period of time.

The primary goal of treatment is to help the person overcome his dependence on alcohol and develop a lifestyle not revolving around its use. Experience to date has been that the chances of improvement seem greatest if total abstinence is the goal. As many as two-thirds of the people who seek help recover from alcoholism, a figure that compares favorably with the results of treatment for other psychological or behavioral problems.

It is almost universally recognized today that alcoholism affects others besides the alcoholic individual--especially those close to the drinker. To meet this need, Al-Anon Family Groups were set up to assist the families--principally spouses--and more recently Alateen came into existence to help the adolescent children of alcoholic persons.

X. CAN ALCOHOL PROBLEMS BE PREVENTED?

Problem drinking and alcoholism can never be controlled solely by treating people. The long-range goal must be prevention; and this requires education, both in the schools and in the adult community, to develop the Nation's habits of mederation in the use of alcoholic beverages and to encourage respect for those who choose to abstain. It also requires investigation and testing of such social policies as control of distribution and availability, excise taxes, etc., as well as study of the effective prevention policies of other cultures.

One immediate step that we as individuals can take toward preventing alcohol problems in our own social circles is assuming the responsibilities that we as hosts and hostesses have to our friends. At dinner parties and social gatherings, food should be served both before and with drinks. As an alternative to alcoholic beverages, soft drinks--including low-calorie beverages--should be made available. These can be supplemented by nonalcoholic punches, fruit juices, tea,and coffee. The guest who does not choose to drink alcoholic beverages should never be cajoled or shamed into doing so, whether he is an abstainer, a recovered alcoholic, or a social drinker who recognizes he has had enough. One effective method of giving your guests some extra time for alcohol effects to wear off is to close the bar at least 1 or 2 hours before you plan to break up your party. This is the time to drink coffee and other nonalcoholic beverages and to serve your own special highlight dish of meat or seafood.

BASIC FUNDAMENTALS OF ALCOHOL AND ALCOHOLISM

TABLE OF CONTENTS

	Page
Introduction	1
I. Alcohol, the Beverage	1
II. Physiological Effects	2
III. Alcoholism Defined	4
IV. Alcoholism: Types	5
V. Causes of Alcoholism	6
VI. Tolerance	8
VII. Progressive Symptoms	9
VIII. Treatment	12
A. Emergency Treatment	12
B. Inpatient Treatment	14
C. Follow-up Treatment	15
D. Deterrent Therapy	16
E. Miscellaneous Therapies	17
F. Alcoholics Anonymous	18

BASIC FUNDAMENTALS OF ALCOHOL AND ALCOHOLISM

INTRODUCTION

"We deal with alcohol -- cunning, baffling, powerful," says the "Big Book" of Alcoholics Anonymous.

So be it. But the cunning, bafflement and power have often been embellished, by those who exploit it for their own ends. "Grab for all the gusto you can get!" urges the beer advertisement. "There's death in the cup -- so beware!" warns the tectotalist.

As a result, so many prejudices and old wives tales have been fostered by alcohol and alcoholism that John Doe has found himself groping in a fog of misunderstanding.

The alcoholism counselor, if he is to function effectively, must cut through the smoke screens and camouflage. Only in that way can he distinguish the true from the false and win the confidence of his patients, their families and their associates. And once he feels reasonably informed, there will be new facts and findings to assimilate and adapt to as research keeps marching on.

I. ALCOHOL, THE BEVERAGE

The history of man's use of alcohol may be boiled down to two sentences. Historically, there is every evidence that man learned how to brew beer before he learned how to bake bread. Go we have had alcohol, the beverage, with us through the ages and will probably continue to have it to the end of time -- legislation and condemnation notwithstanding.

The alcohol contained in the beverage alcohol is called ethyl alcohol (C_2H_5OH), also known as ethanol. There are many other types of alcohol -- such as methyl or wood alcohol, isopropyl or rubbing alcohol, both unfit for human consumption.

First, to examine some popular misconceptions:

Alcohol is not a stimulant. On the contrary, it is an anesthetic. As explained in the next section, it puts judgment and inhibitions to sleep so that emotions and desires are allowed to function unrestrained, giving a false sense of stimulation.

Alcohol is not an aphrodisiac, it does not stimulate one's appetite for sex. Although one or two drinks may lower the individual's inhibitions and facilitate the expression of repressed sexual desires, in larger amounts alcohol -- being an anesthetic -- tends to curb sexual desire and, in the male, may even impair his ability to perform.

Alcohol is an addictive drug. As with all other addictive drugs, the excessive use of alcohol leads to an increased tolerance for it. In the early stages of the disease, the alcoholic can consume much more than the non-alcoholic. Also, withdrawal symptoms often occur with abstinence. One of the more widely known examples is delirium tremens. However, it must be stressed that, as with all other addictive drugs, not all users become addicted. In the case of alcohol, only about 6 to 7 per cent of all drinkers become alcoholics.

Alcohol does not necessarily stimulate one's appetite for food. As a sedative, alcohol taken in small quantity before a meal may help one "unwind" and thus add to his enjoyment of the food by temporarily alleviating his emotional frustrations and worries. Some drinks (aperitifs) contain substances (strychnine, quinine, etc.) specifically for the appetite stimulating effects. In larger amounts, it suppresses the appetite, because one ounce of alcohol supplies 200 calories to the body. As a result, a heavy drinker may forego meals and rely on alcohol for his needed energy. But alcohol is a very poor substitute for food since it does not supply the proteins, vitamins and minerals necessary to good health.

Drinking in moderation does not in itself cause disease. But prolonged, excessive use of alcohol may lead to illnesses in several ways. They can be the direct result of the toxic effects of the drug on living tissue -- e.g., fatty deposits in the liver, heart muscle, etc. They can be the result of poor nutrition -- the lack of proteins, vitamins and minerals mentioned above. Or they can be the result of lowered resistance to infectious diseases -- i.e., the inhibition of the antibody building, defense mechanisms of the body.

By itself, alcohol is not a killer. It is virtually impossible for a man to deliberately "drink himself to death." When the concentration of alcohol in the blood reaches .50 per cent, it affects the portion of the brain that controls breathing and heartbeat, and death follows. But the drinker loses consciousness when the concentration reaches .40 per cent, at which point he can drink no more.

There is no alcoholic "drink of moderation." Beer, wine, and spirits all contain alcohol. It may take more beer (4%) than 100 proof whiskey (50%) to reach the same state of intoxication. But the effect of the alcohol is the same. The "moderation" rests in the drinker.

II. PHYSIOLOGICAL EFFECTS

When one takes a drink -- be it man or woman, alcoholic or non-alcoholic -- the brain and body respond in a systematic manner.

About 10 percent of the alcohol is eliminated through the lungs, kidneys and pores of the skin. The remaining 90 percent is directly absorbed into the blood stream through the walls of the stomach and small intestine. No other digestive processes are involved.

Once in the blood stream, it is distributed to the body tissues.

En route, the alcohol passes through the liver, where it is oxidized and transformed into energy. But even a healthy liver can only oxidize about three-quarters of an ounce per hour. So the excess accumulates in the blood and continues to circulate.

In the blood, alcohol reaches the brain. Here it has a sedative and an anesthetic effect.

The first part of the brain to be affected is the frontal lobe of the cerebrum. This is the seat of reasoning, conscious thinking, memory, self-control. As the frontal lobe is gradually anesthetized by the alcohol, inhibitions disappear. The man forgets his limitations and becomes Mr. Big. No transient ambition is beyond his capacities. The anxieties of day-to-day living evaporate and the world is his friend. This is the false "stimulation" referred to before.

As the concentration of alcohol in the blood increases, other areas of the brain arc affected. The motor area of the cerebrum and the cerebellum control motor activity, muscular coordination and equilibrium. The drinker becomes clumsy and he begins to have trouble walking and keeping his balance. The speech, hearing and vision centers of the brain become affected, which result in slurred speech, dulled hearing and blurred vision. When the sensory area is affected the drinker "feels no pain," thus being deprived of a frequently lifesaving alarm system.

Finally, the medulla -- the portion of the brain connected to the spinal cord -- is affected. This is responsible for the vital functions of the body, including heartbeat, blood flow and breathing. Depending upon the concentration of the alcohol, the drinker will lose consciousness, go into shock, or die.

Thus a drinker's behavior and capabilities are directly related to the alcoholic concentration in his bloodstream. Such being the case, the drinking "capacity" of one man can vary from that of the next. The body fluids inside a 250-pound mailroom clerk. Other things being equal, more alcohol is required to raise the football player's concentration to .40%, or to any other given degree. So the amount of liquor considered "excessive" for one man may not be "excessive" for the next.

But football player or mailroom clerk, a drinker's behavior pattern generally conforms to the following levels of concentration:

.06% Feeling of warmth, relaxation, less concern with minor irritations.

.08% Legal point of intoxication

.09% Buoyancy, exaggerated emotion and behavior, talkative or morose.

.12% Impairment of fine coordination, slight to moderate unsteadiness in standing or walking.

.15% Abnormality of gross bodily function and mental facilities

.30% Stupor

.40% Unconsciousness, possible state of shock

.50% Death

There are, of course, other physiological effects resulting from drinking, many of which are noted below, under "Progressive Symptoms."

Both alcoholics and non-alcoholics, however, are liable to suffer irritation of the throat, esophagus and stomach lining through excessive drinking of undiluted liquors. Painful alcoholic gastritis can result from the latter

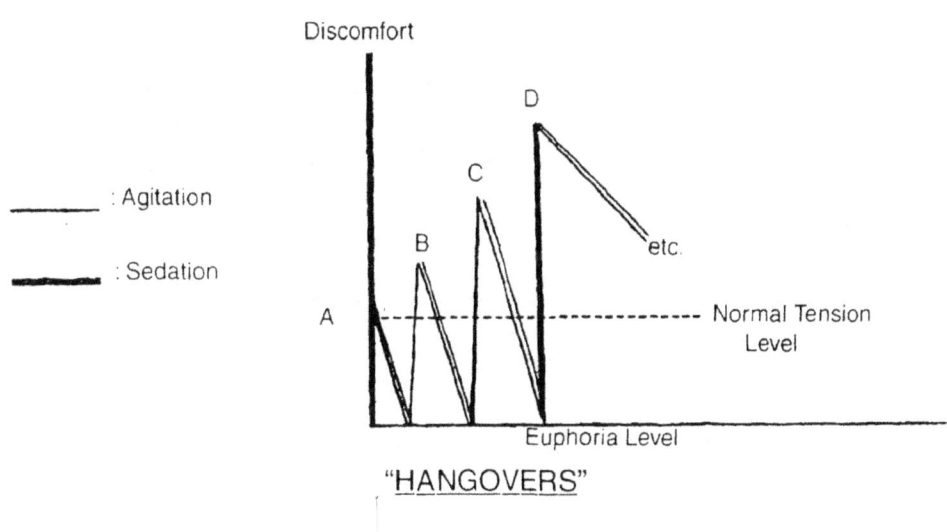

"HANGOVERS"

Then there is that transient hell through which any drinker can pass after he has imbibed too much "the hangover."

All sedatives, including alcohol, have a double-barreled effect. One is the tranquilizing effect which causes men and women to drink. The other is an irritating effect resulting in "psychomotor hyperactivity" which lasts many hours longer and which accounts for the "morning after" distress.

In the accompanying schematic diagram, assume that a man on his way to a party is somewhat nervous and normally anxious (point "A"). He takes a stiff drink to alleviate his anxiety and induce a sense of euphoria. At this stage the sedative effect of the alcohol is intense enough to mask the agitating effect. But within a relatively short period of time, the sedative effect of the alcohol is gone and he is left with only the psychomotor agitation, which gradually accelerates to point "B." He decides upon another drink to rectify matters. Now he needs even more sedation -- first, to get back to his normal state, and then more to become euphoric again. So the process of alternating sedation and agitation continues to points "C," "D" and so on -- until he either goes to bed himself or is carried there by his friends.

In actuality, the party-goer would surely refuel at the first suspicion that his euphoria was wearing off. But he would still awaken the following morning with an accumulation of the agitating effects of his drinks, which last about twelve hours from the time of imbibing. He has three choices: to sweat them out; to take a milder sedative to allay some of the pain; or to have some "hair bf the dog that bit him." The last is rather dangerous. He might find himself back on the same merry-go-round again.

III. ALCOHOLISM DEFINED

Thus far everything has applied to all the men and women who drink any alcoholic beverages at all.

What about the alcoholic? What about the 6 to 7 per cent of those drinkers -- the 1 out of 14 or 15 -- who have lost control of their drinking? What distinguishes them from the others?

There are hundreds of definitions of alcoholism. The technical one published by the World Health Organization reads as follows:

"Any form of drinking which in its extent goes beyond the traditional and customary 'dietary' use or the ordinary compliance with the social drinking customs of the whole community concerned, irrespective of the etiological factors leading to such behavior, and irrespective also of the extent to which such etiological factors are dependent upon heredity, constitution, or acquired physio-pathological and metabolic influences."

Shorter descriptions of the alcoholic include:

"One who repeatedly seeks to change reality through the use of alcohol."

Or

"One who suffers because of uncontrolled compulsive drinking."

For the alcoholism counselor, the following definition may serve as a useful yardstick in evaluating a client's status:

"An alcoholic is one whose drinking interferes with his health, his job, his relations with his family, or his community relationships and yet he continues to drink."

The interference need only be felt in one of the above areas of living for a person's classification as an alcoholic.

The fact that the alcoholic "continues to drink" implies loss of control, which is a characteristic of the illness.

The definition applies to men and women alike. Although it was once thought that male alcoholics outnumbered female alcoholics about five to one, it is now agreed that the number of women is much closer to that of men. Many private physicians who treat both men and women alcoholics say the ratio is about fifty-fifty.

And the definition applies to all social and economic "classes." Only 3 per cent of the alcoholics in the United States are found on Skid Row. The other 97 per cent stretch from waterfront saloons to Main Street and the Hall of Congress.

IV. ALCOHOLISM: TYPES

Since the alcoholic is usually the last to recognize his illness, he often challenges the doctor or counselor with:

"I only drink weekends (or paydays)!" or

"I can go months without touching a drop!" etc.

Such protests may be true. Nevertheless, he can still fall into one of the classifications of alcoholics that have been arrived at by many specialists in the field.

Probably the best known classification is that of the late Dr. E. M. Jellinek, former consultant to the World Health Organization. He identified various types of alcoholics with Greek letters:

Alpha: This man or woman relies upon the effect of alcohol to boost morale,
    bolster self-confidence or relieve emotional pain. He might be regarded as a "social drinker" except for the fact that he often drinks too much at the wrong times, among the wrong people, and is thereby apt to affront others.

The Alpha type does not lose control and can abstain when necessary. However, his drinking can give rise to family squabbles, occasional absenteeism from work, and be a drain on the family budget.

Alpha drinkers may develop into full-fledged Gamma alcoholics (see below). Hence, they are considered by many to be "pre-alcoholics," and should be treated accordingly to forestall that possibility.

Beta: This alcoholic gets sick. He does not become addicted and he suffers no withdrawal symptoms if he stops in tine.

But his poor nutritional habits -- i.e., substituting alcohol for necessary proteins, minerals and vitamins -- lead to such medical complications as peripheral neuritis, cirrhosis of the liver and gastritis. When hospitalized his ailments are all too often treated without regard to the drinking habits that have caused them.

Gamma: These are the alcoholics who most frequently need help from alcoholism clinics and such organizations as Alcoholics Anonymous. Their psychological dependence upon alcohol has grown into a physical dependence. They have lost control over their drinking, and they suffer withdrawal symptoms when they abstain. In early and middle stages of the illness, their tolerance for alcohol is much greater than that of the non-alcoholic. But in late stages their tolerance abruptly decreases to the point where even a single drink can make them ill. (See "Tolerance" and "Progressive Symptoms," below.)

Delta: The Delta alcoholic maintains a steady concentration of alcohol in his bloodstream during his waking hours. Usually he has grown up where alcohol is an all-purpose beverage, served at all meals. But he can be a business executive whose eye openers and three-martinis-for-lunch have become a ritual, or "the little old lady" whose daily quota of dry sherry is a must. Seldom visibly intoxicated, the Delta alcoholic will suffer withdrawal symptoms when forced to abstain. For example, when hospitalized for several days prior to surgery, they may develop delerium tremens.

Epsilon: This is the so called binge drinker, who will go for a long period weeks, months, or even a year without a drink. But once he starts, it is explosive. He continues drinking until he goes into a stupor. If the binges continue with increasing frequency, he may become a Gamma alcoholic.

Dr. Jellinek wrote that there are many other types of alcoholism, more than there are letters in the Greek alphabet. But the above five are the ones the alcoholism counselor is most likely to encounter.

Despite the protests of many alcoholics -- particularly the Gammas, Deltas, and Epsilons -- that they "can take it or leave it" or "only drink on payday," there is one common denominator. Consciously or subconsciously, they are forever looking forward and planning for the next drink, be it tomorrow, next week, or six months from now. This is not conducive to the "comfortable sobriety" that leads to recovery.

V. CAUSES OF ALCOHOLISM

Those engaged in scientific research have yet to establish that there is any hereditary influence in a person's susceptibility to alcohol addiction.

Nor is there any physical basis for alcoholism. However, as already noted, there can be a growing physiological dependence upon alcohol as the disease progresses.

Psychological and personality factors play an important role.

While heredity apparently has no part in determining the possibilities of a youngster's becoming an alcoholic in later years, his environment can. Many surveys indicate that about half the adult alcoholics interviewed have at least one alcoholic parent. Other children may be so repelled by the ugly topsyturvydom of parental drinking that they go through life without touching a drop although they may suffer other emotionally crippling effects.

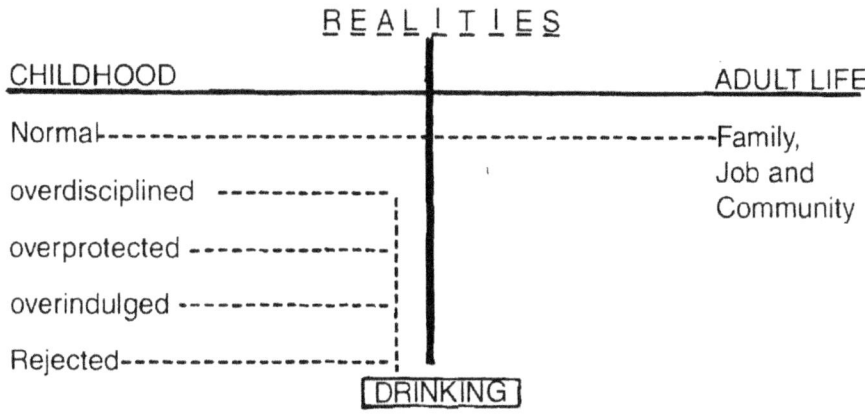

CHILDHOOD EXPERIENCES

More important is the manner in which the child is taught to face reality. As the accompanying "Childhood Experiences" chart indicates, the "normal" child with "normal" parents sees them tackle the problems and decisions in everyday living as they arise. Other things being equal, he will do the same with his lesser difficulties and continue to do so with the big ones in adulthood.

But if the parents overdiscipline, overprotect or overindulge him, he will be more apt to shy away when confronted by any situation that demands his decision or constructive action. Later in life, he discovers that alcohol offers him temporary escape. This discovery eventually leads into habit. As he takes flight in the bottle more and more often, he can develop such a physiological dependency upon it that he is well on the way to full-fledged alcoholism.

The same liability faces the rejected child. Knowing he is not wanted, he is bound to feel a sense of inadequacy. Unless that is overcome, his so called solution to his problems may eventually be the same.

Of course, all alcoholics did not start out in life as overdisciplined, overprotected, overindulged or rejected children. The death of a loved one,

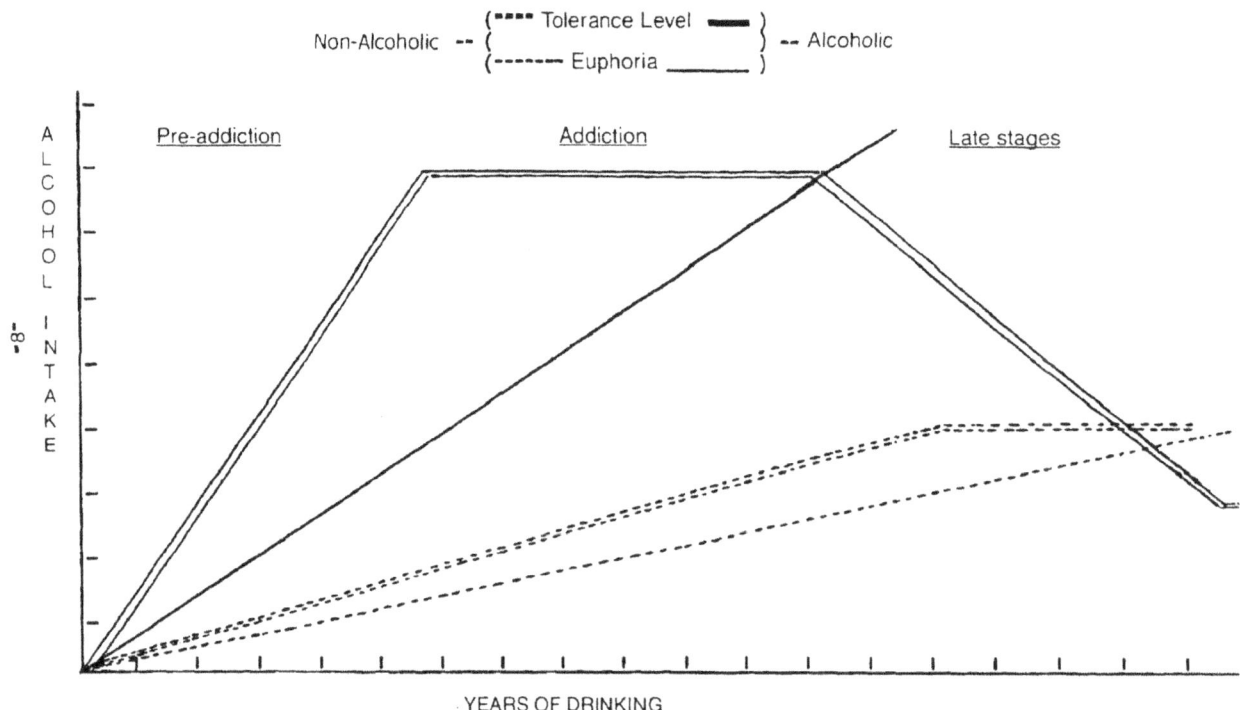

ALCOHOLIC AND NON-ALCOHOLIC TOLERANCE CURVES

unavoidable hard times, another's disloyalty, incessant physical pain, etc., can provoke feelings of inadequacy or frustration at any time from the nursery to the grave. When a person repeatedly turns to alcohol as an escape from his anxieties, great or small, he becomes a potential alcoholic.

In short, the onset of alcoholism is not determined by how much a man drinks, but why he drinks.

VI. TOLERANCE

Once embarked, the alcoholic's course is irreversibly charted -- unless he turns to total abstinence at some point along the way. In that case, he can arrest the progress of his illness. He cannot turn back. He cannot retrim his sails for social drinking.

The accompanying diagram of "Alcoholic and Non-Alcoholic Tolerance" indicates the general course the illness takes.

The "alcohol intake" level refers to the amount consumed at any one occasion. As noted above, what is excessive intake for one person is not necessarily excessive for the next. Among other things, it varies according to the physique of the individual.

The "years of drinking" are also relative. The time it takes a novice drinker to become an addict can be anywhere from one to twenty years.

The "euphoria level" is the point at which the drinker reaches Cloud Nine, forgets his inhibitions, and revels in his own fancied charm as well as that of others.

The "tolerance level" is the point at which he gets sick and can drink no more.

Both the alcoholic and non-alcoholic start their drinking histories with one thing in common it takes little alcohol to put them in high spirits and little more to make them sick.

As time passes, both require more alcohol to reach either level. But the alcoholic needs more and more. Because of the greater significance he gives to drinking, during pre-alcoholism years he may learn how to space his drinks and to some extent control his behavior. But he cannot manipulate his tolerance level. That is biologically determined.

There comes the time when the alcoholic's tolerance levels off. This is usually marked by a loss of control -- give him one drink and he is "off to the races." He has become addicted, physiologically dependent upon alcohol. From this point on, he continues to need more and more to escape everyday reality and regain a sense of euphoria. But his "capacity" before getting sick remains the same. As a result he can handle fewer and fewer drinks after he begins to feel carefree. But he cannot stop in that desirable state of bliss. He is compelled to keep drinking until he is physically unable to drink anymore.

Eventually there comes the day when he drinks just as much, but feels no sense of well-being at all. He only gets sick. (This is the point on the diagram where the tolerance and euphoria lines meet.) Desperately, he goes on benders in search of the alcoholic euphoria he is never to know again. He continues drinking, but gets sick sooner because his tolerance level is plunging down. He discovers that he cannot even keep up with the non-alcoholic friends whom he used to drink under the table any day in the week. One unproductive drink, maybe two, and he is through. His brain and the rest of the body have taken all the alcoholic abuse they can.

VII. PROGRESSIVE SYMPTOMS

The behavioral characteristics of the alcoholic are as progressive as his tolerance to alcohol and the course of the disease itself. They often enable the counselor to determine the relative status of a patient's addiction.

An inventory of some of those symptoms follows. They are not necessarily in precise chronological order. Some may never be experienced by an individual alcoholic. But most of them are experienced and, in toto, are mileposts along the way.

PRE-ADDICTION:

The road to alcoholism begins when drinking is no longer social but a means of psychological escape from the tensions and inhibitions. Although the eventual problem drinker is still in reasonable control, his habits begin to fall into a definite pattern:

1. <u>Gross drinking behavior</u>: He begins to drink more heavily and more often than his friends. "Getting tight" becomes a habit. When drunk, he may develop a "big shot" complex, recklessly spending money, boasting of real and fancied accomplishments, etc.

2. <u>Blackouts</u>: A "blackout," temporary loss of memory, is not to be confused with "pass-out,"

loss of consciousness. The drinker suffering from a blackout cannot remember things he said, things he did, places he visited while carousing the night before or for longer periods. Even a social drinker can have a blackout. With prospective alcoholics, they are more frequent and develop into a pattern.

3. <u>Gulping and sneaking drinks</u>: Anxious to maintain a euphoric level, he begins to toss off drinks at parties and slyly gulp down extra ones when he thinks nobody is looking. He may also "fortify himself" before going to a party to insure his euphoria. He feels guilty about this behavior and skittishly avoids talking about drinks or drinking.

4. <u>Chronic hangovers</u>: As he grows more and more reliant on alcohol as a shock absorber to daily living, "morning after" hangovers become more frequent and increasingly painful. (See "Physiological Effects," above.)

ADDICTION:

Until now the problem drinker has been imbibing heavily but not always conspicuously. More important, he has been able to stop drinking when he so chose. Beyond this point, he develops the symptoms of addiction with increased rapidity:

5. <u>Loss of control</u>: This is the most common symptom that a drinker's pschological habit has become an addiction. He still may refuse to accept a drink. But once he takes a drink, he cannot stop. A single drink is likely to trigger a chain reaction that will continue without a break into a state of complete intoxication.

6. <u>The alibi system</u>: His loss of control induces feelings of guilt and shame. So he concocts an elaborate system of "reasons" for drinking -- "he just completed his income tax," "he failed to complete his income tax," etc. He hopes these will justify his behavior in the eyes of his family and associates. In reality, they are mostly to reassure himself.

7. <u>Eye-openers</u>: He needs a drink in the morning "to start the day right." His morning" may start at any hour of day or night. So an eye-opener is in fact sedation to ease his jangled nerves, hangover, feelings of remorse, etc., after a period of involuntary abstinence, while he was asleep. He cannot face the upcoming hours without alcohol.

8. <u>Changing the pattern</u>: By now he is under pressure from his family, employer, or both. He tries to break the hold alcohol has on him. At first he may try changing brands -- e.g., from whiskey to beer. That docs not good. Then he may set up his own rules on when he will drink and what he will drink -- e.g., only three martinis on weekends and, of course, holidays. He may even "go on the wagon" for a period. Bat one sip of alcohol and the chain reaction starts all over again.

9. <u>Anti-social behavior</u>: He prefers drinking alone or only with other alcoholics, regardless of their social level. He believes that only they can understand him. He broods over imagined wrongs inflicted by others outside this pale and thinks people are staring at him or talking about him. He is highly critical of others and may become violent or destructive.

10. <u>Loss of friends and job</u>: His continuing anti-social behavior causes his friends to avoid him.

The aversion is now mutual. Members of his family may become so helplessly implicated that his wife leaves him "to bring him to his senses." The same situation develops between him, his employer and fellow" workers. And so he loses his job.

11. <u>Seeking medical aid</u>: Physical and mental erosion caused by uncontrolled drinking leads him to make the rounds of hospitals, doctors, psychiatrists, etc. But because he will not admit the extent of his drinking, he seldom receives any lasting benefit. Even when he does halfway "level" with the doctors, he fails to cooperate in following their instructions and the result is the same.

LAST STAGES:

Until he has reached this point, the alcoholic has had a choice: to drink or not to drink that first drink. Once he began, he lost all control. But in the last stages of alcoholism, he has no choice at all. He <u>must</u> drink:

12. <u>Benders</u>:   He gets blindly and helplessly drunk for days at a time, hopelessly searching for that feeling of alcoholic euphoria he once appreciated. He utterly disregards everything -- family, job, food, even shelter. These periodic flights into oblivion might be called "drinking to escape the problems caused by drinking."

13. <u>Tremors</u>:   In the past his hands may have trembled a bit on "mornings after." But now he gets "the shakes" when he is forced to abstain, a serious nervous condition which racks his whole body. When combined with hallucinations, they are known as the D.T.'s (delerium tremens), often fatal if medical help is not close at hand. During and immediately after an attack, he will swear off liquor forever. He nevertheless comes back for more of the same.

14. <u>Protecting the supply</u>: Having an immediate supply of alcohol available becomes the most important thing in his life to avoid the shakes, if nothing else. He will spend his last cent and, if necessary, sell the coat off his back to get it. Then he hides his bottles so there will always be a drink close at hand when he needs it which can be any hour or minute of day or night.

15. <u>Unreasonable resentments</u>: He shows hostility to others. This can be a conscious effort to protect his precious liquor supply, be it a half-pint on the hip or a dozen quarts secreted about the home. It can also be outward evidence of an unconscious desire to punish himself.

16. <u>Nameless fears and anxieties</u>:   He becomes constantly fearful of things he cannot pin down nor describe in words. It is a feeling of impending doom or destruction. This adds to his nervousness and further underscores the compulsion to drink. These fears frequently crop up in the form of hallucinations, both auditory and visual.

17. <u>Collapse of the alibi system</u>: He finally realizes that he can no longer make excuses nor put the blame on others. He has to admit that the fanciful "reasons" he has been fabricating to justify his drinking are preposterous to others and now ridiculous to himself. This may have occurred to him several times during the course of his alcoholic career. But this time it is final. He has to admit that he is licked; that his drinking is beyond his ability to control.

18. Surrender process: Now if ever, he must give up the idea of ever drinking again and be willing to seek and accept help.

If at this point the alcoholic is unable to surrender, all the signposts point to custodial care or death.

If he has not already suffered extensive and irreversible brain damage, there is a strong likelihood that some form of alcoholic psychosis will develop.

The amnesia and confabulation of Korsakoff's syndrome and the convulsions and comas of Wernicke's disease are possibilities.

Death may come in advanced cases of cirrhosis of the liver, pancreatitis, or hemorrhaging varices of the esophagus.

Or he may arrange his own death by suicide. After all, the suicide rate among alcoholics is three times the normal rate of self-extermination.

VIII. TREATMENT

There is as yet no cure for alcoholism.

The alcoholic is fortunate that the disease is treatable, that it can be arrested. But treatment is of no avail unless that addicted patient subscribes to total abstinence from drinking alcohol in any form. As pointed out above, once he has lost control, he will never regain it.

Also, the sooner the progress of the illness is recognized and arrested, the easier the return to a comfortable and contining sobriety and the less physical and mental deterioration.

The treatment of alcoholism falls into three overlapping lines of action designed for three overlapping objectives:

1. Emergency treatment: Immediate medication, etc., designed to avert physical disaster or even death.

2. Inpatient treatment: "Drying out." To alleviate the nervous and physical abnormalities resulting from prolonged and excessive drinking.

3. Follow-up treatment: Psychological rehabilitation necessary for continued sobriety.

Much of the data in the next two sections is for the alcoholism counselor's information only. The prescription and administration of medication and therapeutic procedures are the sole responsibility of authorized medical personnel. However, the counselor should be aware of general practices in order to help the patient and his family arrive at decisions.

A. EMERGENCY TREATMENT

Both acute alcoholic intoxication and many of the withdrawal symptoms which follow can call for prompt treatment in the emergency room of a general hospital.

However, before making a diagnosis of alcohol intoxication, the staff must rule out skull fracture, subdural or subarachnoid hemorrhage, cardio-vascular injury, and diabetic or insulin shock. These are quickly ascertained by laboratory and X-ray tests. Even though blood tests may indicate a high concentration of alcohol in the bloodstream, they do not veto the possibility that other factors may be the primary cause of his condition.

Once alcohol intoxication is diagnosed, it must be remembered that alcohol is in itself a powerful sedative. If the patient is in a stupor or in a comatose state, he should not be given any further sedation.

In cases where <u>treatment for psychomotor agitation</u> (e.g., "the shakes") is indicated, a tranquilizing drug such as Librium is highly effective in reducing tension. Many doctors feel that 100 mgs. given intramuscularly, then followed by smaller amounts taken orally every three or four hours for twelve to twenty-four hours, allow the body to adjust to the abrupt withdrawal of alcohol. Other tran-quilizers such as Thorazine, Sparine, Mellaril, Vistaril, Atarax, etc. are equally effective. An old standby, paraldehyde, has been largely eclipsed by newer drugs because of its habituating properties. Narcotics and barbituates should definitely be avoided because of even more habituating properties. They can only add further addictions to the addiction which already exists.

More serious and sometimes fatal are alcoholic coma, convulsions, hallucinosis and delirium tremens.

Before making a diagnosis of alcoholic coma, the following conditions must be ruled out: skull fracture, subdural or subarachnoid hemorrhage (bleeding in the membranes surrounding the brain), cardio-vascular accident (heart attack), uremia, insulin shock and diabetic coma.

One of the main dangers in alcoholic coma is a respiratory failure, followed by circulatory collapse. It may be necessary to maintain adequate airway to the lungs, use artificial respiration, and/or administer stimulants to the central nervous system. Another danger is the inhalation of vomited matter, which can cause lung abscess or pneumonia. Possible fractures and lacerations resulting from falls must also be considered.

<u>Alcoholic convulsions</u> ("rum fits") closely resemble the grand mal seizures of epilepsy. The examining physician should make certain by electroencephalogram (EEG) if necessary -- that the patient is not suffering from the latter disorder. The primary concern is that he does not injure himself in falling or thrashing about, or by biting or swallowing his tongue, which can cause him to choke to death. A spoon, a leather belt or any device he cannot bite through should be inserted between his teeth. Valium is a useful drug in controlling the attack. To prevent such attacks, Dilantin, an anticonvulsant, is prescribed for alcoholics with a history of seizures.

<u>Alcoholic hallucinosis</u> usually occurs after a patient has been detoxified The hallucinations can be either auditory or visual, with the former more common. They are not as frightening as the fantastic figments encountered during D.T.'s and the patient is usually oriented as to time, place and the existing situation. There is danger of suicide and the patient should be watched.

<u>Delirium tremens</u> (D.T.'s) is a withdrawal symptom which can occur many days after the alcoholic has stopped drinking and, when not immediately treated, can be fatal. As the name implies, it combines visual and auditory hallucinations with extreme tremors and even grand mal type convulsions. Unlike alcoholic hallucinosis, the patient is completely disoriented. His

hallucinations take the form of grotesque human and animal ghouls which threaten him from every side. He should be treated in a well lighted room because every shadow can conjure up another evil menace to panic him. An attending nurse, counselor or other aide should not argue about the existence of these phantasms -- only reassure the patient that nobody will harm him. Librium, Vistaril, chlorpromazines and other tranquilizers are used in treatment.

(The gravity of D.T.'s cannot be overemphasied. In a situation where a patient shows signs of impending D.T.'s and no medical help is available, he can be given an ounce or two of whiskey or fortified wine. This will help to stave off the attack until he can be handed over to a hospital emergency room.)

Coma, convulsions, hallucinosis and D.T.'s are definite medical emergencies and should be treated in the hospital until the patient has fully recovered from the immediate crisis.

In other cases of acute phases of chronic alcoholism, if the patient is not too ill he may be discharged in the care of a cooperative family or interested person who will follow medical instructions.

In any event, the patient must be directed to follow up his emergency room treatment by seeing his family doctor, coming back to the hospital's outpatient clinic, or arranging for continued treatment at a public or private alcoholism clinic. This is for his own protection as well as that of the hospital and personnel who attended him.

B. <u>IMPATIENT TREATMENT</u>

Then there are the hundreds, even thousands of non-emergency patients whose prolonged and excessive drinking has left them so mentally and physically "run down" that they are incapable of adequately dealing with their responsibilities at home or on the job. Simply to let them sleep off their drunks or give them tranquilizers to cushion their shakes and then send them on their ways is inviting trouble. Most of then will wander into the nearest tavern or liquor store and promptly find themselves in worse trouble than they were before -- back again in "the revolving door."

What they need is "drying out," both physical and mental. They need to start repairing the damage the persistent drinking has done to their bodies. They need to disentangle their confused thinking before they can even grasp the meaning of any new program of rehabilitation.

For these persons the best solution is six to eight days hospitalization. In this way, constant care and medication is assured. If they suffer withdrawal symptoms -- such as hallucinosis or D.T's -- there is professional help at hand for immediate treatment, or even to avert the attacks. Above all, they are removed from the temptation of sneaking drinks that often undo the good of treatment at home.

Patients are usually kept on bed rest for the first twenty-four hours after admission, during which they are given routine laboratory and X-ray tests. There will be psychomotor agitation as the patient's body adjusts to the abrupt withdrawal of alcohol. Tranquilizers such as Librium, Sparine, Mellaril, Thorazine, Vistaril, or Atarax will keep him in a state of quiet suspense for the first 36 to 48 hours and are gradually tapered off as his condition improves.

At the same time steps are taken to correct the vitamin-mineral deficiency which has been building up over the days, weeks, or months the patient has been drinking instead of eating. He is put on a high protein diet and multivitamins. Orange juice, with a dash of sodium chloride in it, is kept at his bedside. And in cases of severe dehydration, he is given "Philadelphia cocktails" intravenously, which contain a glucose-saline solution, insulin, and vitamins.

As this period of rest and recuperation progresses, his thinking begins to straighten out. This is the time to lay the groundwork for follow-up treatment. He must be made to realize that recovery from chronic alcoholism is not an overnight or eight-day procedure. The damage has been years in the making. Even with his sincere cooperation, it takes one or two years to make basic psychological and physical repairs. This is the time to line him up for continuing treatment at an outpatient clinic, Alcoholics Anonymous, or other therapeutic agencies.

During this period, the patient may also be started on Antabuse (see "Deterrent Therapy," below).

C. FOLLOW-UP TREATMENT

The chronic alcoholic cannot stay sober without help. (One hears of the person who "did it on his own," but one seldom meets him in the flesh.)

The alcoholic needs support. He should have the encouragement of family and friends, if he has any left. But the support of family and friends can be erratic and is not to be found in some areas where he needs help the most.

He constantly needs to remember that he is an alcoholic who cannot afford to take a drink without unfortunate results just as the diabetic cannot afford to forget his ailment and his insulin, or the epileptic his Dilantin.

For years the alcoholic has been committing physical and mental hara-kiri and he may need prolonged medical or psychiatric help.

Alcoholism can be expensive; and, therefore, the patient may be broke. Alcoholism loses jobs; he may need employment. Alcoholism causes dissension; he may seek reconciliation with his family. And so on.

Unless he is spiritually barren, he can be kept reminded of his vulnerability in Alcoholics Anonymous, as well as find understanding and moral support (see below). But if he is in need of professional help and advice in addition to awareness and understanding, an alcoholism clinic is probably his one best resource.

The many roles played by outpatient clinics are described in the next chapter. In brief, their primary concerns are medical and psychiatric services, and individual and group counseling. These are geared to meet the needs of alcoholics at large as well as hospital dischargees.

The medical and psychiatric services can range from consultation and referrals to critical treatment-on-the-spot, depending upon facilities.

The medical and psychiatric services can range from consultation and referrals to critical treatment-on-the-spot, depending upon facilities.

Individual counseling is available to help the patient work out solutions to his very personal problems. This service is hot intended to act as an employment or public welfare resource. But the counselor should be able to refer the patient to appropriate agencies in the community to meet these and other special needs.

Group counseling or "group therapy," to use the term in its broad non-professional sense is the outpatient clinic's major contribution to continued treatment once a patient has emerged from the mental and physical distress of intoxication, and withdrawal.

Continued sobriety can only be achieved by changing the alcoholic's attitude and teaching him new ways of dealing with the frustrations that drove him to drink.

In this type of treatment, the patient is assigned to a small, ongoing group of fellow alcoholics who discuss their common "hang-ups" -- i.e., frustrations and temptations which led to their past drinking -- and what they are doing to meet them without resorting to alcohol. A trained leader -- usually a psychiatrist, psychiatric nurse, social worker or counselor -- merely keeps the discussion within bounds. At first, the new patient is inclined to confine his participation and mental note-taking to alcohol, its use and misuse. As he becomes better acquainted with the other members of the group, he finds himself more and more involved in the discussion of more stressful areas of personal and social functioning. Accordingly, the way is cleared for greater insight into his own personality and behavior and those elements which have contributed to his alcoholism. He is then better able to adapt himself to a more meaningful way of living without recourse to alcohol.

Many psychiatrists feel that group therapy is far more effective than individual psychotherapy. Because of the alcoholic's habit of "sneaking" drinks, protecting his supply, and feelings of guilt, he becomes more and more of a "loner" as his illness progresses. In group treatment he once again becomes physically and psychologically involved with other people. Thus, he is pried loose from the isolation, he has built up for himself not by choice, but because his disease demanded it.

(Both individual and group counseling are more fully discussed in Chapter III.)

D. DETERRENT THERAPY

Disulfiram (Antabuse) is a drug often prescribed to deter the alcoholic from drinking. It is no "cure." It does not erase the desire to drink. But it does make the consequences of drinking the slightest amount of alcohol so agonizing that even the most confirmed dipsomaniac will abstain so long as it remains in his system.

Normally the liver oxidizes alcohol into acetaldehyde which, in turn, breaks down into acetic acid and next into carbon dioxide and water. Acetaldehyde is a poison. Necessary for its breakdown is a enzyme (acetaldehyde dehydrogenase) which the disulfiram blocks. When this happens, the acetaldehyde rapidly accumulates and within a few minutes, the patient becomes violently ill. He becomes extremely hot and flushed. His blood pressure rises rapidly and a splitting headache develops. Concurrently, he develops a pain in the chest which spreads into the left arm, his heart pounds rapidly, and he finds it difficult to breathe. Suddenly, his blood pressure falls and. he may become sick to the stomach and even collapse. He then falls into a deep sleep.

The attack may last up to four hours; but the patient shudders at the thought of experiencing it again.

However, Antabuse has no effect upon the body unless alcohol is taken. It needs a detonator to start the chain reaction. And the only detonator is a drink.

Thus, it acts as or silent policeman to protect the patient's abstinence. The average practicing alcoholic cannot envision life without his favorite beverage to sustain him. Once he starts on an Antabuse regimen, he discovers that sobriety is not only attainable and endurable, but that it can be more agreeable than the way things were with alcohol.

By itself, Antabuse is no panacea to bring about and maintain sobriety. But taken regularly, it acts as a shield against impulsive "slips" which can be serious setbacks in continuing treatment. Once the patient takes his daily dose, he has no decisions to make about drinking or not drinking for the next 72 hours. And it keeps him sober to profit from whatever form of follow-up therapy he may be undergoing.

On the other hand, if a patient who claims that he is "on Antabuse" drinks with no ill effects, the therapist knows that he is not taking his medication as prescribed. It can be reasonably assumed that he has not yet achieved the motivation necessary for any program of recovery.

Because of the reactions that occur when alcohol is taken on top of Antabuse, the patient must have a physical examination before the drug can be prescribed. (Contraindications include uncontrolled hypertension (high blood pressure), coronary heart disease, late stages of cirrhosis, severe pancreatitis, psychoses or brain damage, and sometimes pregnancy.) The patient is given a card to carry with him so he will not be given medication containing alcohol in the event of an emergency. Antabuse should not be administered until 72 hours have elapsed since the patient's last drink; nor should he drink again until at least 72 hours after taking his last pill.

E. <u>MISCELLANEOUS THERAPIES</u>

There are many other types of therapy, most of which the alcoholism counselor will probably never hear about. But there arc several of which he should be aware:

<u>Lysergic acid (LSD) therapy</u>: Research continues on this still unproved method of treatment. Thus far the effectiveness apparently rests in the degree of rapport established between the patient and the individual therapist who attends him on his "trips."

<u>Hypnosis</u>: Used in certain types of psychiatric and psychosomatic illnesses, some practitioners believe hypnosis can be employed in the treatment of alcoholism. Up to now the results have not been very successful.

<u>Conditioned response therapy</u>: The most common of many procedures is to add an emetic to a patient's favorite brand of alcoholic beverage. After several nauseating experiences, he is automatically supposed to develop a distast for the stuff. Chief drawbacks are: (1) that frequent "reconditioning" is necessary; and (2) that patients can often switch to other brands and continue drinking without ill effects.

Psychodrama: This is a form of group therapy wherein the patients act out psychic conflicts. Because of the highly emotional nature of these conflicts, psychodrama should only be employed under the close supervision of a psychiatrist or specially trained psychodrama therapist.

F. ALCOHOLICS ANONYMOUS

Alcoholics Anonymous is a fellowship of problem drinkers who have banded together in an effort to help themselves and other problem drinkers attain sobriety.

Their program is best summed up in "Twelve Steps" which the members are urged to follow:

1. We admitted we were powerless over alcohol -- that our lives had become unmanageable.
2. Cane to believe that a Power greater than ourselves could restore us to sanity.
3. Made a decision to turn our will and our lives over to the care of God as we understood Him.
4. Made a searching and fearless moral inventory of ourselves.
5. Admitted to God, to ourselves, and to another human being the exact nature of our wrongs.
6. Were entirely ready to have God remove all these defects of character.
7. Humbly asked Him to remove our shortcomings.
8. Made a list of all persons we had harmed, and became willing to make amends to them all.
9. Made direct amends to such people wherever possible, except when to do so would injure them or others.
10. Continued to take personal inventory and when we were wrong promptly admitted it.
11. Sought through prayer and meditation to improve our conscious contact with God as we understood Him, praying only for knowledge of His will for us and the power to carry that out.
12. Having had a spiritual awakening as the result of these steps, we tried to carry this message to alcoholics, and to practice these principles in all our affairs.

While "God" is frequently mentioned in these steps, A.A. members are quick to point out that they "adhere to no particular creed or religion" and welcome agnostics into the fellowship. But the spiritual element does play an important role in the "therapy."

Undoubtedly, A.A. has been responsible for many recoveries in the United States and in other countries. This is not surprising in view of its half million members including those not affiliated with any one group and the profusion of those groups, which are to be found in practically any sizable community in the country. With "no dues or fees in A.A.," with no rosters kept (to insure anonymity), with no record of those who may attend one or two meetings and then disappear from sight, it is impossible to estimate the percentage of recoveries. But by the sheer weight of the number of alcoholics exposed, any head-count would be high.

A.A. meetings are either "open" or "closed." Anyone interested in the program, alcoholic or non-alcoholic, can attend the former. Closed meetings are for alcoholics only. They are usually sessions in which the participants discuss more intimate alcoholic experiences. Both meetings are presided over by members chosen on a rotating, week-to-week basis -- i.e., no special training is involved.

One consideration in a sick alcoholic's limiting his treatment to A.A. is the fact that there is no medical or psychiatric screening. A "Twelfth Step worker" enthused over his own improvement, may be apt to disregard an underlying mental or physical disorder that is contributing to the woes of the person who has called for help. But on the whole, A.A.'ers are becoming increasingly aware of the physiological and psychiatric complications of the disease. More realize that "first things come first" and that physical and mental blocks must be overcome before the ailing alcoholic is ready to comprehend the spiritual.

Many clinic patients regularly attend A.A. meetings, just as many A.A. members find additional support in clinical therapy and Antabuse.

All reliable resources must be used in treating the alcoholic. So the alcoholism counselor should keep schedules of area A.A. meetings on hand at all times. Alcoholics Anonymous has proved its worth.

COUNSELING THE ALCOHOLIC

CONTENTS

I. PHILOSOPHY AND PRINCIPLES	1
II. THREE STAGES OF RELATIONSHIP	1
III. THE INITIAL INTERVIEW	2
IV. THE CONTINUING RELATIONSHIP	4
V. GROUP COUNSELING	5
VI. GROUP THERAPY AND A. A.	7

COUNSELING THE ALCOHOLIC

I. PHILOSOPHY AND PRINCIPLES

The alcoholic who is not ready to undergo treatment will often protest,. "Only an alcoholic can help an alcoholic!"

That is not true.

But the counselor -- alcoholic or non-alcoholic --who would help the man or woman whose life is disintegrating because of drinking should thoroughly understand the physical and emotional pain involved before attempting to establish rapport.

The essential quality is one of empathy, which the dictionary defines as "the capacity for participating in another's feelings or ideas." It differs from sympathy in that the counselor does not become emotionally involved, allowing the patient's joys and sorrows to affect his own ability to evaluate and advise.

The effective counselor must not only be able to understand others. He must have a real desire to understand others, to explore the whys of human behavior. And he must have an unconditional, positive regard for the individual patient -- a blend of warmth, acceptance, regard, interest, and respect.

He must continually work on his own self-awareness. He should recognize his own hang-ups and learn to deal with them. One who is able to do this is better able to be a partner in a helping relationship.

He must always remember that he is a counselor, not an analyst nor a judge. Overconcern with personality theories and counseling techniques will endanger rapport, just as premature attempts to arrive at solutions will surely lead to the patient's being short-changed.

Equipped with a knowledge of the physiological and psychological nature of alcoholism and especially of its progressive symptoms, the trained counselor usually is in a position to assess the general status of the new patient who sits before him. He has a broad idea of the physical pains, emotional distress, and changing attitudes the alcoholic has already suffered. This may be a small start. But it is an important head start in winning acceptance and evolving a program for recovery.

From that point on it is the counselor's job to translate his general observations into full and meaningful particulars about the highly individual person who seeks his help. Once that is accomplished, they can work together towards reasonable decisions and practical steps to be taken.

II. THREE STAGES OF RELATIONSHIP

Effective relationships between alcoholism counselors and their patients can be broken down into three stages:

The <u>first</u> might be called the subjective period. During this, usually the initial interview, the counselor wins the patient's confidence and establishes his empathy with him. He then gathers as much pertinent information as possible -- e.g., personal data, marriage and family status, employment, hospitalizations and arrests, drinking habits, etc.

The <u>second</u> is an objective stage. The counselor points out to the pa-tient his current status in comparison with known patterns and established facts about the disease. He explains what could lie ahead.

The <u>third</u> stage is one of teamwork. The counselor joins with the patient in building a road to recovery and solving the problems still posed by the past.

III. THE INITIAL INTERVIEW

    A. <u>Importance</u>

    The initial interview usually is the most important, not only because "first impressions" tend to linger on, but because it may also be the last.

    For a variety of reasons, the counselor may never again set eyes upon his patient. One of the most common -- particularly in outpatient clinics -- is that the patient is not sufficiently motivated to undergo continuing treatment. At the moment, the prospect of a lifetime without drinking is too frightening. He should nevertheless leave the counselor's office knowing that the door will always be open to him, tomorrow or ten years hence.

    A sense of security is the key to gaining the new patient's confidence so that he will come back.

    So the patient must be satisfied that the counselor will respect whatever confidences he may choose to divulge. He must be reasonably confident that the counselor is not going to berate him as he has been berated in the past. He must be assured that he can lower his defenses and receive understanding instead of recrimination.

    The counselor cannot expect to be told pertinent confidences unless the patient has confidence in him.

    B. <u>The Contract</u>
    Also in the initial interview, a "contract" should be established.

    The patient must be aware that alcoholism is an illness -- not a sin or a sign of weakness of character. Whether or not he is suffering from that illness will be up to him to decide, if he has not already done so.

    If the answer is yes, he has two choices: to accept treatment or to continue drinking. If he chooses the latter, probably, eventually, it will result in custodial care or death.

However, if he sincerely wants to recover, he must accept the fact that he is a sick man who can no longer drink. The counselor and his colleagues cannot do this for him. But they can help him help himself.

Such are the essentials of the initial contract. The counselor can make them clear in any way that best befits the situation or the patient's general attitude at the time. But unless the patient subscribes to them, any recovery program is courting failure.

C. <u>Eliciting Patient History</u>

The primary concern in a counselor-patient relationship is "Where do we go from here?" But significant facts about the patient's past and present are necessary for any reliable estimate of the situation.

In the course of time, counselors develop their individual methods of eliciting this information. So it would be presumptuous here to advance any hard-and-fast rules about interviewing new patients as one would instruct a student in the operation of a computer. However, there are certain basic principles to be considered.

The truism that "the quality of the answer depends upon the quality of the question" is universally accepted. The patient must be made to feel that he has the interviewer's undivided attention. He can perceive the presence or lack of empathy not only by the questions asked, but also by the counselor's overall manner. The tone of voice can be more persuasive than the questions themselves. Questions that reflect accusation and suspicion on the part of the counselor arouse resentment and suspicion in the patient and can quickly erase whatever rapport has been established in the beginning.

Even the pacing should be adjusted to the patient. Too slow a pace may suggest a difficulty in understanding on the part of the counselor. Too fast a pace can imply lack of interest.

Some questions must of necessity be pointed and direct e.g., date of birth, marital status, employment, etc. Those are to be expected. Other pointed questions - such as those dealing with the patient's parental and childhood background - are more readily answered if the purpose in asking them is explained. But, in general, pithy questions are preferable to those that can be answered yes or no. They can lead to greater insight into the patient's personality.

D. <u>Problems and Solutions</u>

Then there is the question that slams the door. The patient "clams up." More often than not it touches upon a painful memory which triggers the frigid reaction. It is useless to pursue the point at that time. The counselor can come back to it later in the interview or, as often happens, the patient will inadvertently supply the answer while responding to another evocative question.

In the same category are evasions and obvious lies. Few alcoholics will admit to having more than "a couple of beers" before their accidents, arrests, or other plights. The first meeting is no time to break down their defenses. Usually "the truth will out" -- that the patient had a pint and a half of whiskey between the two beers -- before the interview is over. The counselor should accept both the lie and its disproval without comment. The same holds true for other camouflages thrown up by the patient.

Nor are all answers verbal. The counselor should listen to what the patient does not say, as well as to what he says. The omissions in his explanations and comments are frequently more revealing than the explanations themselves. At the same time, physical clues can also be expressive of the emotional attitude -- e.g., the sweaty palms arising from fear or a sense of guilt, the folded arms of contrariness, the tears of sheer frustration and self-pity.

The most empathic alcoholism counselor in the world could not hope for a perfect batting average among all the applicants who come to him for aid. Perfect rapport cannot be arranged by an admission desk. Sometimes a patient might better be counseled by a worker in the next room or one down the hall. Or he may gravitate to a new group leader, even after weeks of individual counseling by the person who first interviewed him. In such cases, the counselor should have no hesitancy in "letting the patient go."

E. Problems that the Counselor Cannot Solve

The counselor must be able to distinguish between the patients he can help and those he cannot. He should recognize his own capabilities and limitations. It may be that a difficult family or financial situation or some other involved personal problem is causing or substantially contributing to the patient's drinking. When it is apparent that the cause, whatever it may be, is beyond the counselor's ability to help, he should refer the patient to an agency which can.

IV. THE CONTINUING RELATIONSHIP

Most of the above observations also apply to the continuing counselor-patient relationship. Of course, once the ice has been broken in the initial interviews and confidence established, the alcoholic is not apt to revert to lies and evasions with his counselor or physician. If he has normal intelligence, he will have found out that frankness best paves the way for significant planning and decisions.

Nor are there any precise ground rules to guide the counselor in an ongoing relationship. Success lies in adapting himself to the patient's attitude and, through empathy, helping him to plan ways and means of reaching the goals he sincerely wants to reach. In other words, the counselor has to "play it by ear."

A. Basics

But there are several basic "rules of thumb."

In planning ways and means of reaching objectives, final decisions should be made by the patient, not by the counselor.

One must remember that the average alcoholic comes glutted with unasked-for advice -- opinionated guidance supplied by family, parents, employer, best friend, and well-meaning companions. The patient is tired of advice.

So even if the counselor should know the answers, he should forego the role of mastermind. Better he discuss the pros and cons until the patient can view himself and his situation in the cold light of reality and decide for himself what had best be done to remedy matters. This is not to say that the counselor cannot offer alternatives, nor should he allow the patient to decide upon a potentially disastrous course of action. But when the patient himself makes the final decision or believes that he made it -- it becomes a strictly personal matter. It is no longer advice from family, parents, employer, or best friend. It is his own decision and, as such, he has greater confidence in the chances for success, especially with the counselor and his resources to lend support.

B. Constructive Forces

Besides being surfeited with advice, the average alcoholic comes oppressed with feelings of guilt and inferiority and loss of self-respect. The counselor should search out the constructive forces in his client. He must believe in them and their potentialities. And then he must make the patient realize them and believe in them, too. He can always cite the truism that every man is superior to the next man in some respect -- physically, psychologically, or intellectually. Once that asset is recognized, it can become another steppingstone in planning the road to recovery.

One of the beneficial by-products of counseling is catharsis the process by which repressed emotions and memories are brought to consciousness and released. It is an outpouring of emotionally painful thoughts which the patient has been harboring inside himself with perhaps no one available to console or consult, and which he has futile-ly been attempting to drown in drink. The counselor-patient relationship offers an opportunity for such purgative relief.

Catharsis should be fostered, but not forced. As he listens, the counselor should be alert to responses by the patient which reflect feeling rather than mere recollection, emotions rather than intellect. Strongly felt sentiments can reveal themselves at almost any time e.g., while talking about the family's reaction to his drinking, difficulties on the job, strained relation in the community. The bald recital of an occurrence may impulsively be punctuated with the patient's emotional reaction to the event. This is the time for the counselor to encourage him to express his feelings instead of just facts. But his questions and comments should be leading rather than probing, persuasive rather than pressing. Otherwise the patient may crawl back into his private world and slam the door behind him.

V. GROUP COUNSELING

As a general rule alcoholics are more effectively treated in group therapy than in the traditional one-to-one counselor-patient relationship.

This does not mean that the patient's need for individual counseling is completely superseded when he becomes a member of a group. Strictly personal problems may arise. Help from outside resources may be needed. Periods of uncertainty and depression may threaten his new self-command. In such cases, he may need individual counseling for support.

But for ongoing therapy the group affords a climate which the alcoholic has been avoiding for months or even years. Hiding his drinking habits from others or protecting his supply, he has usually become a loner. As participant in a group, he again becomes a member of society a society in miniature, perhaps, but nevertheless, a cooperative body with common aims and interests. It evokes intercommunication and, hopefully, interaction with others so necessary in again facing up to reality and normal living.

This escape from isolation is only one of many benefits a patient can derive from group therapy. The interpersonal relationships with others faced with the same illness gradually reduces his own sensitivity. He finds understanding, reassurance, and support. As time goes on, he gains greater insight into the origins and evolution of his behavior patterns. He is re-educated in ways of adapting himself to reality. And, because the environment is real, not artificial, he can test many of those ways within the group itself.

A. Role of the Group Leader

The group leader -- be he alcoholism counselor, social worker, or psychiatrist -- must always remember that the group belongs to its members. His primary mission is to be a good listener, with any outward participation kept to a minimum. The members must feel that they are the ones who are choosing the questions for discussion, arriving at the answers, settling any conflicts or confrontations.

However passive his role may appear to be, the leader must see to it that the discussion does not wander too far away from the subject. He should encourage participation by the silent minority, if any. He should act to relieve tensions and mediate debates. And, at all times, he should be noting the actions and reactions of the individual members, for these are clues to their progress in the recovery program.

While all these duties might seem to conflict with the leader's role as passive observer, he can usually delegate action to others.

Every group is made up of as many different personalities as there are members. They unconsciouly tend to assume various roles which they continue to play week after week. The leader can usually count upon them to function as needed. Among them are: The
- Initiator--introduces new ideas or subjects for discussion.
- Information-seeker -- asks for pertinent facts.
- Information-giver, -- always ready to supply those pertinent facts if he can.
- Elaborator -- develops others' comments and ideas.
- Orienter -- raises questions about the direction of discussion.
- Coordinator -- tries to pull ideas and suggestions together.
- Tester -- checks whether the group is ready for decision.
- Opinion-giver -- states what he believes to be the consensus of the group.
- Such members -- and other members in other roles -- are the group leader's advocates.

B. Measuring the Success of the Group

Superficially, it might seem easiest to measure the success of any group by the faithful attendance of its members and its attraction of new members.

But the true effectiveness of a group is best reflected in its contribution to its members' recovery. From time to time, the leader should ask himself these questions:

Has our group created an atmosphere in which constructive progress can be made?

Has it achieved real communication among members?

Do the members freely give and freely receive help?

Are the conditions such that each member can make his own special contribution?

Does it allow conflict and confrontation to be resolved into creative problem solving?

Has it evolved acceptable ways of making decisions?

If the leader can answer yes to all of these questions, he and the group are accomplishing their mission. If not, he had better diagnose the shortcomings and repair them.

VI. GROUP THERAPY AND A.A.

One frequently hears Alcoholics Anonymous vaguely referred to as "group psychotherapy."

In reality, there are many basic differences between the two methods of treatment. But a layman's misunderstanding can be forgiven since both have one aim among others -- to help the alcoholic stop drinking.

The counselor should be aware of these differences because the confusion is a common one.

A. <u>Differences Between the Two Methods</u>

In balancing method, it is best to disregard A.A.'s open meetings, where the general public is invited to attend, and limit comparisons to A.A.'s closed meetings, for alcoholics only.

Both A.A. and clinical groups are open to all alcoholics regardless of race, sex, or socio-economic status. While the latter are deliberately kept heterogeneous, members of A.A. tend to gravitate to groups composed of racial and socio-economic peers.

Both stress confidentiality. Outside visitors are not allowed. A.A. closed meetings do not permit the non-alcoholic spouses of members to attend. Clinical groups, recognizing alcoholism as a family disease, urge participation by members' families.

So long as alcoholic patients are under clinical treatment, they are required to attend group meetings, which are usually limited in size -- preferably six to nine participants. A.A. members are not required to attend meetings. Nor are there any limitations as to size. Hence, the same group can vary greatly from week to week in both numbers and make-up.

Leadership in clinical groups is vested in a trained psychotherapist or alcoholism counselor who unobtrusively steers discussion, mediates differences, and, when called upon, answers pertinent questions concerning alcohol and alcoholism. A.A. groups are presided over by a chairman, usually selected weekly on a rotating basis. The only requirement is to be an abstaining alcoholic.

The cornerstone of A.A. therapy is belief in a "God as one understands Him" and reliance upon His power to effect "a spiritual awakening" which will support a new, continuing life without alcohol. Catharsis and reparation for past wrongs committed against others are intended to alleviate guilt. Identification with other members who have succeeded in the program is stressed. Abstinence is the goal.

Clinical therapy, on the other hand, centers on psychological aspects. The alcoholic's nonrational and fantastic life theme is brought out and, through inter-communication and interaction with other group members, is eventually accepted by the patient and hopefully altered. The strengthening of relationships with other group members develops a sense of responsibility both for himself and for others. Full sobriety, not merely abstinence, is the goal.

In A.A., life membership is encouraged for continuing support. In clinical therapy, the successful member eventually leaves the group and stands on his own.

There are other differences, but these are the basic ones. The two therapies do not contravene one another. For many patients, they complement each other. When such is the case, the alcoholic can profitably embrace both.

PARENTS' GUIDE FOR THE PREVENTION OF YOUTHFUL ALCOHOL, TOBACCO & DRUG USE

Do you know your son's or daughter's friends?

During middle and high school years, fitting in with friends becomes extremely important. But, who will most likely ask your child to try beer, cigarettes or other drugs? A friend. How does it feel to say "no" to a friend? It is the alcohol, tobacco and other drugs that are being rejected, not necessarily the friend. As parents, it is important to emphasize that our kids CAN say "no" and keep their friends, sometimes. Their friends may even follow their lead and say "no" too.

Is it OK for parents to introduce their kids to alcohol occasionally, but only at home?

No. In fact, the younger a person is when introduced to alcohol, the more difficult it becomes to stop. The truth is that if a person begins drinking alcohol at the age of 15, they are 4 times more likely to develop alcohol dependence than those who begin at age 21. If kids reach the age of 21 without drinking or smoking, the chance is almost zero that they will ever develop a serious drug problem. "Learning how to drink" during adolescence is not a rite of passage nor a "part of growing up". When school-age youth are allowed to drink at home, they are more likely to use alcohol and other drugs outside the home, **and** are at risk to develop serious behavioral and health problems related to substance use.

What is alcohol poisoning and binge drinking?

Alcohol poisoning, or acute intoxication, is a drug overdose which kills over 4,000 kids every year and can cause irreversible brain damage in those who survive. Some teens drink with the purpose of getting drunk. They drink fast, or binge drink, attempting to get as much alcohol in them as possible. **Binge drinking** is defined as five or more beers or drinks for boys and four or more beers or drinks for girls at one sitting at least once in a two week period. Binge drinking is increasing among teens.

The signs of alcohol overdose include mental confusion, stupor, difficulty being aroused, slow or irregular breathing, low body temperature, bluish skin color. Be aware that someone who is passed out from drinking can die. If the thought of alcohol overdose is in your mind, call 911 and do not leave the person alone.

What you should NOT do. Do not give the person food, do not let the person sleep it off, do not give them a cold shower. **NEVER ENCOURAGE VOMITING** due to the risks of blocking the trachea or causing someone to inhale (aspirate) the material that has been vomited which can lead to life-threatening complications.

A MATTER OF CONCERN

For Students

I don't drink or use drugs. I just smoke cigarettes. What's the big deal?

Your initial decision to smoke tobacco is a critical incident because that choice often leads to other risky behaviors. The Center for Disease Control has found that kids who smoke are 3 times more likely to use alcohol, 8 times more likely to use marijuana and an astounding 22 times more likely to use cocaine than non-smokers.

How can I say "no" to alcohol, tobacco and other drugs?

Your ability to say "no" is the simplest way to prevent the use of alcohol, tobacco and other drugs. The more prepared you are, the better able you will be to handle high-pressure situations that involve drinking, smoking or other drug use. Here are some suggestions:

What can you say when you are at a party and a friend offers you a cigarette, beer or other drugs?

- No, I don' t want any...Forget it, I don't need it.
- I'm not into that kind of stuff.
- My mom and dad trust me not to try that.
- No, my parents will ground me for a month. It's not worth it.
- I want to stay eligible for the team, or the play...etc.
- Back off. Why do you keep pressuring me when I've said "no"?

What could you do if you find yourself in a house where kids are passing around beers and parents are nowhere in sight? Leave.

Call home and ask to be picked up. A prearranged code phrase such as, "I forgot about practice tomorrow," or "I have a terrible stomach ache, can you come get me?" will make it easy for your mom or dad to know you need help.

Be calm and confident. The first time you say "no" is the hardest. It's easier with practice. Often a person trying to get you to join them in using a substance will take a weak "no" as a possible "yes". Don't argue, don't discuss. Say "no" and show that you mean it, then it will be less likely that you will be asked again.

Do most kids in high school use alcohol or other drugs?

No. That is a myth. *Most* kids are not using alcohol, tobacco, or other drugs and it's perfectly normal not to. The trick is to not make smoking, drinking or using other drugs your ticket to fitting in. Find two or three kids who do not drink and with whom you would like to be friends. This will make the transition into high school easier.

The Brain

"Wiring"

Until recently, it was thought that brain development and growth were completed in late childhood. However, it is now clear that the brain continues to develop throughout adolescence up until at least a person's early twenties. The part of the brain that undergoes the most change during adolescence is an area behind the forehead called the prefrontal cortex. Additionally, there are changes in the central core of the brain occurring at the same time. In these regions the prefrontal cortex, which is the brains voice of reason and decision-maker and the hippocampus, which is responsible for memory and many types of learning, are especially sensitive to alcohol and other drugs. The chronic presence of drugs in the growing brain can damage the way it develops. Listed below are 4 drugs and information about what they can do to kids' brains.

Tobacco
Nicotine is a highly addictive drug and it is in all tobacco products, not just cigarettes. Nicotine is a powerful drug that affects the chemistry of the brain regulating thinking and feelings. A recent study involving about 15,000 teens suggests that in addition to the many reported known health risks, teens who smoke are at a significant increased risk for depression—a serious clinical problem which affects nearly 10% of adolescents. Addiction to nicotine also frequently leads to other forms of drug addiction.

Alcohol
In the past, scientists believed that younger brains were more resilient than adult brains and were able to escape many of the worst ills of alcohol. On the contrary, new studies indicate that the younger the brain is, the more it may be at risk. Alcohol consumption by young people has a dramatic impact on their ability to learn. Alcohol impairs mental function in young drinkers more than in adults. Research shows kids who drink a lot of alcohol may lose 10% of their brainpower—the difference between a pass or a fall in school—or in life.

Marijuana
The single most important negative consequence of marijuana use is that it impairs the ability of the brain to store new information—to learn. It takes 8 days to remove 90% of the active ingredients from a person's body. This impairment is often unrecognized by the user. Marijuana also impairs finely controlled and coordinated movements such as those involved in athletics or playing music. This drug often reduces a person's motivation and can cause a sense of anxiety, fear or panic.

Ecstasy
The first use of Ecstasy can cause seizures, brain injury or death. It is a powerful chemical that enters the brain and causes the release of massive amounts of the brains natural chemical serotonin. The best medical research is showing that Ecstasy is a neurotoxin. Repeated use kills part of the nerve cells that release serotonin and it is not known when or if recovery occurs.

Middle School Years-The Bridge to Adolescence

When should I start to talk to my children about alcohol and other drug use?
It is never too early. Start when they are curious and begin to ask questions. By late elementary school or early middle school, children may begin to see classmates smoking or drinking. Most kids who become users began using alcohol, tobacco or other drugs at age 11 or 12 or began to inhale household products to get high in 6th or 7th grade. Middle school kids need a clear no-use message, factual information and strong motivation to resist pressures to try alcohol, tobacco or other drugs. Appropriate new information might include: ways to identify specific drugs (see Drug Chart section) and the dangers and consequences of use (see Negative Effects and Legal section).

Do you know your preteen?

If your children feel comfortable talking openly with you, you'll have a greater chance of guiding them toward healthy decision making. With younger kids, ages 10-13, ask questions like "Have you heard about any kids drinking or smoking or using drugs? / Why do you think kids drink or use drugs? / How do you feel about this?" Avoid questions that have a simple "yes" or "no" answer. A parent's disapproval of youthful alcohol or other drug use is the key reason children choose not to drink, smoke or use other drugs.

Peer pressure and fitting in

During the middle school years, fitting in with friends becomes extremely important. Kids increasingly look to friends and the media for clues on how to behave. We, as parents, often feel shoved aside. However, we need to help our kids sort out the facts from fiction. Studies show that even during the teen years, parents have enormous influence on their children's behavior.

Family interaction

Parents have more influence on their kids' decisions about drinking, smoking or using other drugs **before** they begin to use alcohol, tobacco or other drugs. Use family traditions, daily structure and routines to reinforce your values and shared responsibilities. Give family time top priority even though you're all busy. Among kids whose parents stay on top of their behavior through adolescence, less than 10% drink at all, never mind drink excessively.

Internet sense

Stay in close touch with your kids as they explore the Internet's sites and chat rooms. It's important at this age to emphasize the concept of credibility. Kids need to understand that not everything they see on the Internet is true or valuable, just as not all advice they get from their peers is valuable or true. It's 3:45 pm—do you know where your kids are in cyberspace?

WHY AND WHY NOT

Why Kids Use Alcohol, Tobacco and Other Drugs

There is no single answer to the question "Why do kids use alcohol, tobacco and other drugs?" The answers are many and varied, and can depend upon a variety of social, emotional, physical, and environmental factors. They may include:

The influence of peer acceptance
The powerful influence of fitting in with one's peers is well known. For preteens and teenagers the acceptance of the peer group is of overriding importance. Gaining the acceptance of the group may include indulging in risky behavior, including alcohol, tobacco or other drug use. The potential risks may not be apparent to the adolescent, and this behavior may be viewed as essentially harmless because "everybody's doing it."

The need to escape anxiety
Young people are frequently ill at ease in social situations. In order to cope with these uncomfortable feelings, they may be tempted to use alcohol, tobacco or other drugs in order to lessen their stress and to give them a false sense of confidence in their dealings with others.

The desire to feel good, to relax, or to seek excitement
In general, individuals who use mind-altering substances do so for the reasons cited above, or they may simply be seeking an escape from the pressures of everyday life. Adolescents, in particular, may be interested in using alcohol, tobacco or other drugs to achieve a feeling of well being and relaxation.

To satisfy curiosity or to reduce boredom
Young people are eager to try new experiences, especially those that are supposed to be for adults only. Kids who are not actively involved in extracurricular activities in addition to their studies may find themselves with time on their hands. For these individuals, alcohol, tobacco and other drugs may be seen as one way to pass the time.

As relief from an intolerable situation or as a means of masking low self esteem and/or depression
Some kids are dealing with serious problems in their home or school environments. The psychological toll that these problems take on the adolescents' self esteem may push them to self-medicate using alcohol, tobacco or other drugs as a way to escape their difficulties.

Why Kids Should Not Use Alcohol, Tobacco and Other Drugs

Preteens and teenagers should not use alcohol, tobacco or other drugs at all. Here are some reasons why:

It's illegal
Recognizing that alcohol is a powerful drug that must be used responsibly, state governments have imposed a limit of 21 years of age for its possession and use. The

use of narcotics or other drugs unless prescribed by a physician is illegal under any circumstances. It is also illegal for a prescription drug to be used by anyone other than the person for whom the drug is prescribed. The sale to and use of tobacco products by minors is illegal. (See Legal Consequences)

Certain individuals have a biological predisposition to addiction

The most serious problem with the use of alcohol, tobacco or other drugs by young people is the possibility that they may have a biological predisposition to become addicted to these substances, especially if their relatives are addicted. While it is true that not everyone who drinks, smokes or uses other drugs will become addicted, inevitably there are some who will. There is no way to predict who the vulnerable ones will be, and the extent to which their addiction will compromise their future success in life. It is important to inform kids about any family history of alcoholism or other drug dependencies.

The use of alcohol, tobacco and other drugs delays the maturation process

When kids use alcohol, tobacco or other drugs as a crutch in social situations, they severely hamper their ability to develop the necessary social skills and self-confidence to be successful in their dealings with others.

Alcohol, tobacco and other drugs have a more powerful effect on the growing body than on that of an adult

Because certain drugs, and alcohol in particular, are depressants, their effects on the developing nervous system and brain are more pronounced. Intoxication may come very quickly, and lead to impulsive and irrational behavior that is not tempered by adult judgment.

Impaired judgment may lead to regrettable, or even dangerous situations

Alcohol or other drug-induced highs have been responsible for countless injuries and deaths by car crashes, falls, fighting, drowning, or alcohol poisoning. Impaired judgment can lead to serious situations that may range from the destruction of property to promiscuous sex, unintended pregnancies, and the spread of sexually transmitted diseases, including AIDS.

SIGNS AND SYMPTOMS

Four Basic Stages of Alcohol, Tobacco and Other Drug Use

It is a difficult task to readily identify signs of alcohol, tobacco or other drug use in your kids. Some of the signs and symptoms may be "normal" adolescent behavior. If more than a few of the signs are present, however, this is not "normal" and is an indication of a problem. You know what is typical behavior for them and what is not. Trust your judgment.

Listed below are the four major stages of substance abuse. Any "use" of alcohol, tobacco or other drugs by kids is considered "abuse". There is no definitive line separating each stage.

Initial use
The user learns he/she can produce a euphoric feeling from using alcohol, tobacco or other drugs.
Drugs: Tobacco, alcohol, marijuana, ecstasy and inhalants.
Use: Occasional weekend use.
Behavior: No obvious change in personality.

Regular use
The user deliberately and actively seeks the "good" feelings produced by alcohol, tobacco or other drugs.
Drugs: Tobacco, alcohol, marijuana, ecstasy, inhalants, uppers and downers.
Use: Moves from occasional weekend to every weekend use.
Behavior: Obvious changes in personality. Lying, displays of anger, may be more confrontational with parents/adults, change in friends. May lose interest in extracurricular activities.

Daily use
Achieving the "high" is the sole obsession and preoccupation.
Drugs: Tobacco, alcohol, marijuana, ecstasy, inhalants, uppers/downers, cocaine, heroin.
Use: Daily, frequently during the day. Solitary use. Overdoses occur.
Behavior: Lying, stealing, problems with the law, job loss, failure at school, loss of original friends. Depression, suicidal thoughts.

Complete dependency
Increased levels of drugs are needed to start and finish the day.
Drugs: Tobacco, alcohol, marijuana, ecstasy, inhalants, uppers/downers, cocaine, heroin.
Use: Constant. It is an addiction. Compulsive. The user has no control over use at this point. He or she is addicted and requires intensive medical intervention.
Behavior: Total deterioration of physical health. Weight loss, chronic cough, and memory loss. Blackouts, flashbacks, frequent feelings of helplessness.

Symptoms of Alcohol, Tobacco and Other Drug Use

All parents today, whatever their social or economic status, need to be aware that a serious alcohol, tobacco and other drug problem exists among many preteens and teenagers and that their own sons or daughters are vulnerable.

Addiction is the repetitive compulsive use of a substance that occurs despite negative consequences to the user. Addiction is a disease—it is chronic and progressive and it requires professional treatment.

Listed below are some common problem areas, as well as changes that you may have noticed in your children. If you have a concern or think there may be a problem, seek the help of a substance abuse counselor or medical doctor.

Academic Performance
Slipping grades
Tardy or absent often
Excuses for incomplete assignments
Short attention span/difficulty concentrating
Change in attitude toward coaches and teachers
Change in motivation to perform

Alcohol and Other Drug Curiosity
Talks about alcohol and drug use
Change in attitude about tobacco use
Starts smoking cigarettes
Interested in music/literature on pro-drug use
Wears hats, shirts, jewelry etc. with alcohol/drug logos
Evidence of drug paraphernalia
Hostility in discussing alcohol/drugs

Behavioral Changes
Lack of interest in personal appearance
Withdrawal, isolation, fatigue, depression, anxiety
Aggressive, rebellious behavior
Lack of cooperation; defies rules
Increased friction with family
Begins to make up own rules
Difficult to engage in usual conversation
Increased need for money
Comes home late and sneaks off to bed
Lying, stealing

Peer Relations
Change in friends
Vague about whereabouts
Phone calls from friends who are "new"
Sudden status with peers
Avoids old friends

Physical Changes
Blood shot eyes/dilated pupils
Weight loss or gain
Dazed look
Runny nose, frequent colds
Coughing
Bruises
Spurts of snack-food hunger
Loss of appetite
Forgetful
Sleeping more than usual

Physical Evidence
Empty beer cans around house
Matches and lighters
Rolling papers
Sudden concern for privacy of things
Mouthwash, gum, breath sprays
Burning incense
Unfamiliar smell on clothing
Disappearance of alcohol from home
Eye drops (Visine or Murine)
Pipes or bongs
"Stash cans" often disguised as soda or beer cans
People telling you that your child is drinking, smoking or using other drugs

THE NEGATIVE EFFECTS

The Gateway Drugs

The most widely used drugs in America are nicotine, alcohol and marijuana, and among kids 12-17, inhalants. Each is destructive in its own right. The use of any one of them seems to "open the door" to involvement with other drugs. Tobacco, alcohol, marijuana and inhalants are referred to as "gateway drugs" in that individuals rarely use potent drugs such as cocaine or heroin without first having used tobacco, alcohol, marijuana and/or inhalants. Many people who become addicted to these drugs began using during adolescence.

Tobacco
- The peak time for the initiation of smoking is in sixth and seventh grades.
- 90% of all adult smokers began at or before age 18.
- Each year, one million teens begin smoking. They are the prime targets of tobacco advertisers and 1/3 of them will die from a tobacco-related illness.
- 1,200 people die every day in the U.S. from tobacco-related illnesses.
- Nicotine is highly addictive and new research shows that kids exhibit serious symptoms of addiction within weeks or just days of first smoking.

Alcohol
- One 12 oz. beer has the same amount of alcohol as 1.5 oz. whiskey, 5 oz. of wine, or a wine cooler.
- Among kids who begin drinking at age 13, 43 percent will go on to develop alcoholism.
- Children of alcoholics have a 4 to 10 times greater risk of becoming alcoholics than children of non-alcoholics.
- Over one-third of America's alcoholics (4.7 million) are under 21. In fact, more than one quarter of eighth graders in the U.S. have already been drunk.

Marijuana
- The potency of marijuana today can be much stronger than that used in 1965 due to refinements in the plants.
- At least 18 percent of eighth graders have used marijuana. By the time a teen reaches 17 years of age, 6 out of 7 have friends who use marijuana and 7 out of 10 can buy marijuana within a day.
- Most affected are the centers of the brain that regulate a person's highest levels of thought, behavior and cognitive functioning. *Simply put: every marijuana smoker is dumber than before he began.*
- THC, the principal intoxicating chemical, is stored for weeks in the fatty tissues of the body, including the brain.
- Marijuana inhibits nausea and allows a person to consume large quantities of alcohol without getting sick. As a consequence, death due to alcohol overdose has escalated among teens.

Inhalants
- 20 percent of eighth graders have used inhalants at least once.

- Inhalants can be fatal on the first use or cause permanent damage to the brain, central nervous system or other organs.
- Young teens may inhale common household substances such as aerosol propellants (spray starch), cleaning solvents, gasoline, glue or paint thinners because they are easy to get and inexpensive.

Consequences

Arrested psychological development

The major task of adolescents is to grow into responsible adults. Kids need to learn how to accept and handle their emotions: joy, excitement, anger, frustration, anxiety, disappointment, sadness and fear. They also need to learn how to celebrate, relax and feel accepted, be part of a group and yet be an individual. Kids learn these skills through trial and error and repetition over time. Alcohol, tobacco or other drug use short-circuits this entire process and stunts or prevents normal development. When kids are "high" they cannot learn to manage their feelings. Although they may feel relaxed and feel part of the group, they are not actually doing the hard work it takes to develop and integrate these adult skills. *They may mature physically, but their emotional and psychological maturity may be greatly delayed.*

Date rape

Typically occurs because one or both parties are under the influence of alcohol or other drugs. Date rape is a crime. It is criminal for someone to have sex with a person who is mentally or physically incapable of giving consent. To have sex with a person who is drugged, intoxicated, passed-out, incapable of saying "no" or is unaware of what is happening around them is to commit rape. Teens think that a potential rapist is someone who is a crazy guy or a weirdo, yet date rape happens on dates with students who are popular, good-looking and smart without regard to social class, race, or economic status. (see Drug Chart for Date Rape Drugs) Sexual exploitation, pregnancy or sexually transmitted diseases may result due to loss of judgment and lowered inhibitions.

Car crashes

The use of alcohol and other drugs reduces a person's normal reaction time, thereby increasing chances of crashes. Driving under the influence of alcohol or having passengers who are drunk can result in the loss of driver's license and insurance coverage.

Confusion

Parents who allow their kids to drink or use other drugs are unintentionally sending the message, "I don't care about you" or "I'm not willing to do whatever it takes to protect you." Schools and the media stress the dangers of alcohol, tobacco and other drugs, but peer pressure and advertising can encourage kids to try these substances. These conflicting messages are confusing. Kids, whose parents do not have strong underage drinking rules, are more likely to have been drunk in the last 2 weeks. Parents' admissions about their own teenage alcohol/drug usage only adds to the confusion.

Lost opportunities

May include suspension or expulsion from school, rejection for summer or full time employment as many corporations require passing drug tests, risk of arrest, incarceration or costly fines due to violent, illegal acts.

Tobacco risks

People who smoke are more prone to a variety of illnesses such as colds, ear and sinus infections. Their wounds heal less easily. They wrinkle and age more rapidly. Besides bad breath, they have more tooth decay, gum disease and persistent coughs. Exercise tolerance and physical performance can drop. Kids who smoke are more likely to use alcohol, marijuana and other illicit drugs in the future.

Depression and Suicide

Depression

More than 11 million children and adolescents in the general population suffer from depression at any given point in time. Kids under stress, who experience loss, or who have attention disorders are at a higher risk for depression. Depression also tends to run in families. Depressed adolescents may be more likely to use alcohol, tobacco or other drugs as a way to feel better.

Depression is defined as an illness when the feelings of depression persist and interfere with a person's ability to function. Unfortunately, it often takes a young person's suicide attempt for the problem to surface. For the many families of the 15,000 children who kill themselves each year, the problem surfaces too late.

The following behaviors may be warning signs of depression that can lead to suicide:

    Increased sadness, tearfulness, moodiness, anger or irritability
    Decreased interest in activities; or inability to enjoy previously favorite activities
    Persistent boredom; low energy
    A major change in eating and/or sleeping patterns
    Social isolation, poor communication, difficulty with relationships
    Extreme sensitivity to rejection or failure
    Frequent absences from school or poor performance in school; poor concentration
    Giving away favorite possessions

Suicide

More than 8 out of 10 kids who threaten suicide attempt it. Suicide is the second leading cause of death among youths aged 15 to 19 and is often associated with alcohol and other drug use and depression. Two thirds of suicidal teens report poor relationships with their parents. Although these are alarming statistics, suicide is preventable.

If suicide appears imminent, do not waste time feeling guilty, angry or upset. ACT! Call a suicide or crisis intervention hotline, the psychiatric unit at your local hospital or a trusted family practitioner. Do not wait for a return phone call. If you cannot reach the first person, call someone else. Never wait to see if your adolescent feels better in the morning. Most teen suicides take place al home in the late afternoon or evening with family members present.

Talk to your children. The idea that talking about suicide encourages it is false and dangerous. The truth is that once the depressing and frightening thoughts inside your child's head are out in the open, they become less threatening.

Reassurance and expressing concern and understanding for your children's anguish is a huge first. Let them know that whatever the problem(s) may be, your love for them is not conditional and you will work through this with them. Don't give up. Someone once said that suicide is a permanent solution to a temporary problem.

HELP

What Can I Do if I Think My Son or Daughter is Using Alcohol, Tobacco or Other Drugs?

Most parents have a sixth sense about how their kids act and feel. Learning the difference between "the symptoms of growing up" and the warning signs of alcohol and other drug use is not always easy. Recognizing a problem is the first big step. Asking for help is the next one.

Be wary of denial

Denial is a way of coping with painful situations that allows a person to avoid dealing with a problem.

There is the element of shame and inadequacy associated with alcohol and other drug use. Many adults feel helpless and assume that they can take care of the problem within the family itself However, now is the time to reach out for professional and community based help. Confront the problem; it is never too late nor too early.

Confronting the problem

Agree on a course of action with your spouse or other adult family member BEFORE talking with your preteen or teen. Be open and honest with your feelings, but do not let anger or fear overwhelm your effectiveness to communicate.

Do let your child know that you do not condone his or her behavior.
Do tell your child that you value him or her and will be a supportive advocate.
Do set new guidelines and limits for your child's behavior.
Do become more aware of your child's activities.

If your preteen or teenager is under the influence of alcohol or other drugs:
Right now:

Do try to remain cool and calm.
Do try to find out what he or she has taken and under what circumstances.
Do call a doctor or take your child to the hospital if he or she is incoherent and/or seriously ill.
Do tell your child that you will talk about the matter the next day.
Don't shout, excuse, or use physical force. This can only make matters worse.

The next day:

Do talk with your preteen or teen as soon as possible.
Do have your child assume responsibility for his or her actions, including cleanup.
Do try to find out the circumstances under which he or she came to use, including the people they were with.
Don't name call, belittle, blame or threaten. Mutual respect should be safeguarded.
Don't discuss anything with your child if you are too angry, or unable to talk without losing your temper.
Don't ask why. Work with what happened and what you know.
Do seek help from community supports: medical, mental health, religious, legal and self-help groups.
Do enforce consequences, e.g. loss of privileges.

COMMUNICATION

Communicating With Your Preteen and Teenager: Foster Self Respect

Internal control helps preteens and teenagers make safer decisions, but high self-esteem is what allows them to believe in and stick by their good choices. A child who has a positive self-image is one who will most likely have the courage to resist peer pressure to drink, smoke or use other drugs. In order to encourage non-use among our children, it is important to build good relationships with them based upon mutual respect.

Make time for your son or daughter
Find an activity you enjoy doing together and pursue it.

Listen, really listen
Because parents have so much to do and so little time, they often try to listen while doing other tasks. Put your chores aside so your child knows you're really paying attention. Don't do all the talking or give long lectures.

Encourage independent thinking
Eventually your child will make a decision about whether to smoke, drink or use drugs. Wanting to be accepted by peers is a major reason kids try these substances. Help them practice making decisions on their own. Let them know it is OK to act independently from others and to think for themselves.

Praise your kids for who they are, not just for their accomplishments
When parents are quicker to praise than to criticize, kids feel good about themselves, and develop the self-confidence to trust their own judgment.

Tolerate differences
Build strong family relationships by openly encouraging your children to talk freely about their lives, problems, school and work. Talk about topics where all people do not have the same opinion.

Give preteens and teenagers responsibility for their own problems
Allow your kids to experience the consequences of their behavior even though these consequences may be uncomfortable or embarrassing.

Remove the stigma of failure from your home
Young people need to understand that the only failure is in not trying. Mistakes are not failures. Mistakes simply provide us with new information that can help us to succeed. We all need the freedom to be imperfect.

Encourage outside interests
Kids who are involved in after school activities and sports develop friendships and interests that will help to keep them away from alcohol, tobacco and other drugs. Preteens and teens who learn to have fun, as well as cope with stress in healthy ways, will be less likely to turn to artificial substances to relax.

Establish Guidelines

Many parents hesitate to discuss alcohol, tobacco and other drug use with their children. Some of us believe that our kids won't use alcohol, tobacco or other drugs. Others delay because we don't know what to say or how to say it, or we are afraid of putting ideas into our children's heads. However, many young people in treatment programs say that they had used alcohol, tobacco or other drugs for at least 2 years before their parents knew about it.

Take a firm stand against any form of tobacco, alcohol or other drug use

Do not accept getting high or drunk as normal at any age. Exercise parental authority and responsibility. Be persistent.

Know where your son or daughter is

Let them know where you can be reached at all times in case of emergency. Assure them that they can telephone you for a ride home whenever they need to, at any time, for any reason, without your asking any questions. Pick a code phrase that your child can use as a cue for you to come and pick them up—"I have a headache" or "Tomorrow I'm supposed to start work on that huge project..." When you pick up your teen, if it is not too late, do something fun together.

Do not serve alcohol to underage kids and don't allow kids to bring tobacco, alcohol or other drugs into your home

Set reasonable limits to help your child say "No". Establish guidelines, rules and curfews both for weekdays and for weekends that must be followed. State clearly the rules and values of your family and what the consequences are if they are ignored.

Teach resistance skills

Help your children develop coping strategies for dealing with problem situations. Talk through strategies with them for saying "no", and make sure they know whom to call upon if help is needed. Provide them with phone numbers and cab fare to carry with them. Advance planning can give them a way out of a difficult situation.

Be willing to be unpopular

Try to accept that there will be times when your kids won't like what you say—or will act as though they don't like you. Being your child's friend should not be your primary role during this time in their lives. It's important to resist the urge to win their favor or try too hard to please them. Inflammatory remarks such as, "You don't understand... I am the only one who..." are simply tactics kids use to get you to relent and say yes when you want to say no. Be consistent. Hold your ground.

Be at home while your preteens or teens are getting ready to go out

When they are leaving, remind them of your expectations that they not drink, smoke or use other drugs. Give them the confidence to stay in control.

Be awake

When your son or daughter comes home after an evening out, wait up for them or ask them to awaken you when they arrive. It will be easier for you to determine if they have been smoking, drinking or using other drugs.

Communicating With Other Parents Network Frequently

The best offense in the battle against alcohol, tobacco and other drug use among preteens and teens is to know what's going on. Most parents have heard the whining refrain, 'All the other kids' parents let them..." This persuasive and manipulative phrase may result in making you feel alone in your decision making. It is never too early or too late to turn the tables and really find out what other parents are doing. We, as parents, do more to shape our kids' views than any other single influence in their lives.

Get to know your son's or daughter's friends
If your child is associating with kids who are using tobacco, alcohol or other drugs, your child is at risk.

Get to know the parents of your child's friends
You can become involved with other parents through the Parents' Organization, sports or drama activities, volunteering, etc. Develop a "united front" and discuss concerns openly.

Be a good role model
Set good examples in your own life. Believe that kids can understand and accept that there are differences between what adults may do legally and what is legal for adolescents. Keep that distinction sharp.

Call to confirm the activities your preteen or adolescent plans to attend
Find out if parties will be parent-supervised. When in doubt, consider asking the parents hosting the party for their assurance that they will serve no alcohol and that they will not permit guests to bring alcohol.

Ask for help
Give permission to other parents to call you if they see your son or daughter participating in activities they know you would not approve of. Encourage your children to ask for help if one of their friends is experiencing difficulties with tobacco, alcohol or other drug use by telling you, talking with their parents or speaking directly with the friend.

Provide help
Call the parents of any boy or girl at any event whom you perceive to be high, stoned or drunk. It takes a brave parent to call another with bad news. Be willing to provide a ride to protect the teen or to call the police if necessary.

Know what to do if you suspect a problem
Realize that no adolescent is immune to alcohol, tobacco or other drugs. Learn what other people are observing. Trust your gut. If you think there might be a problem, there probably is. Remember addiction is a disease, not a cause for shame. Seek professional help immediately.

A PARENT'S REPORT CARD—GO FOR STRAIGHT A'S
Be **Aware** of their attitudes.
Be **Alert** to their environment.
Be **Around** their activities.
Be **Assertive** in your parenting.
Be **Awake** when they come home.

THE FIVE BASIC A'S OF PREVENTION

Communicating With the School: Work Together

All of the schools in the "Community of Concern" encourage parents to become involved with the school and our children's activities. As the primary educators of our children, the schools and parents form a unique partnership.

Take advantage of volunteer opportunities
One of the best ways to learn what is going on at school and to get to know other parents is to volunteer at the school. The Parents' Organizations provide a myriad of ways for parents to become involved. You can sign up by calling Parents' Organization's members to offer your time. Their names and telephone numbers are listed in the Student Telephone Directory or can be obtained from the school.

Know the school's Substance Abuse Policy...
...and actively support the policy.

Talk with the school counselor, chaplain, principal or dean of students...
...if you suspect a problem with alcohol, tobacco or other drug use because it is usually easier to take care of a problem in the earlier stages.

During High School
Some kids talk about "learning to drink responsibly" before they get to college. Learning to be responsible *about* drinking does not require learning how to drink. Parents may think about introducing their kids to alcohol at home. Stop and think. Studies show that the younger kids are when they start to drink, the more likely they will develop problems with addiction in the future.

Furthermore, the legal drinking age is 21. If you say to your child, "It's OK to break the law as along as you do it here with me", you are sending them a basic message that individuals can decide whether or not or when to obey the law and when to ignore it. Instead, we can educate our kids about the medical, legal and other consequences of underage drinking so that they may make responsible decisions *about not* drinking.

Beyond High School
According to the National Center of Addiction and Substance Abuse at Columbia University, "Did you know that the average college student spends more money on alcohol than on books? The consequences of campus alcohol abuse are devastating: 95 percent of violent campus crime is alcohol-related, and, in at least 73 percent of reported campus rapes, either the perpetrator, the victim, or both have been drinking. Students who drink most heavily receive the lowest grades.

While alcohol is the top substance of abuse in college, for most students alcohol abuse started well before they graduated from high school. Only 14 percent of students began drinking in college; 71 percent first used alcohol before age eighteen. Students who first used alcohol before college binge drink far more often than those who began drinking later." It's important to remember that most college kids are under 21 and still not legally eligible to drink. Many parents are beginning to hold the colleges accountable.

PARTIES AND THE SOCIAL SCENE

Parties

Parties or "get togethers" are a major part of the high school social scene. They can be an enjoyable way for kids to meet and socialize. However, without proper planning and careful supervision, parties can be a disaster waiting to happen. The following guidelines will help you keep parties both more fun and safe.

When the party is at your house
  Before the party:
- Set the ground rules. Your son or daughter needs to know what you expect.
- Limit party attendance. Curb the "open party" situation.
- Designate the "off-limits" rooms in your house.
- Know your legal responsibilities. Include your child in this feeling of responsibility.
- Set a time for the party to end.
- Remove any family liquor from areas accessible to party guests.
- Invite other couples to help chaperone.

  At the party:
- Be present and visible. Don't be pressured into staying out of sight. Greet guests as they arrive.
- Occasionally check on food and soda and monitor your yard.
- No smoking, no alcohol, no drugs.
- No leaving the party and then returning.
- Backpacks and coats must be left at the door.
- Consider checking contents of backpacks.
- Open cans or containers cannot be brought into the party.
- Don't hesitate to call police if unwanted guests refuse to leave.
- Never allow anyone you suspect is under the influence of drugs or alcohol to drive.
- Call their parents, a cab, or ask a sober adult to drive them home.

When the party is elsewhere
- Call the host parent to be sure that a parent will be present and get assurance that alcohol and drugs will not be permitted.
- Know how your child will get to and from the party.
- Discuss in advance the possible situations your preteen or teen might encounter and how to handle them. Make sure he or she has a phone number where you can be reached should they want to leave the party early.
- Be awake for your child's return or have him or her awaken you. This gives you an opportunity to assess whether or not your child has been using drugs or alcohol.
- Verify any plans to stay overnight with the host parents. Be wary of impromptu sleepovers.

- Establish firm, clear rules against driving under the influence of drugs or alcohol or riding with someone who has been drinking or using drugs.

If the parents are out of town

Tell a neighbor about your scheduled absence and leave instructions to protect yourself against "surprise parties." Leave a number where you can be reached. Inform your preteen or teenager of your preparations.

The Social Scene

When the party is nowhere and everywhere

Teenage parties whose destinations are parks or open fields are of grave concern because of their isolation and lack of supervision. Typically they are most prevalent during warmer weather, well organized with large amounts of alcohol, a cover charge, and lots of teenagers.

Insist that your teen keep you posted of any change in plans. Parents must realize that once kids start driving, their plans change rapidly and frequently. They may start at an "agreed upon" party and before long, move onto several different locations without your permission. This possibility might bear discussion so a plan consistent with your family's rules can be agreed upon.

"Raves"

These all night dance parties with loud "techno" music are set up in warehouses, fields or stadiums and are frequently advertised as alcohol-free, giving parents a false sense of security. "Club drugs", such as Ecstasy, are often readily available at "raves". Ecstasy's stimulant effects enable users to dance for long periods thereby increasing the body's core temperature. This can lead to hypertension, dehydration or heart or kidney failure.

Homecoming, Holiday Dances, School Dances and Prom

These social events often include group transportation using commercial limousine or bus services. This can be an attractive option, as long as the vehicle is not used as an opportunity to drink. If your son or daughter and their friends are planning to use group transportation, consider the following:

Take responsibility for hiring the transport company yourself. Do not give this responsibility to your child. Some counties have approved limousine lists.

Inform the transport company they are to make no stops to or from the event other than the stops you have pre-authorized. Be firm that you will hold them accountable to ensure that no alcohol is illegally consumed by minors.

All bags must be kept in the trunk to ensure that no alcohol is brought on board by any young men or women.

Celebrations off-campus

The week after school ends, thousands of students, many unchaperoned, gather at local resorts. For many students, this is a time to relax and have fun with friends after exams or graduation. For far too many, it is a time of near non-stop drunkenness and sexual promiscuity. Many parents who look upon these occasions as an innocent "rite of passage" for high school students regret their mistake. If you are thinking of allowing your son or daughter to take part in large group celebrations, consider the following:

Provide responsible chaperoning. You are the best chaperones of your children. However, other parents whose judgment you trust and whose values you share are a reasonable alternative.

Don't ask young adults, including relatives, to chaperone. They are a poor choice, as they often buy alcohol for the minors under their care.

Offer an alternative. Father/son or mother/daughter outings, special privileges…etc.

Alcohopops
Be Alert. "Starter suds" are alcoholic beverages that resemble non-alcoholic lemonades, fruit punches and soft drinks. These sweet, fruity beverages disguise the taste of alcohol and contribute to underage drinking.

LEGAL CONSEQUENCES

Civil Damages, Enforcement Policy and Criminal Penalties

Civil Damages

A person who supplies alcohol or drugs to a minor, or who allows alcohol or drugs to be used by a minor when he or she is in a position to prevent that use, may be liable for damages resulting from the minor's impairment. For example, a person who supplies alcohol to minors or hosts a party where drinking is allowed could be assessed for significant damages if the minor, driving while impaired, should have an accident causing injury to himself or others or to property.

Enforcement Policy

With the heightened awareness of the problems created by underage individuals use of alcohol and other drugs, authorities are not inclined to look the other way at offenses. For example, in come counties, zero tolerance is the procedure. Where underage individuals are consuming alcohol at a party, all those in attendance, whether drinking or not, will be subject to civil citations.

Criminal Penalties—Tobacco

All 50 states and DC prohibit the sale of tobacco products to minors. Retailers who sell tobacco products to kids under 18 are subject to fines; as are persons who distribute to or buy tobacco products for kids. More than 44 states also have laws that penalize kids for buying, possessing or using tobacco products with fines, community service, or loss of driving privileges.

Criminal Penalties—Use of Controlled Dangerous Substances

In many states "Possession or Sale of Controlled Substances" is classified as a Felony. Penalties range from prison sentences to heavy fines or both. Penalties for "Sale on School Property or Within 1000 Feet of Any School" and "Distribution to Persons Under 18" are severe.

Criminal Penalties—Alcohol and Marijuana

State	Forged ID	Purchase/Possession of Alcohol By a Minor	Purchase/Furnish Alcohol For a Minor	Possession of Marijuana
AK	Fine up to $5,000, Jail up to 1 yr., DL revoked	Purchase/Fine up to $5,000, Jail up to 1 yr., Possession/Fine $100	Fine up to $5,000, Jail up to 1 yr.	Fine $1,000, Jail 0-90 days
AL	Fine $50-500, Jail up to 3 mo., LS 3-6 mo.	Fine $50-500, Jail up to 3 mo., LS 3-6 mo.	Fine up to $1,000, Jail up to 6 mo.	Fine up to $2,000, Jail up to 1 yr., LS up to 6 mo.
AR	Fine up to $500, Jail up to 90 days, possible probation	Fine $100-500, and/or probation or essay	Fine upto$1,000, Jail up to 5 yrs.	Fine $1,000, Jail 0-1 yr.
AZ	Fine up to $2,500, Jail up to 6 mo., LS	Fine up to $500, Jail up to 30 days	Fine up to $2,500, Jail up to 6 mo.	Fine $750-150,000, Jail-probation
CA	Fine up to $1,000, Jail up to 6 mo., LS up to 1 yr., CS 24-32 hrs.	Fine $250 and CS up to 32 hrs., LS up to 1 yr.	Fine $1,000 CS up to 24 hrs.	Fine $1,000, Jail-appear court

State	Forged ID	Purchase/Possession of Alcohol By a Minor	Purchase/Furnish Alcohol For a Minor	Possession of Marijuana
CO	Fine up to $1,000, Jail up to 12 mo.	Fine up to $1,000, AE, SAP, LS, JO, CS	Fine up to $1,000, Jail up to 12 mo.	Fine up to $100, Jail up to 15 days
CT	Fine $50-500, Jail up to 30 days, LS	Fine $200-500, Jail up to 30 days, LS	Fine up to $1,500 and/or jail up to 18 mo.	Fine up to $1,000, Jail up to 1 yr.
DE	Fine $100-500, Jail up to 30 days	Fine up to $100 or LS 30 days	Fine up to $500, Jail up to 30 days, CS-40 hrs.	Fine $1,150, Jail 0-6 mo.
DC	Fine up to $300, Jail up to 30 days, LS up to 1 yr.	Fine up to $300, Jail up to 30 days, LS	Fine up to $1,000, Jail up to 180 days	Fine up to $1,000, Jail 0-180 days
FL	Fine up to $500, Jail up to 60 days, CS-40 hrs., LS 6 mo.	Fine up to $500, Jail up to 60 days, LS up to 1 yr.	Fine up to $500, Jail up to 60 days, CS-40 hrs., LS	Fine up to $1,000, Jail 0-1 yr.
GA	Fine up to $1,000, Jail up to 12 mo.	Fine up to $300, and/or Jail up to 6 mo., LS	Fine up to $1,000, Jail up to 1 yr.	Fine $1,000, Jail 0-1 yr.
HI	Fine up to $10,000, Jail up to 5 yrs.	Under 18-family court, 18-21 petty misd.-penalty varies by county	Fine up to $2,000, Jail up to 6 mo.	Fine up to $1,000, Jail 0-1 yr.
ID	Fine up to $3,000, Jail up to 60 days	Fine up to $1,000, LS up to 1 yr., AE, SAP	Fine up to $1,000, Jail up to 60 days	Fine $1,000, Jail 0-1 yr.
IL	Fine up to $500, CS up to 25 hrs., LS	Fine up to $2,500, Jail up to 12 mo., LS, SAP	Fine up to $2,500, Jail up to 12 mo.	Fine $500, Jail 0-30 days
IN	Fine up to $500, Jail up to 60 days, LS up to 1 yr.	Fine up to $500, Jail up to 60 days	Fine up to $1,000, Jail up to 60 days	Fine $5,000, Jail 0-1 yr.,
IA	Fine up to $200, LS up to 1 yr.	Fine up to $200, LS up to 1 yr., CS	Fine up to $500, Jail	Fine up to $1,000, Jail up to 6 mo., rehab. serv.
KS	Fine up to $500, CS up to 100 hrs.	Fine $200-500, CS-40 hrs., SAP	Fine min. $200, Jail	Fine $2,500, Jail 0-1 yr.
KY	Fine up to $500, Jail up to 1 yr., LS-up to 6 mo., SAP	Fine up to $500, Jail up to 1 yr.	Fine up to $500, Jail up to 1 yr.	Fine $500, Jail 90 days to 1 yr.
LA	Fine up to $2,000, CS-30 hrs.	Fine up to $250, Jail 6 mo., LS, SAP	Fine up to $500, Jail up to 6 mo.	Fine $500, Jail 0-6 mo.
ME	Fine $100-500	Fine $100-300, CS, LS	Fine up to $1,000, Jail	Fine $400, Jail 0-1 yr.
MD	Fine $500, Jail up to 2 mo., Fake drivers lic. up to 12 points	Fine $500, AE, SAP, CS-20 hrs.	Fine up to $1,000, Jail up to 2 yrs.	Fine $1,000, Jail 0-1 yr.

State	Forged ID	Purchase/Possession of Alcohol By a Minor	Purchase/Furnish Alcohol For a Minor	Possession of Marijuana
MA	Fine $300, LS-180 days	Fine up to $300, LS up to 180 days	Fine up to $2,000, Jail up to 6 mo.	Fine $500, Jail 0-6 mo.
MI	Fine up to $100, Jail up to 90 days, LS up to 90 days	Fine up to $500, SAP, CS	Fine up to $2,500, Jail up to 90 days, CS	Fine $1,000, Jail 0-1 yr. or Probation
MN	Fine up to $100, LS	Fine up to $100	Fine up to $100, CS	Fine $200, SAP
MS	Fine up to $200, Jail 5-30 days, CS up to 30 days	Fine up to $100	Fine up to $2,000, Jail up to 1 yr.	Fine up to $1,000, Jail 0-1 yr.
MO	Fine $500	Fine $500-1,000, Jail 6 mo.-1 yr., LS, SAP	Fine up to $1,000, Jail up to 1 yr.	Fine $1,000, Jail 0-1 yr.
MT	Fine $500 and/or Jail 6 mo., LS 6 mo.	Fine up to $100, LS up to 90 days, CS, SAP	Fine up to $500, Jail up to 6 mo.	Fine $100-500, Jail 0-6 mo.
NE	Fine up to $500, Jail up to 3 mo.	Fine up to $500, Jail up to 30 days, CS up to 10 days, LS	Fine up to $1,000, Jail up to 1 yr.	Fine up to $500, Jail up to 7 days, SAP
NV	Fine up to $1,000, Jail up to 6 mo., CS	Fine up to $1,000, Jail up to 6 mo., CS	Fine up to $1,000, Jail up to 6 mo., CS	Fine $5,000, Jail 1-4 yrs.
NH	Fine up to $500, LS up to 60 days	Fine up to $250, LS 90 days - 1 yr.	Fine up to $2,000, Jail up to 12 mo.	Fine $1,000, Jail 0-1 yr.
NJ	Fine up to $500, LS-6 mo., SAP	Fine at least $500, LS-6 mo., SAP	Fine $500, LS-6mo.	Fine $1,000, Jail 0-6 mo.
NM	Fine up to $1,000, Jail 2-5 days, CS-60 hr.	Fine up to $1,000, Jail up to 60 days, CS up to 50 hrs., SAP LS up to 3 mos., AE	Fine up to $1,000, Jail up to 5 days, CS, LS up to 1 yr.	Fine up to $1,000, Jail up to 1 yr., Eligible for probation
NY	Fine up to $100, CS up to 30 hr., LS up to 3 mo., SAP	Fine up to $100, CS up to 30 hr., SAP	Fine up to $500, Jail up to 5 days	Fine $500, Jail 0-3 mo.
NC	Fine at court's discretion, Jail up to 45 days, LS 1 yr.	Fine min. $250 Jail and/or probation, CS up to 25 hrs., LS	Fine $2,000 (over 21), Jail 0-2 yrs., CS up to 150 hrs.	Jail 30 days-6 mo., CS
ND	Fine $1,000, Jail 30 days	Fine $1,000, Jail 30 days, AE	Fine up to $2,000, Jail up to 1 yr.	Fine $1,000, Jail 0-30 days
OH	Fine up to $1,000, Jail up to 6 mo., LS up to 1 yr., CS	Fine $1,000, Jail up to 6 mo., LS up to 1 yr.	Fine $500-1,000, Jail up to 6 mo.	Fine $250 Jail 0-30 days
OK	Fine up to $50, LS 1 yr. or until 21 yrs. of age	Fine up to $100 and/or jail 30 days, SAP, AE, CS 20 hrs.	Fine up to $5,000, Jail up to 5 yr., Lic. revoked	Fine $500, Jail 0-1 yr.

State	Forged ID	Purchase/Possession of Alcohol By a Minor	Purchase/Furnish Alcohol For a Minor	Possession of Marijuana
OR	Fine $300, CS, LS-1 yr., SAP if 18-21 yrs. old	Fine up to $300, SAP	Fine at least $350, Jail at least 30 days	Fine $500-1,000
PA	Fine up to $300, Jail up to 90 days, AE, LS, SAP	Fine $500, LS-90 days, SAP	Fine $1,000-2,000, Jail up to 1 yr.	Fine $500 and/or Jail up to 30 days
RI	Fine $150-1,000, LS-3 mo.-1 yr.	Fine $100-500, LS 3 mo.	Fine up to $1,000, Jail up to 6 mo.	Fine $200-500, Jail up to 1 yr.
SC	Fine $100-200, Jail up to 30 days, LS	Fine up to $200, Jail up to 30 days, LS	Fine up to $200, Jail up to 30 days, LS	Fine $100-200, Jail 0 to 30 days
SD	Fine $200, Jail up to 30 days, LS-30 days-1 yr.	Fine $200 and/or jail-30 days, LS-30 days-1 yr., SAP	Fine $1,000 and/or jail 0-1 yr., LS 30 days-1 yr.	Fine $100, Jail 0-30 days
TN	Fine $50-500, Jail 5-30 days, LS, CS-20 hrs.	Fine $50-500, Jail 5-30 days, CS 20 hrs.	Fine $50-2,500, Jail 11 mo. 29 days, CS-up to 30 days	Fine min. $250, Jail 0-1 yr.
TX	Fine $250-2,000, Jail up to 180 days, CS-8-40 hrs., LS, SAP	Fine $250-2,000 and/or Jail up to 180 days, CS 8-40 hrs., LS, SAP	Fine $250-2,000 and/or jail up to 180 days, CS 8-40 hrs., LS	Fine $2,000, Jail 0-180 days
UT	Fine up to $1,000, Jail up to 6 mo., LS	Fine up to $1,000, Jail up to 6 mo., LS	Fine up to $2,500, Jail up to 1 yr.	Fine $1,000, Jail up to 6 mo.
VT	Fine up to $50	Fine up to $500, Jail up to 30 days	Fine $200-1,000, Jail up to 2 yrs.	Fine $500 and/or Jail up to 6 mo.
VA	Fine $100-500	Fine $500, CS-50 hrs, LS up to 1 yr.	Fine $2,500, Jail up to 1 yr.	Fine $500, Jail up to 30 days
WA	Fine up to $1,000, Jail up to 90 days	Fine up to $1,000, Jail up to 90 days	Fine up to $2,500, Jail up to 90 days	Fine $1,000, Jail 1-90 days
WV	Fine up to $50 and/or jail 72 hrs. or 1 yr. probation	Fine up to $50 and/or Jail 72 hrs. or 1 yr. probation	Fine up to $100, Jail up to 10 days	Fine $1,000, Jail 90 days to 6 mo.
WI	Fine at least $300, CS, LS	Fine $250-500, LS, CS	Fine up to $500, Jail up to 90 days, LS 3-30 days	Fine up to $1,000, Jail up to 6 mo.
WY	Fine up to $750 and/or jail up to 6 mo.	Fine up to $750, Jail 6 mo., LS	Fine up to $750, Jail up to 6 mo.	Fine up to $1,000, Jail up to 1 yr.

AE- Alcohol Evaluation, CS- Community Service, LS- License Suspension, SAP-Substance Abuse Program
Laws and penalties change and are interpreted and enforced differently even in the same legal jurisdiction. Listed penalties increase with subsequent offenses. Information contained in this report is for informational purposes only. Special Thanks to Sunanda K. Holmes, Esquire

RESOURCES

National 24-Hour Hotlines
AIDS Hotline	800-342-2437
Alcohol and Drug Helpline	800-821-4357
National Runaway Switchboard	800-621-4000
We Tip (to anonymously report selling or trafficking of illicit drugs)	800-782-7463

Information

Al-Anon/Alateen (www.al-anon.alateen.org) — 800-356-9996
　Provides support for families and friends of alcoholics.

Alcoholics Anonymous (www.alcoholics-anonymous.org) — 212-870-3400
　Provides help for those concerned about their drinking.

American Council for Drug Education (www.acde.org) — 800-488-3784
　Scientifically accurate information on illegal drugs.
　(www.drughelp.org)

Best Friends Foundation (www.bestfriendsfoundation.org) — 202-237-8156
　Provides alcohol/drug curriculum information.

Campaign for Tobacco-Free Kids (www.tobaccofreekids.org) — 202-296-5469
　Provides information to protect kids from tobacco addiction.

Caron Adolescent Treatment Center (www.caron.org) — 800-678-2332
　Provides treatment for addictions.

Community of Concern (www.communitiesofconcern.org) — 301-493-5000
　Provides information on this booklet, activities and awards.

Detection (www.phamatech.com) — 888-635-5840
　Provides drug-testing information for parents.

Father Martin's Ashley (www.fathermartinsashley.com) — 800-799-4673
　Provides addiction treatment services.

Hazelden Foundation (www.hazelden.com) — 800-257-7800
　Provides information and treatment for addictions.

National Clearinghouse for Alcohol and Drug Information — 800-662-HELP
　(www.health.org)
　Gives local referrals for treatment and provides publications.

Partnership for a Drug-Free America — 212-922-1560
　(www.drugfreeamerica.org)
　Answers questions frequently asked by parents.

PTA (www.pta.org) — 800-307-4782
　"Children First"—website of the National PTA

Toughlove (www.toughlove.org) — 800-333-1069
　National self-help group for parents and children.

U.S. DOE—Safe and Drug Free Schools — 202-260-3954
　(www.ed.gov/offices/OESE/SDFS)
　Provides funding and technical support for school based programs.

Local Resources

You do not need to be alone when dealing with your son or daughter's alcohol, tobacco or other drug issues. Reach out for help. A good place to start is the counseling department at your child's school.

DRUG CHART

Common Drugs of Use

Type of Drug	Drug Name	Street Name	Description	DEA Schedule#/ How Its Used	Related Paraphernalia	Signs and Symptoms of Use
Cannabis	MARIJUANA Hashish, Hash Oil	Pot, grass, reefer, weed, sinsemilla, joint, blunts, MJ	Like dried oregano leaves, stems and seeds	I, Swallowed, smoked	Rolling papers, pipes, bongs, baggies, roachclips, cigars "blunts"	Sweet burnt odor, slow reactions, red eyes, impaired memory
Depressants (Depress the nervous sys.)	ALCOHOL Beer, wine, distilled spirits (whiskey, vodka, gin, rum, brandy)	Booze, juice, brew, 40's	Liquid	Not Scheduled Swallowed	Flask, bottles, cans, alcopops	Impaired judgment, mood changes, lowered inhibitions
	BARBITURATES Amyl, Seconal, Nembutal	Barbs, downers, yellow jackets, reds, blue devils	Tablets, powder	II, III, Swallowed, injected	Syringe, needles	Confusion, fatigue, impaired coordination, slurred speech
	TRANQUILIZERS Valium, Librium	Tranks, downers, candy	Tablets	IV, Swallowed	Pill bottles	Drowsiness, dizziness
Narcotics	HEROIN, MORPHINE	Dreamer, junk, smack, horse	White to brown powders, tablets, liquid	I, Injected, smoked, snorted	Syringes, spoon, lighter, needles	Lethargy, loss of skin color, needle marks, constricted pupils, staggering gait
	OXYCONTIN	Killers, OC, Oxy, Oxycotton	Tablet	II, Chewed, snorted, injected	Razor blades	Sedation, dizziness, dry mouth, sweating
Stimulants (Stimulate the nervous sys.)	AMPHETAMINES Amphetamine, Dextroamphetamine, Methamphetamine	Speed, uppers, bennies, crank, crystal, black beauties, crosses, wide-eye ice	Variety of tablets, crystal-like rock salt	II, Swallowed, injected, smoked, snorted	Syringe, needles	Excess activity, irritability, nervous, tremor, impulsive behavior, dilated pupils,
	METHYLPHE-NIDATE	Ritalin, JIF, vitamin R, R-ball	Tablets	II, Swallowed, snorted, injected straws	Razor blade, glass surfaces,	Unusual alertness, excitation, insomnia, loss of appetite
	COCAINE/ CRACK	Coke, snow, toot, blow, white lady, flake, vitamin "C"	White powder	I, Snorted, injected, swallowed, smoked	Razor blade, mirrors, glassy surfaces, straws	Dilated pupils, talkativeness, euphoric short-term high, depression, oily skin
	TOBACCO/ NICOTINE	Smokes, butts, cigs, cancer sticks/snuff, dip, chew	Dried brown organic material	Not Scheduled. Smoked or chewed	Spit cups, cigar cutters, lighters, matches	Short of breath, respiratory illness, lung, oral or other cancers

Type of Drug	Drug Name	Street Name	Description	DEA Schedule #/ How Its Used	Related Paraphernalia	Signs and Symptoms of Use
Hallucinogens (Alters perceptions of reality)	PCP (Phencyclidine)	Angel dust, hog, peace pill, tic/tac, zoot	White powder or tablet, liquid, capsule	I, II, Smoked, snorted, injected, swallowed	Tin foil, can be applied to leafy material i.e. mint, parsley, tobacco	Impaired motor function, numbness, unpredictability, panic, aggression
	LSD (Lysergic Acid Diethylamide)	Acid, cubes, blotter, microdot, yellow sunshine, gel tabs	Odorless, colorless, tasteless powder, tablet, liquid	I, Swallowed, sugar cubes or licked off blotter paper	Blotter papers, thin squares of gelatin	Dilated pupils, altered states of perception/feeling, flashbacks
	MESCALINE Psilocybin	Mesc, cactus, magic mushroom, shrooms	Brown discs, tablets, natural mushrooms (fried or dried)	I, Swallowed, smoked, chewed	Dried mushroom brewed as tea	Same as LSD, nervousness, paranoia
Inhalants (Substances inhaled by nose/mouth)	Air Freshener, correction fluid, aerosols, airplane glue, gasoline, marking pens, amyl and butyl nitrate	Glue, kick, bang, huff, poppers, whippets, texas shoe-shine, jac blaster	Chemicals that produce mind-altering vapors	Not scheduled, Inhaled nasally or mouth, often with the use of paper or plastic bags	Cleaning rags, empty spray cans, tubes of glue, baggies, aerosol cans, large balloons	Bad breath, altered vision, slowed thought, headache, depletion of oxygen, spots or sores near mouth or nose
Steroids	Anabolic	A's, stackers, gym candy, juice arnolds, weight trainers	Tablet	III, Swallowed, injected	Used in large quantities to add muscle strength	Aggression, 'Roid rage'
Club Drugs/ Designer Drugs	MDMA, MDA, MDEA (Stimulant/ Hallucinogen)	Ectasy, X, XTC, Peace, E	Branded tablets	I, Swallowed	Glow sticks, candy pacifiers	Anxiety, teeth clenching, paranoia, hyperthermia
Date Rape	Rohypnol (Depressant)	R-Z, roofies, Mexican valium, spanish fly	Tasteless, odorless, dissolves easily in beverages, carbonated	IV, Swallowed, added to drinks	Drinks, soda cans	Small amounts cause unconsciousness and/or amnesia
	GHB (Depressant)	Grievous Bodily Harm, Georgia Home Boy	Clear liquid, capsule	I in 6 states; Schedule # pending in 44 states. Swallowed, dissolved in drinks	Drinks, soda cans	Drowsiness, loss of reflexes, headache

Drug Enforcement Administration (DEA) Schedule—Tiered System for Regulating Psychoactive Drugs—Schedule I/II high potential for abuse. Schedule I—no approved medical use. Schedule II—available by non-refillable prescription. Schedule III/IV—available by prescription, with restricted refills. Schedule V—available over the counter. (U.S. Department of Justice)